SMITH WIGGLESWORTH

On Manifesting the Divine Nature

ABIDING IN POWER
EVERY DAY OF THE YEAR

SMITH WIGGLESWORTH

On Manifesting the Divine Nature

ABIDING IN POWER
EVERY DAY OF THE YEAR

DESTINY IMAGE® PUBLISHERS, INC.

P.O. Box 310, Shippensburg, PA 17257-0310

"Promoting Inspired Lives."

This book and all other Destiny Image, Revival Press, MercyPlace, Fresh Bread, Destiny Image Fiction, and Treasure House books are available at Christian bookstores and distributors worldwide.

For a U.S. bookstore nearest you, call 1-800-722-6774.

For more information on foreign distributors, call 717-532-3040.

Reach us on the Internet: www.destinyimage.com.

ISBN 13 TP: 978-0-7684-0334-3

ISBN 13 Ebook: 978-0-7684-8567-7

For Worldwide Distribution, Printed in the U.S.A.

1 2 3 4 5 6 7 8 / 17 16 15 14 13

Acknowledgments

A special thanks to Tony Cauchi for gathering and stewarding the many sermons and articles attributed to Smith Wigglesworth. Without Tony's great work, the world would not have access to Smith's wonderful teachings and ministry. Tony hosts the Revival Library (www.revival-library.org) and Smith Wigglesworth (www.smithwigglesworth.com) websites. He studied with the Elim Bible College and was awarded a Diploma in Theology from London University. He lives in Hampshire, England with his wife, Liz. They have two married children and five grandchildren.

Behold, I have longed after thy precepts:
quicken me in thy righteousness.

Psalm 119:40

SATISFACTION IN THE SPIRIT OF GOD

He...shall be satisfied (Isaiah 53:11).

Beloved, we may be so endued by the Spirit of the Lord in the morning that it is a tonic for the whole day. Think of it! God can so thrill us with new life that nothing ordinary or small will satisfy us after that. There is a great place for us in God where we won't be satisfied with small things. We won't have any satisfaction unless the fire falls, and whenever we pray we will have the assurance that what we have prayed for is going to follow the moment we open our mouth.

Oh, this praying in the Spirit! This great plan of God for us! In a moment we can go right in. In where? Into His will. Then all things will be well.

We should always be awake to what God has for us. Awake to take! Awake to hold it after we get it! How much can you take? We know that God is more willing to give than we are to receive. How shall we dare to be asleep when the Spirit commands us to take everything on the table? It is the greatest banquet that ever was and ever will be—the table where all you take only leaves more behind. This fullness cannot be exhausted! How many are prepared for a lot? Come into the Spirit, to the banquet table, and be filled to satisfaction!

SAFEGUARDED BY THE WORD OF GOD

Thy word have I hid in mine heart, that I might not sin against thee (Psalm 119:11).

The Word of God must have first place. It must not have a second place. In any measure that we doubt the Word of God, from that moment we have ceased to thrive spiritually and actively. The Word of God is not only to be looked at and read, but also received as the Word of God so it becomes life right within our life.

By the grace of God I want to impart the Word and bring you into a place where you will dare to act upon the plan of the Word, where you will breathe life by the power of the Word so that it is impossible for you to go on under any circumstances without His provision. The most difficult things that come to us are to our advantage. When we come to the place of impossibilities, it is the grandest place for us to see the possibilities of God.

Put this right in your mind and never forget it. You will never be of any importance to God till you venture into the impossible. God wants people to be daring. I do not mean foolish daring. "Be filled with the Spirit," and when we are filled with the Spirit, we are not so much concerned about secondary things. God is concerned with first things first. "Seek ye first the Kingdom of God" (Matt. 6:33).

All things evil, unclean, and satanic in any way are objectionable things to God, and we are to live above them, to destroy them, to not allow them to have any place. Jesus didn't let the devil answer back. We must reach the place where we will not allow anything to interfere with the plan of God.

LIFE THROUGH THE WORD

Thy word have I hid in mine heart, that I might not sin against thee (Psalm 119:11).

None of you can be strong in God unless you are diligently and constantly hearkening to what God has to say to you through His Word. You cannot know the power and the nature of God unless you partake of His inbreathed Word. Read it at morn and at night and at every opportunity you get. After every meal, instead of indulging in unprofitable conversation round the table, read a chapter from the Word and then have a season of prayer. I endeavor to make a point of doing this no matter where or with whom I am staying.

The Psalmist said that he had hid God's Word in his heart, that he might not sin against Him; and you will find that the more of God's Word you hide in your heart, the easier it is to live a holy life. He also testified that God's Word had quickened him; and, as you receive God's Word into your being, your whole physical being will be quickened and you will be made strong. As you receive with meekness the Word, you will find faith springing up from within. And you will have life through the Word.

The Word of God must have first place. It must not have a second place. We must be rooted in the Word of God. In any measure that we doubt the Word of God, from that moment we have ceased to thrive spiritually and actively. The Word of God is not only to be looked at and read but received as the Word of God to become life right within our life. "Thy word have I hid in mine heart, that I might not sin against thee" (Ps. 119:11).

An Ordinary Calling

...When the number of the disciples was multiplied...their widows were neglected in the daily ministration. Then the twelve called the multitude of the disciples unto them, and said...Look ye out among you seven men of honest report, full of the Holy Ghost and wisdom, whom we may appoint over this business (Acts 6:1-3).

The twelve told the rest to search for seven men to look after the business end of things. They were to be men of honest report and filled with the Holy Ghost. These were just ordinary men who were chosen, but they were filled with the Holy Spirit, and this infilling always lifts a man to a plane above the ordinary. It does not take a cultured or a learned man to fill a position in God's church; what God requires is a yielded, consecrated, holy life that He can make into such a flame of fire. Baptized with the Holy Ghost and fire!

The multitude chose seven men to serve tables. They were doubtless faithful in their appointed tasks, but we see that God soon had a better choice for two of them. Philip was so full of the Holy Ghost that he could have a revival wherever God put him down. Man chose him to serve tables, but God chose him to win souls. Oh, if I could only stir you up to see that as you are faithful in performing the humblest office, God can fill you with His Spirit and make you a chosen vessel for Himself and promote you to a place of mighty ministry in the salvation of souls and in the healing of the sick. There is nothing impossible to a man filled with the Holy Ghost. It is beyond all human comprehension. When you are filled with the power of the Holy Ghost, God will wonderfully work wherever you go. When you are filled with the Spirit, you will know the voice of God.

GLORIFYING GOD

...and they chose Stephen, a man full of faith and of the Holy Ghost... (Acts 6:5).

Look at Stephen. He was just an ordinary man chosen to serve tables, but the Holy Ghost was in him, and he was full of faith and power and did great wonders and miracles among the people. There was no resisting the wisdom and the spirit by which he spoke. How important it is that every man shall be filled with the Holy Spirit.

You have no conception what God can do through you when you are filled with His Spirit. Every day and every hour you can have the divine leading of God. To be filled with the Holy Ghost means much.

Stephen's opposers were unable to resist the wisdom and spirit by which he spoke, and so, full of rage, they brought him to the council. And God filled his face with a ray of heaven's light. It is worth being filled with the Spirit, no matter what it costs. Read the seventh chapter of Acts, the mighty prophetic utterance by this holy man. Without fear Stephen tells them, "Ye stiffnecked and uncircumcised in heart and ears, ye do always resist the Holy Ghost..." (Acts 7:51). And when they heard these things they were cut to the heart.

There are two ways of being cut to the heart. Here they gnashed their teeth and cast him out of the city and stoned him. On the day of Pentecost, when they were cut or pricked at the heart they cried out, "What shall we do?" They took the opposite way. The devil, if he can have his way, will cause you to commit murder. If Jesus has His way, you will repent.

LIFE IN THE HOLY GHOST

For in him we live, and move, and have our being... (Acts 17:28).

You enter into a realm of illumination, of revelation, by the power of the Holy Ghost. He reveals the preciousness and the power of the blood of Christ. I find by the revelation of the Spirit that there is not one thing in me that the blood does not cleanse. I find that God sanctifies me by the blood and reveals the efficacy of the work by the Spirit.

Oh, this life in the Holy Ghost! This life is one of deep, inward revelation, of transformation from one state to another, of growing in grace and in all knowledge and in the power of the Spirit, the life, and the mind of Christ. These things are being renewed in you, along with constant revelations of the might of His power. It is only this kind of thing that will enable us to stand.

We have to learn the power of the breath of the Holy Ghost. If I am filled with the Holy Ghost, He will formulate the word that will come into my heart. The sound of my voice is only by the breath that goes through it. God will move upon the people to make them see the glory of God just as it was when Jesus walked in this world, and I believe the Holy Ghost will do special wonders and miracles in these last days.

The secret for the future is living and moving in the power of the Holy Ghost. One thing I rejoice in is that there need not be an hour or a moment when I do not know the Holy Ghost is upon me. Oh, this glorious life in God is beyond expression; it is God manifest in the flesh. Oh, this glorious unction of the Holy Ghost—that we move by the Spirit. He should be our continual life.

Everything He Said Came to Pass

And Jesus entered into Jerusalem, and into the temple: and when he had looked round about upon all things, and now the eventide was come, he went out unto Bethany with the twelve. And on the morrow, when they were come from Bethany, he was hungry: and seeing a fig tree afar off having leaves; he came, if haply he might find any thing thereon: and when he came to it, he found nothing but leaves; for the time of figs was not yet. And Jesus answered and said unto it, No man eat fruit of thee hereafter for ever. And his disciples heard it (Mark 11:11-14).

Jesus was sent from God to meet the world's need. Jesus lived to minister life by the words He spoke; He said to Philip, "…he that hath seen me hath seen the Father…the words that I speak unto you I speak not of myself: but the Father that dwelleth in me…" (John 14:9-10).

I am persuaded that if we are filled with His words of life and the Holy Ghost, and Christ is made manifest in our mortal flesh, then the Holy Ghost can really move us with His life, His words, till we are as He was in the world. We are receiving our life from God, and it is always kept in tremendous activity. Divine life works in our whole nature as we live in perfect contact with God.

Jesus spoke and everything He said must come to pass. That is the great plan. When we are filled only with the Holy Spirit, and we won't allow the Word of God to be detracted by what we hear or by what we read, then comes the inspiration, then the life, then the activity, then the glory! Oh, to live in it! To live in it is to be moved by it. To live in it is to be moved so that we will have God's life and personality in the human body.

Into the Treasure House of the Most High

For where your treasure is, there will your heart be also (Luke 12:34).

The way into the treasure house of the Most High is through the authority of the living Word. The Kingdom of Heaven is open to all believers. He has called us and brought us into divine association with heaven, if we will dare to believe, for all things are possible to him that believes.

When we believe, like Abraham who believed God, we shall find the Holy Ghost's tremendous ability to change weakness into strength, character, and power, and to make all things new. The result is a life yielded and absorbed by divine authority, so that we are standing on the principles of God. May God increase the numbers who dare to believe under all circumstances, who dare to believe God on the authority of the Word.

I depend upon the Holy Ghost to bring us into revelation. Oh, the breath of God! There is no room for weakness when we see this mighty incoming life through the Spirit. We need to have the hearing of faith, always soaring higher, understanding the leading of the Spirit.

There is something mighty in believing God. Have you found it? God said He would cover Abraham with His righteousness, holiness, and integrity of faith because Abraham believed in Him. God loves to see His children when they believe Him. He covers them. It is a lovely covering, the covering of the Almighty. Blessed is the man to whom God imputes righteousness. Beloved, there must be this divine fellowship between God and us.

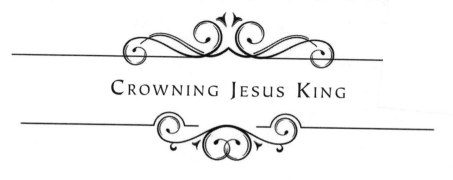

CROWNING JESUS KING

...No man can say that Jesus is the Lord, but by the Holy Ghost (First Corinthians 12:3).

I see the dew of the Spirit. The Holy Ghost sets us apart for God. It brings the blessing of divine order, an ability to crown Jesus King. Then there is the sealing of the Spirit. This great spiritual adjustment gives us the knowledge of the revelation of Jesus as King over all—over our affections, our desires, and our wishes.

When the King is crowned, what tremendous things we find pertaining to the flesh—perpetual divine motion, the power of God sweeping through the regions of weakness. We have new life flowing through us. All the Word of God is yea and amen in faith. Divine actions in the flesh seem mighty and so full of operation until we see God working. Nothing can interfere with the progress of God, the author and finisher of our faith, and no man can call Jesus Lord but in the Holy Ghost.

Don't be fearful. He wants to make us strong, powerful, loyal, and resolute, so that we can rest upon the authority of God. It is only on this line that I can speak. We have seen the King; we have been quickened from death. God has worked special miracles in us all. We are made with one great design and purpose. He has set His seal upon our hearts, so that we might know the hope of our calling and live unto the praise of His glory. Hallelujah!

Ye were sealed with that holy Spirit of promise, which is the earnest of our inheritance until the redemption of the purchased possession, unto the praise of his glory (Ephesians 1:13-14).

GOD WILL VINDICATE YOU

In the world ye shall have tribulation: but be of good cheer; I have overcome the world (John 16:33).

How is it that the moment you are filled with the Holy Ghost that persecution starts? It was so with the Lord Jesus Himself. We do not read of any persecutions before the Holy Spirit came down like a dove upon Him. Shortly after this we find that after preaching in His hometown they wanted to throw Him over the brow of a hill. It was the same with the twelve disciples. They had no persecution before the day of Pentecost, but after they were filled with the Spirit they were soon in prison. The devil and the priests of religion will always get stirred when a man is filled with the Spirit and does things in the power of the Spirit. And persecution is the greatest blessing to a church. When we have persecution we will have purity. If you desire to be filled with the Spirit, you can count on one thing, and that is persecution. The Lord came to bring division, and even in your own household you may find three against two.

The Lord Jesus came to bring peace, but as soon as you get peace within, you get persecution without. If you remain stationary, the devil and his agents will not disturb you much. But when you press on and go the whole length with God, the enemy has you as a target. But God will vindicate you in the midst of the whole thing. In this life, the Lord puts you in all sorts of places and then reveals His power. Will you let Him have your will; will you let Him have you? If you will, all His power is at your disposal.

Living Flames

[Jesus] *saith..."Be not afraid, only believe"* (Mark 5:36).

The people in whom God delights are the ones who rest upon His Word without wavering. God has nothing for the man who wavers, for "let him that wavereth expect nothing from God." I would like us, therefore, to get this verse deep down into our hearts, until it penetrates every fiber of our being: "Only believe! *All things are possible—only believe.*"

He has a plan for every individual life, and if we have any other plan in view, *we miss the grandest plan of all!* Nothing of the past is equal to the present, and nothing of the present can equal the things of tomorrow, for tomorrow should be so filled with holy expectation that we will be living flames for Him. God never intended His people to be ordinary or commonplace; His intentions were that they should be on fire for Him, conscious of His divine power, realizing the glory of the cross that foreshadows the crown.

This is the heritage of the Church—to be so endued with power that God can lay His hand upon any member at any time to do His perfect will. There is no stop in the Spirit-filled life: we begin at the cross, the place of ignominy, shame, and death, and that very death brings the power of resurrection life; and, being filled with Holy Spirit, we go on "from glory to glory." Let us not forget that possessing the baptism in the Holy Spirit means there must be an "ever-increasing" holiness. How the Church needs divine unction—God's presence and power so manifest that the world will know it. When you are filled with the Holy Ghost, you will know when the tide is flowing and when it is ebbing. Have you received the Holy Ghost since you believed? Are you filled with divine power?

CHOSEN FOR ORDINARY SERVICE

And in those days, when the number of the disciples was multiplied, there arose a murmuring of the Grecians against the Hebrews, because their widows were neglected in the daily ministration. Then the twelve called the multitude of the disciples unto them, and said...Look ye out among you seven men of honest report, full of the Holy Ghost and wisdom, whom we may appoint over this business... (Acts 6:1-3).

During the time of the inauguration of the Church, the disciples were hard pressed on all lines; the things of natural order could not be attended to and many were complaining concerning the neglect of the widows in their midst. The disciples therefore decided upon a plan to choose seven men to do the work—men who were "full of the Holy Ghost." What a divine thought! No matter what kind of work was to be done, however menial it may have been, the person chosen must be filled with the Holy Ghost. The plan of the Church was that everything, even of natural order, must be sanctified unto God, for the Church had to be a Holy Ghost church. Beloved, God has never ordained anything less!

The necessity that seven men be chosen for the position of "serving tables" was very evident. The disciples knew that these seven men were *men ready for active service,* and so they chose them. Beloved, are you full of the Holy Ghost and ready for active service? Are you filled with divine power?

Be Vigilant

And the saying pleased the whole multitude: and they chose Stephen, a man full of faith and of the Holy Ghost, and Philip... (Acts 6:5).

There were others chosen to care for the widows, of course, but Stephen and Philip stand out most prominently in the Scriptures. Philip was a man so filled with the Holy Ghost that a revival always followed wherever he went. Stephen was a man so filled with divine power that, although serving tables might have been all right in the minds of the other disciples, God had yet a greater vision for him—*a baptism of fire,* of power, and of divine unction that took him on and on to the climax of his life until he saw right into the open heavens.

Had we been there with the disciples at that time, I believe we should have heard men saying to each other, "Look here! Neither Stephen nor Philip are doing the work we called them to. If they do not attend to business, we shall have to get someone else!" That was the *natural* way of thinking, but divine order is far above our finite planning. When we please God in our daily ministration, we shall always find in operation the fact "that everyone who is faithful in little, God will make faithful in much." We have such an example right here. Stephen was a man chosen to serve tables, but he had such a revelation of the mind of Christ, and of the depth and height of God, that there was no stop in his experience but a going forward with leaps and bounds. Beloved, there is a race to be run; there is a crown to be won. *We cannot stand still!* I say unto you: be vigilant! Be vigilant! Let no man take your crown!

LIVING ABOVE ORDINARY

And Stephen, full of faith and power, did great wonders and miracles among the people (Acts 6:8).

God has privileged us in Christ Jesus to live above the ordinary human plane of life. Those who want to be ordinary, and live on a lower plane, can do so; but as for me, *I will not!* For the same unction, the same zeal, the same Holy Ghost power that was at the command of Stephen and the apostles is at our command. We have the same God that Abraham had, that Elijah had, and we need not come behind in any gift or grace. We may not possess the gifts as abiding gifts, but as we are full of the Holy Ghost and divine unction, it is possible when there is need for God to manifest every gift of the Spirit through us. As I have already said, I do not mean by this that we should necessarily possess the gifts permanently, but there should be a manifestation of the gifts as God may choose to use us.

This *ordinary* man became mighty under the Holy Ghost anointing, until he stood supreme, in many ways, among the apostles. As we go deeper in God, He enlarges our conception and places before us a wide-open door. I am not surprised that this man chosen to serve tables was afterwards called to a higher plane. "What do you mean?" you may ask. "Did he quit this service?" No! But he was lost in the power of God. He lost sight of everything in the natural and steadfastly fixed his gaze upon Jesus, "the author and finisher of our faith," until he was transformed into a shining light in the Kingdom of God. Oh, that we might be awakened to believe His Word, to understand the mind of the Spirit, for there is an inner place of whiteness and purity where we can "see God."

Dare to Believe Christ

Then there arose certain of the synagogue, which is called the synagogue of the Libertines, and Cyrenians, and Alexandrians...disputing with Stephen. And they were not able to resist the wisdom and the spirit by which he spake (Acts 6:9-10).

As you go on in this life of the Spirit, you will find that the devil will begin to get restless and there will be a stir in the synagogue; it was so with Stephen. Any number of people may be found in the "synagogue," who are very proper in the worldly sense—always correctly dressed, the elite of the land, welcoming into the church everything but the power of God.

"The Libertines" could not stand the truth of God. With these opponents, Stephen found himself in the same predicament as the blind man whom Jesus healed. As soon as the blind man's eyes were opened, they shut him out of the synagogue. They will not have anybody in the "synagogue" with their eyes open. As soon as you receive spiritual eyesight, out you go! These Libertines, Cyrenians, and Alexandrians rose up full of wrath in the very place where they should have been full of the power of God, full of divine love, and full of reverence for the Holy Ghost. They rose up against Stephen, this man "full of the Holy Ghost."

Stephen was just as ordinary a man as you and me, but he was in the place where God could so move upon him that he, in turn, could move all before him. He began in a most humble place, and ended in a blaze of glory. Beloved, dare to believe Christ!

Do Not Resist the Holy Spirit

And they were not able to resist the wisdom and the spirit by which he spake (Acts 6:10).

Something had happened in the life of Stephen, chosen for menial service, and he became *mighty for God*. How was it accomplished in him? It was because his aim was high; faithful in little, God brought him to full fruition. Under the inspiration of divine power by which he spoke, they could not but listen—even the angels listened, as he spoke before that council with holy, prophetic utterances. As light upon light, truth upon truth, and revelation upon revelation found their way into their calloused hearts, they gazed at him in astonishment. Perhaps, at times, their hearts became warm and they may have said, "Truly, this man is sent of God."

Stephen spoke with marked wisdom; where he was, things began to move. You will find that there is always movement when the Holy Spirit has control. People were brought under conviction by the message of Stephen, but they resisted. They did anything and everything to stifle that conviction. Not only did they lie, but they got others to lie against this man who would have laid down his life for any one of them. Stephen was used to heal the sick, perform miracles, and yet they brought false accusations against him.

Beloved, if there is anything in your life that in any way resists the power of the Holy Ghost and the entrance of His Word into your heart and life, *drop on your knees and **cry aloud** for mercy*! When the Spirit of God is brooding over your heart's door, do not resist Him. Open your heart to the touch of God. There is a resisting "unto blood" when you are striving *against sin*, and there is a resisting of the Holy Ghost that will drive you *into sin*.

PRICKED TO THE HEART

…We have heard him speak blasphemous words against Moses, and against God (Acts 6:11).

Stephen's accusers could not dispute his ministry, but they still brought public accusations against him. The Holy Ghost always brings persecution. Beginning with Abraham and Moses, Stephen unfolded the truth to his accusers. What a marvelous exhortation! Take your Bibles and read Acts 7. Listen in as the angels listened in. Here is Stephen, speaking under the inspiration of the Holy Ghost, and the men of this council, being "pricked to the heart," rise up as one man to slay him. From his place of helplessness, Stephen looked up and said:

…Behold, I see the heavens opened, and the Son of man standing on the right hand of God (Acts 7:56).

Is that the position that Jesus went to take? No! He went to "sit" at the right hand of the Father, but on behalf of the *first martyr*, the man with that burning flame of Holy Ghost power, God's Son *stood up* in honorary testimony of him who, called to serve tables, was faithful unto death. But is that all? No! I am so glad that it is not all. As the stones came flying at Stephen, pounding his body, crashing into his bones, striking his temple, mangling his beautiful face, what happened? How did this scene end? With that sublime, upward look, this man—chosen for an ordinary task but filled with the Holy Ghost—was so moved upon by God that he finished his earthly work in a blaze of glory, magnifying God with his last breath. Looking up into the face of the Master, he said: *Lord Jesus, forgive them!* "…Lay not this sin to their charge. And when he had said this, he fell asleep" (Acts 7:60).

Friends, it is worth dying a thousand deaths to gain that spirit. My God! What a divine ending to the life and testimony of a man who was chosen to serve tables.

CHILDREN OF GOD

Behold, what manner of love the Father hath bestowed upon us, that we should be called the sons of God... (First John 3:1).

God does not dwell in temples made by hands but in poor and contrite hearts. God is a Spirit, and they that worship Him must worship Him in spirit and in truth, for the Father seeks such to worship Him. The Church is the body of Christ; its worship is heart worship, a longing to come into the Presence of God. He wants us to come to a place of undisturbed rest and peace; only simplicity will bring us there. Jesus said, when He uplifted the baby, "Except you become as little children, you shall in no wise enter the Kingdom of Heaven" (see Matt. 18:2-3). It is not to have the child's mind, but the child's spirit—meekness, gentleness. It is the only place to meet God. He will give us that place of worship.

How my heart cries out for a deep vision of God. The world cannot produce it. We long for a place where we see the Lord, where we know God hears us. We have no fear, just living faith, and we come into the presence of God believing for an answer. In His Presence is fullness of joy, and at His right hand are pleasures for evermore (see Ps. 16:11). God is looking for a people to whom He can reveal Himself.

Sons of God with Power

Beloved, now are we the sons of God, and it doth not yet appear what we shall be: but we know that, when he shall appear, we shall be like him; for we shall see him as he is (First John 3:2).

If you believe, you can be sons of God—in likeness, character, spirit, longings, acts, until all will know you are a son of God. The Spirit of God can change our nature. God is Creator—His Word is creative, and as you believe, a creative power is changing your whole nature. You can reach this altitude only by faith. No man can keep himself. The Almighty God spreads His covering over you and says, "I am able to do all things; and all things are possible to him that believeth."

The old nature is so difficult to manage. You have been ashamed of it many a time, but the Lord Himself will come. He says, "Come unto Me, and I will give thee rest, peace, strength. I will change you, I will operate upon you by My power making you a new creation, if you will believe."

Take your burden to the Lord and leave it there. "Learn of Me; for I am meek and lowly in heart: and ye shall find rest unto your souls" (Matt. 11:29). The world has no rest, for it is full of trouble; but in Him is peace that passes understanding. His inward flow of divine power changes our nature until we can live, move, and act in the power of God.

A KEEN CONSCIENCE

And every man that hath this hope in him purifieth himself, even as he is pure (First John 3:3).

Wherever Jesus went, sin was revealed, and men didn't like sin revealed. You are in a good place when you weep before God and repent over the least thing. If you have spoken unkindly, you realize it was not like the Lord. Your keen conscience has taken you to prayer. It is a wonderful thing to have a keen conscience. It is when we are close to God that our hearts are revealed. God intends us to live in purity seeing Him all the time.

If there is anything wrong, come to the Blood. "If we walk in the light, as He is in the light, we have fellowship one with another, and the blood of Jesus Christ his son cleanseth us from all sin" (1 John 1:7). Jesus was manifested to destroy the works of the devil. We can come into a new experience of God, where God creates in our hearts such a love for Jesus that we are living in a new realm—Sons of God with power, filled with all the fullness of God.

Brothers, sisters, it is vital that we keep pure hearts before God. Purify yourselves and see the face of God. He greatly desires to draw near to you, but you must first purify your heart and your hands.

Create in me a clean heart, O God; and renew a right spirit within me. Cast me not away from thy presence; and take not thy holy spirit from me (Psalm 51:10-11).

UNDISTURBED REST AND PEACE

God is a Spirit: and they that worship him must worship him in spirit and in truth (John 4:24).

We are glad of cathedrals and churches, but God does not dwell in temples made by hands but in the fleshly tables of the heart. Here is true worship. God is a Spirit, and they that worship Him must worship Him in spirit and in truth, for the Father seeks such to worship Him. The Church is the body of Christ. Its worship is heart worship, a longing to come into the Presence of God. He wants us to come to a place of undisturbed rest and peace; only simplicity will bring us there.

Beloved, let us enter into the Sabbath rest of God, for He has made a way for us to receive peace and rest. Draw near to God, and He will draw near to you.

For if Jesus had given them rest, then would he not afterward have spoken of another day. There remaineth therefore a rest to the people of God. For he that is entered into his rest, he also hath ceased from his own works, as God did from his. Let us labour therefore to enter into that rest, lest any man fall after the same example of unbelief (Hebrews 4:8-11).

He longs to show you lovingkindness. And when you are firmly established in His peace, nothing can disturb you. Nothing can cause you a moment's anxiety or fear, because you are at rest in your faith. There is no striving, no worry, no apprehension. No, in the presence of God is fullness of peace, rest, and joy.

Sin Makes a Man Weak

If we walk in the light, as He is in the light, we have fellowship one with another, and the blood of Jesus Christ his Son cleanseth us from all sin (First John 1:7).

The world does not know us, but we are sons of God with power. No man that sins has power.

Remember this—sin dethrones, but purity strengthens. Temptation is not sin, but the devil is a liar and tries to take away our peace. You must live in the Word of God. There is now no condemnation. Who can condemn you? Christ has died. He won't condemn you. He died to save you. Don't condemn yourself. If there is anything wrong, come to the Blood. Jesus was manifested to destroy the works of the devil. We can come into a new experience of God where God creates in our hearts such a love for Jesus that we are living in a new realm—sons of God with power, filled with all the fullness of God.

This is our inheritance through the blood of Jesus—life forevermore. Believe and the Lord will transmit life through you, that you may be waiting for His coming and witnessing unto Him.

The baptism is the last thing. If you do not get this, you are living in a weak and impoverished condition that is no good to yourself or anybody else. Never live in a place less than where God has called you to, and He has called you up on high to live with Him. God has designed that everything shall be subject to man. Through Christ He has given you power over all the power of the enemy.

No Condemnation in Christ

There is therefore now no condemnation to them which are in Christ Jesus, who walk not after the flesh, but after the Spirit. For the law of the Spirit of life in Christ Jesus hath made me free from the law of sin and death (Romans 8:1-2).

God wants us to be holy. He wants us to be filled with a power that keeps us holy. He wants us to have a revelation of what sin and death are, and what the Spirit and the life of the Spirit are.

If you are without condemnation you are in a place where you can pray through—where you have a revelation of Christ. For Him to be in you brings you to a place where you cannot but follow the divine leadings of the Spirit of Christ and where you have no fellowship with the world. I want you to see that the Spirit of the Lord would reveal this fact unto us: if you love the world, you cannot love God, and the love of God cannot be in you. So God wants a straight cut. Why does God want a straight cut? Because if you are "in Christ," you are a "new creation." You are in Him; you belong to a new creation in the Spirit. You walk, therefore, in the Spirit and are free from condemnation.

So the Spirit of the Lord wants you without condemnation, and He desires to bring you into revelation. God wants all His people to be targets, to be lights, to be like cities set on a hill that cannot be hid, to be so "in God" for the world's redemption that the world may know that you belong to God. That is the law of the Spirit.

THE LAW OF THE SPIRIT OF LIFE

I thank God through Jesus Christ our Lord. So then with the mind I myself serve the law of God; but with the flesh the law of sin (Romans 7:25).

What will the law of the Spirit do? The law of the Spirit of life in Christ Jesus will make you free from the law of sin and death. Sin will have no dominion over you. You will have no desire to sin, and it will be as true in your case as it was in Jesus's when He said: "Satan cometh, but findeth nothing in Me" (see John 14:30). He cannot condemn; he has no power. His power is destroyed in the tenth verse. What does it say? "…The body is dead because of sin; but the Spirit is life because of righteousness" (Rom. 8:10). To be "filled with God" means that you are free—full of joy, peace, blessing, endowment, strength of character, molded afresh in God, and transformed by His mighty power till you *live*. Yet it is not you, but another lives in you, and He is manifesting His power through you as sons of God.

Notice these two laws: the law of the Spirit of life in Christ Jesus making you free from the law of sin and death. The same law is in you as was in you before, but it is dead. You are just the same man, only quickened—the same flesh, but it is dead. You are a new creation—a new creature. You are created in God afresh after the image of Christ. Now, beloved, some people come into line with this but do not understand their inheritance and go down; but instead of being weak and going down, you have to rise triumphantly.

God wants to show you that there is a place where you can live in the Spirit and not be subject to the flesh. Live in the Spirit till sin has no dominion. Sin reigns unto death; but Christ reigns, and so we reign in Christ, over sin and death (see Rom. 5:20-21). Beloved, we are reigning in life.

BLESSED REDEMPTION

For what the law could not do, in that it was weak through the flesh, God sending his own Son in the likeness of sinful flesh, and for sin, condemned sin in the flesh: that the righteousness of the law might be fulfilled in us, who walk not after the flesh, but after the Spirit (Romans 8:3-4).

You have to reign. God made you like Himself, and Jesus bought back for us in the Garden of Gethsemane everything that was lost in the Garden of Eden, and He restored it to us in His agony. He bought that blessed redemption. When I think of redemption, I wonder if there is anything greater than the Garden of Eden, when Adam and Eve had fellowship with God, and He came down and walked with them in the cool of the evening. Is there anything greater?

Yes, redemption is greater. How? Anything that is local is never so great. When God was in the Garden, Adam was local. But the moment a man is born again, he is free and lives in heavenly places. He has no destination except the glory. Redemption is greater than the Garden, and God wants you to come into this glorious redemption, not only for the salvation of your soul, but also for your body—to know that it is redeemed from the curse of the law, to know that you have been made free, to know that God's Son has set you free. Hallelujah! Free from the law of sin and death!

I tell you there is redemption. There is atonement in Christ—a personality of Christ to dwell in you. There is a God-likeness for you to attain to—a blessed resemblance of Christ in you, if you will believe the Word of God.

THE LIVING WORD OF GOD

For the law of the Spirit of life in Christ Jesus hath made me free from the law of sin and death (Romans 8:2).

The Word is sufficient for you. Eat it; devour it. It is the living Word of God. Jesus was manifested to destroy the works of the devil. God so manifested His fullness in Jesus that He walked this earth glorified and filled with God.

In the first place, Jesus was with God and was called "the Word." Their cooperation in oneness was so manifest that there was nothing done without the other. They cooperated in the working of power. You must see that before the foundation of the world this plan of redemption was all completed and set in order before the fall.

Notice that this redemption had to be so mighty, and to redeem us all so perfectly, that there should be no lack in the whole redemption. You are born of an incorruptible power—the power of God's Word—by His personality and His nature. You are begotten of God and are not your own. You are now incarnated. You can believe that you have passed from death unto life and become an heir of God, a joint-heir with Christ, in the measure that you believe His Word. The natural flesh has been changed for a new order; the first order was the natural Adamic order, the last order is Christ—the heavenly order.

And now you become changed by a heavenly power existing in an earthly body; a power that can never die. It can never see corruption, and it cannot be lost. If you are born of God, you are born of the power of the Word and not of man. You are born of a power that exists in you, a power of which God took and made the world that you are in. It is the law of the Spirit of life in Christ Jesus that makes us free from the law of sin and death. Did you accept it?

NOTHING BUT THE BLOOD OF JESUS

...and the blood of Jesus Christ his Son cleanseth us from all sin (First John 1:7).

There is no power that can convert men except the power of the blood of Jesus. Men try without it; science tries without it; all have tried without it; but all are left shaking on the brink of hell—without it. Nothing can deliver you but the blood of the Lamb. Free from the law of sin and death by the Spirit of life in Christ Jesus (see Rom. 8:2). Clean hearts and pure lives.

Brothers, the carnal life is not subject to the will of God, neither can it be. Carnality is selfishness—uncleanness. It cannot be subject to God. Flesh will not believe. It interferes with you. It binds and keeps you in bondage. But, beloved, God destroys carnality. He destroys the work of the flesh. How? By a new life that is so much better, by a peace that passes all understanding, by a joy that is unspeakable and full of glory.

Everything that God does is too big to tell. It cannot be told. His grace is too big. His love is too big. Why, it takes all heaven. His salvation is too big to be told. One cannot understand. It is so vast, mighty, and wonderful—so "in God." God gives us the power to understand it. Yes, of course, He does. Do you not know that ours is an abundant God? His love is far and above all that we could ask or think (see Eph. 3:20). Hear! After you were illuminated—Glory to God—you were quickened by the Spirit. Now we are looking forward to a day of rapture when we will be caught up and lifted into the presence of God.

THE SAME QUICKENING SPIRIT

But if the Spirit of him that raised up Jesus from the dead dwell in you, he that raised up Christ from the dead shall also quicken your mortal bodies... (Romans 8:11).

Christ Jesus has borne the cross for us—there is no need for us to bear it. He has borne the curse, for "cursed is every one that hangeth on a tree" (Gal. 3:13). The curse covered everything. When Christ was in the grave, the Word says that He was raised from the grave by the operation of God through the Spirit. The Spirit quickened Him in the grave, and so the same Spirit dwelling in you shall quicken your mortal bodies. Jesus rose by the quickening power of the Holy Ghost. He will also quicken your mortal body.

If you will allow Jesus to have control of your bodies, you will find that His Spirit will quicken you, will loose you; He will show you that it is the mortal body that has to be quickened. Talk about divine healing! Everyone who is healed by the power of God—especially believers—will find their healing an incentive to make them purer and holier. If healing were only to make you whole, it would be worth nothing. Divine healing is a divine act of the providence of God coming into your mortal bodies and touching them with almightiness. Could you remain the same? No. The moment you yield yourself, the Bible becomes a new Book; it becomes revelation, so that we have the fullness of redemption going right through our bodies in every way until we are filled with all the fullness of the Godhead.

Filled with God! Yes, filled with God,
Pardoned and cleansed and filled with God.
Filled with God! Yes, filled with God,
Emptied of self and filled with God!

DEAD TO SELF

...I die daily (First Corinthians 15:31).

A young monk came one day to his father superior and asked: "Father, what is it to be dead to self?" The father replied: "I cannot explain it now; but I have a duty for you to perform. Brother Martin died last week and is buried in the churchyard of our order. Go to his grave, standing close beside it, repeat in a loud voice all the good things you ever heard of him. After this, say all the flattering things you can invent; and attribute to him every saintly grace and virtue, without regard to truth; and report the result to me."

The young monk went to do his bidding, wondering what all this could mean. Soon he returned and the father asked him what had transpired. "Why, nothing," replied the young man. "I did as you told me and that was all." Did Brother Martin make no reply?" asked the superior. "Of course he did not, for he was dead," said the monk. The elder shook his head thoughtfully, saying: "That is very strange. Go again tomorrow at the same hour, and repeat at the graveside all the evil you ever heard concerning Brother Martin. Add to that the worst slander and character assassination your mind can imagine and report the result to me."

Again the young man obeyed and brought back the same report. He had heaped unlimited abuse on the head of Brother Martin and yet had received no reply. "From Brother Martin you may learn," said the father, "what it is to be dead to self. Neither flattery nor abuse has moved him, for he is dead. So the disciple who is dead to self will be insensible to these things, hearing neither voice of praise nor retaliation. All personal feeling will be lost in the service of Christ."

SATISFIED BY GOD

Thou wilt shew me the path of life: in thy presence is fullness of joy; at thy right hand there are pleasures for evermore (Psalm 16:11).

Some people only come with a very small thought concerning God's fullness, and a lot of people are satisfied with a thimbleful, and you can just imagine God saying, "Oh, if they only knew how much they could take away!" Other people come with a larger vessel, and they go away satisfied, but you can feel how much God is longing for us to have such a desire for more, such a longing as only God Himself can satisfy.

I suppose you women would have a good idea of what I mean from the illustration of a screaming child being taken about from one to another, but who is never satisfied till it gets to the bosom of its mother. You will find that there is no peace, no help, no source of strength, no power, no life, nothing can satisfy the cry of the child of God but the Word of God. God has a special way of satisfying the cry of His children. He is waiting to open to us the windows of heaven, until He has so moved in the depths of our hearts that everything unlike Him has been destroyed. There need no one in this place go away dry, dry. God wants you to be filled.

My brother, my sister, God wants you today to be like a watered garden, filled with the fragrance of His own heavenly joy, till you know at last you have touched immensity. The Son of God came for no other purpose than to lift and lift, and mold and fashion and remold, until we are just after His mind.

STREAMS OF LIFE

There is a river, the streams whereof shall make glad the city of God, the holy place of the tabernacles of the most High (Psalm 46:4).

May God save me from ever wanting anything less than a flood. I will not stoop for small things when I have such a big God. Through the blood of Christ's atonement we may have riches and riches. We need the warming atmosphere of the Spirit's power to bring us closer and closer until nothing but God can satisfy, and then we may have some idea of what God has left after we have taken all that we can. It is only like a sparrow taking a drink of the ocean and then looking around and saying, "What a vast ocean! What a lot more I could have taken if I had only had room."

Don't you know that you could be dying of thirst right in a river of plenty? There was once a vessel in the mouth of the Amazon River. They thought they were still in the ocean, and they were dying of thirst, some of them nearly mad. They saw a ship and asked if they would give them some water, for some of them were dying of thirst, and they replied, "Dip your bucket right over; you are in the mouth of the river." There are people today in the midst of a great river of life, but they are dying of thirst, because they do not dip down and take it. Dear brother, you may have the Word, but you need an awakened spirit. The Word is not alive until the Spirit of God moves upon it, and in the right sense it becomes Spirit and life when His hand alone touches it.

Oh, beloved, there is a stream that makes glad the city of God. There is a stream of life that makes everything move. There is a touch of divine life and likeness through the Word of God that comes nowhere else. There is a death that has no life in it; and there is death-likeness in Christ that is full of life.

WRESTLING WITH GOD

And Jacob was left alone; and there wrestled a man with him until the breaking of the day. And when he saw that he prevailed not against him, he touched the hollow of his thigh; and the hollow of Jacob's thigh was out of joint, as he wrestled with him. And he said, Let me go, for the day breaketh. And he said, I will not let thee go, except thou bless me. And he said unto him, What is thy name? And he said, Jacob. And he said, Thy name shall be called no more Jacob, but Israel: for as a prince hast thou power with God and with men, and hast prevailed. ...And he blessed him there. And Jacob called the name of the place Peniel: for I have seen God face to face, and my life is preserved (Genesis 32:24-30).

The next morning as the sun rose, Jacob "...halted upon his thigh" (Gen. 32:31). You may ask, "What is the use of a lame man?" It is those who have seen the face of God and have been broken by Him, who can meet the forces of the enemy and break down the bulwarks of satan's kingdom. The Word declares, "...the lame take the prey" (Isa. 33:23). On that day Jacob was brought to a place of dependence upon God.

Oh, the blessedness of being brought into a life of dependence upon the power of the Holy Spirit. Henceforth we know that we are nothing without Him; we are absolutely dependent upon Him. I am absolutely nothing without the power and unction of the Holy Ghost. Oh, for a life of absolute dependence! Through a life of dependence there is a life of power. If you are not there, get alone with God. If need be, spend a whole night alone with God, and let Him change and transform you. Never let Him go until He blesses you, until He makes you an Israel, a prince with God.

Jacob's Blessing

I will not let thee go, except thou bless me (Genesis 32:26).

When you get alone with God, what a place of revelation it is. What a revelation of self we receive. And then what a revelation of the provision made for us at Calvary. It is here that we get a revelation of a life crucified with Christ, buried with Him, raised with Him, transformed by Christ, and empowered by the Spirit. Oh, that we might spend all nights alone with God! We are occupied too much with the things of time and sense. We need to spend time alone in the presence of God. We need to give God much time in order to receive new revelations from Him. We need to get past all the thoughts of earthly matters that crowd in so rapidly. It takes God time to deal with us. If He would only deal with us as He dealt with Jacob, then we should have power with Him and prevail.

Jacob deceived his brother Esau out of his birthright. Esau was furious and vowed to kill Jacob, so Jacob fled in fear of his life. Jacob was not dry-eyed the night he returned. Hosea tells us, "...he wept, and made supplication..." (Hos. 12:4). He knew that he had been a disappointment to the Lord, that he had been a groveler, but in the revelation he received that night he saw the possibility of being transformed from a supplanter to a prince with God. Jacob knew that if God went without blessing him, Esau could not be met. You cannot meet the terrible things that await you in the world unless you secure the blessing of God.

You must never let go. Whatever you are seeking—a fresh revelation, light on the path, some particular thing—never let go. Victory is yours if you are earnest enough. If you are in darkness, if you need a fresh revelation, if your mind needs relief, if there are problems you cannot solve, lay hold of God and declare, "I will not let thee go, except thou bless me" (Gen. 32:26).

THE BENEFIT OF BLESSING

And he said, Thy name shall be called no more Jacob, but Israel: for as a prince hast thou power with God and with men, and hast prevailed (Genesis 32:28).

God means to have people who are broken. The divine power can only come when there is an end of our own self-sufficiency. But when we are broken, we must hold fast. If we let go then we shall fall short.

Jacob cried, "...I will not let thee go, except thou bless me...." And God blessed him, saying, "...Thy name shall be called no more Jacob, but Israel: for as a prince hast thou power with God and with men, and hast prevailed" (Gen. 32:28). Now a new order begins. The old supplanter has passed away, there is a new creation: Jacob the supplanter has been transformed into Israel the prince.

When God comes into your life, you will find Him enough. As Israel came forth, the sun rose upon him, and he had power over all the things of the world and power over Esau. Esau met him, but there was no fight now; there was reconciliation. They kissed each other. How true it is, "When a man's ways please the Lord, he maketh even his enemies to be at peace with him" (Prov. 16:7). Esau inquired, "What about all these cattle, Jacob?"

"Oh, that's a present."

"Oh, I have plenty; I don't want your cattle. What a joy to see your face again!"

What a wonderful change! The material things did not count for much after the night of revelation. Who worked the change? God.

INTO THE ORBIT OF
HIS OWN PERFECT WILL

For it is God which worketh in you both to will and to do of his good pleasure (Philippians 2:13).

Can you hold on to God, as did Jacob? You certainly can if you are sincere, if you are dependent, if you are broken, if you are weak. It is when you are weak that you are strong (see 2 Cor. 12:10). But if you are self-righteous, if you are proud, if you are high-minded, if you are puffed up in your own imagination, you can receive nothing from Him. If you become lukewarm instead of being at white heat, you can become a disappointment to God. And He says, "...I will spue thee out of my mouth" (Rev. 3:16).

But there is a place of holiness, a place of meekness, a place of faith, where you can call to God, "I will not let thee go, except thou bless me" (Gen. 32:26). And in response, He will bless you exceedingly abundantly above all you ask or think.

Sometimes we are tempted to think that He has left us. Oh, no. He has promised never to leave us, and He will not fail. Jacob held on until the blessing came. We can do the same.

If God does not help us, we are no good for this world's need. We are no longer salt; we lose our savor. But as we spend time alone with God, and cry to Him to bless us, He re-salts us and re-empowers us; but He brings us to brokenness and moves us into the orbit of His own perfect will. Oh, the blessedness of being brought into a life of dependence upon the power of the Holy Spirit. It is through a life of dependence that you find a life of power. If you are not there, get alone with God. If need be, spend a whole night alone with God and let Him change and transform you. Never let Him go until He blesses you, until He makes you an Israel, a prince with God.

THE POWER OF THE BLOOD

Beloved, believe not every spirit, but try the spirits whether they are of God... (First John 4:1).

Beloved, you have to be in a position to test the spirits to determine whether they are of God. Why should we test them? You can always test the spirits for this reason—so you will be able to tell the true revelation, and the true revelation that will come to you will always sanctify the heart; it will never have an *if* in it. When the devil came to Jesus, he had an *if. If* thou be the Son of God; *if* thou wilt worship me. The Holy Ghost never comes with an *if.* The Holy Ghost is the divine orator of this wonderful Word.

Take your position in the first epistle of John and declare, "...greater is he that is in [me], than he that is in the world" (1 John 4:4). Then recognize that it is not yourself that has to deal with the power of the devil, but the Greater One who is in you. Oh, what it means to be filled with Him. You can do nothing of yourself, but He that is in you will win the victory. Your being has become the temple of the Spirit. Your mouth, your mind, your whole being becomes exercised and worked upon by the Spirit of God.

You cannot get near God but by the blood; it is impossible. The blood is the only power that can make a clear road into the Kingdom for you. It is the blood of Jesus.

Oh, thank God for Jesus. I want you to notice that Jesus wants you to be so under His power, so controlled by and filled with the Holy Ghost, that the power of authority in you will resent all evil. Every believer should reach a place in the Holy Ghost where he has no desire except the desire of God. The Holy Ghost has to possess us till we are filled and led—yes, divinely led by the Holy Ghost. It is a mighty thing to be filled with the Holy Ghost.

A LIFE OF LOVE AND LIBERTY

Therefore leaving the principles of the doctrine of Christ, let us go on unto perfection; not laying again the foundation of repentance from dead works, and of faith toward God, of the doctrine of baptisms, and of laying on of hands, and of resurrection of the dead, and of eternal judgment (Hebrews 6:1-2).

What would you think of a builder who was continually pulling down his house and putting in fresh foundations? Never look back if you want the power of God in your life. You will find out that in the measure you have allowed yourself to look back you have missed what God had for you. The Holy Ghost shows us that we must never look back to the law of sin and death from which we have been delivered. God has brought us into a new order of things, a life of love and liberty in Christ Jesus that is beyond all human comprehension.

Many are brought into this new life through the power of the Spirit of God, and then, like the Galatians who ran well at the beginning, they try to perfect themselves on the lines of legalism. They go back from the life in the Spirit to a life on natural lines. God is not pleased with this, for He has no place for the man who has lost the vision. The only thing to do is to repent. Don't try to cover up anything. If you have been tripped up on any line, confess it out, and then look to God to bring you to a place of stability of faith where your whole walk will be in the Spirit.

Take the place of knowing that you are a son of God and remember that, as your hope is set in Christ, it should have a purifying effect on your life. The Holy Spirit says, "Whosoever is born of God doth not commit sin; for His seed remaineth in him: and he cannot sin, because he is born of God" (1 John 3:9). There is life and power in the seed of the Word that is implanted within.

POWER IN THE WORD OF GOD

Whosoever is born of God doth not commit sin; for his seed remaineth in him: and he cannot sin, because he is born of God (First John 3:9).

As your hope is set in Christ it should have a purifying effect on your life. There is life and power in the seed of the Word that is implanted within. God is in that "cannot," and there is more power in that Word of His than in any human objections. God's thought for every one of us is that we shall reign in life by Jesus Christ.

We cannot be to the praise of His glory until we are ready for trials and are able to triumph in them. We cannot get away from the fact that sin came in by nature, but God comes into our nature and puts it into the place of death, that the Spirit of God may come into the temple in all His power and liberty, so that right here in this present evil world satan may be dethroned by the believer.

Satan is always endeavoring to bring the saints of God into disrepute, bringing against them railing accusations, but the Holy Ghost never comes with condemnation. He always reveals the blood of Christ. He always brings us help. The Lord Jesus referred to Him as the Comforter who would come. He is always on hand to help in the seasons of trial and test. The Holy Ghost is the lifting power of the Church of Christ. And Paul tells us that we "…are manifestly declared to be the epistle of Christ…written not with ink, but with the Spirit of the living God; not in tables of stone, but in fleshy tables of the heart" (2 Cor. 3:3). The Holy Ghost begins in the heart, right in the depths of human affections. He brings into the heart the riches of the revelation of Christ, implanting a purity and holiness there, so that out of its depths praises well up continually.

INTO THE PLACE OF SONSHIP

Finally, brethren, whatsoever things are true, whatsoever things are honest, whatsoever things are just, whatsoever things are pure, whatsoever things are lovely, whatsoever things are of good report; if there be any virtue, and if there be any praise, think on these things (Philippians 4:8).

In this new life in the Spirit, in this new covenant life, you love the things that are right and pure and holy, and you shudder at all things that are wrong. Jesus was able to say, "...the prince of this world cometh, and hath nothing in me" (John 14:30). And the moment we are filled with the Spirit of God we are brought into like wonderful condition, and as we continue to be filled with the Spirit, the enemy cannot have an inch of territory in us.

Do you not believe that you can be so filled with the Spirit that a man who is not living right can be judged and convicted by your presence? As we go on in the life of the Spirit, it will be said of us, "In whose eyes a vile person is contemned..." (Ps. 15:4). Jesus lived and moved in this realm, and His life was a constant reproof to the wickedness around. "But He was the Son of God," you say. God, through Him, has brought us into the place of sonship, and I believe that if He has a chance with the material, the Holy Ghost can make something of us and bring us to the same place.

THE LAW OF THE SPIRIT OF LIFE

For the law of the Spirit of life in Christ Jesus hath made me free from the law of sin and death (Romans 8:2).

We must move from everything of the letter. All that we do must be done under the anointing of the Spirit. The trouble has been that we as Pentecostal people have been living in the letter. Believe what the Holy Spirit says through Paul—that all this ministration of condemnation that has hindered your liberty in Christ is done away. The law is *done away!*

As far as you are concerned, all that old order of things is forever done away, and the Spirit of God has brought in a new life of purity and love. The Holy Ghost takes it for granted that you are finished with all the things of the old life when you become a new creation in Christ. In the life in the Spirit, the old allurements have lost their power. The devil will meet you at every turn, but the Spirit of God will always lift up a standard against him.

Oh, if God had His way, we would be like torches, purifying the very atmosphere wherever we go, moving back the forces of wickedness.

And if Christ be in you, the body is dead because of sin; but the Spirit is life because of righteousness. But if the Spirit of him that raised up Jesus from the dead dwell in you, he that raised up Christ from the dead shall also quicken your mortal bodies by his Spirit that dwelleth in you (Romans 8:10-11).

ENTERING INTO SABBATH REST

For he that is entered into his rest, he also hath ceased from his own works, as God did from his (Hebrews 4:10).

Oh, this is a lovely rest! The whole life is a Sabbath. This is the only life that can glorify God. It is a life of joy, and every day is a day of heaven on earth. There is a continued transformation in this life. Beholding the Lord and His glory, we are changed into the same image from glory to glory, even by the Spirit of the Lord. There is a continued unveiling, a constant revelation, a continual clothing from above. I want you to promise God never to look back, never to go back to that which the Spirit has said is "done away." I made this promise to the Lord that I would never allow myself to doubt His Word.

There is one thing about a baby: it takes all that comes to it. A prudent man lets his reason cheat him out of God's best, but a baby takes all that its mother brings and tries to swallow the bottle and all. The baby can't walk, but the mother carries it; the baby cannot dress itself, but the mother dresses it. The baby can't even talk.

So in the life of the Spirit, God undertakes to do what we cannot do. He carries us along, He clothes us, and He gives us utterance. Would that we all had the simplicity of the babes.

At the same time came the disciples unto Jesus, saying, Who is the greatest in the kingdom of heaven? And Jesus called a little child unto him, and set him in the midst of them, and said, Verily I say unto you, Except ye be converted, and become as little children, ye shall not enter into the kingdom of heaven. Whosoever therefore shall humble himself as this little child, the same is greatest in the kingdom of heaven (Matthew 18:1-4).

Be Ready

He that hath an ear, let him hear what the Spirit saith unto the churches;
He that overcometh shall not be hurt of the second death (Revelation 2:11).

God has so many things for us in this day that we must be ready. That is the reason why I try to provoke you to holiness, to an intensity of desire, to an inward cry after God.

O Lord, help me! Help me, so that I may earnestly contend, leaving all things before me and pressing forward to the prize.

Are you ready today? Are you anxious today? Are you willing today? Oh, it was wonderful that they were willing in the day of their visitation. It is lovely to be in a place where we can say, "Mine eyes have seen thy salvation."

Are you ready? What for? To be so moved this afternoon by the power of God that this day shall be eclipsed on every line because of God taking you on with Him.

Are you ready? What for? To so lose yourself in God today that you will not claim your earthly rights but claim the rights of your heavenly Father.

Are you ready? What for? That you may so cry aloud that the Lord Himself will be the only One who can satisfy the desire of your heart.

THE PLACE OF REIGNING

Man shall not live by bread alone, but by every word that proceedeth out of the mouth of God (Matthew 4:4).

If you are going on with God, you cannot be fed with natural bread. The people who are going on with God have to have the bread that comes down, and you know it is very fresh every day. It is very special bread because it just meets the need of every heart. The disciples knew it. They were listening to His voice. He was saying marvelous words, yet they knew that there was such a freshness about it that they said, "Even give us this bread."

Now this is the bread that came down from heaven—the Son of God, who gave His life for the world. Remember that He has so wonderfully overcome the power of satan and all the powers of disease and all the powers of sin till there is a perfect place in Christ Jesus where we may be free from sin, sickness, disease, and death. It is one of the greatest positions that God has for us.

There is therefore now no condemnation to them which are in Christ Jesus, who walk not after the flesh, but after the Spirit. For the law of the Spirit of life in Christ Jesus hath made me free from the law of sin and death (Romans 8:1-2).

You see it is as clear, as definite, and as personal as it could be. As we enter into these divine, personal plans today, we will find that sin is dethroned, disease can't hold its seat, death has lost its sting, and victory is in Christ Jesus. How? It is accomplished by reigning in life with Christ Jesus. To reign in life means that you are over every human weakness on every line. To reign means to say that you are on the Rock and everything else is under your feet.

BELIEVE AND BE HEALED

But Simon's wife's mother lay sick of a fever, and anon they tell him of her. And he came and took her by the hand, and lifted her up; and immediately the fever left her, and she ministered unto them (Mark 1:30-31).

When Jesus went into Peter's mother-in-law's house, what did He really do? Did He cover her up with a blanket and put a hot water bottle to her feet? If He did not do that, why didn't He do it? Because He knew her illness was caused by demons that had all the heat of hell in them. He did the right thing: He rebuked the fever and it left. Oh, what would happen if everybody in this place would repent today! Talk about blessings! The glory would fall so they couldn't get out of the place. We need to see that God wants us to be blessed, but first of all He wants us to be ready for the blessing.

The God who told Moses to make a pole and put a brazen serpent upon it, so that whoever looked at it could be healed, now says, "The brazen serpent is not on the pole, Jesus is not on the cross, so now *believe*, and you shall be healed if you *believe*."

You cannot look to the cross, you cannot look to the serpent, but you can believe, and if you believe you can be healed. God desires that you put your faith in Him.

God means you to be helped today. I more and more see that the day of visitation of the Lord is upon us, that the presence of the Lord is here to heal. I have been preaching faith in healing so that you may definitely claim your healing.

HOLY PERSECUTION

Then this Daniel was preferred above the presidents and princes, because an excellent spirit was in him; and the king thought to set him over the whole realm. Then the presidents and princes sought to find occasion against Daniel concerning the kingdom; but they could find none occasion nor fault; forasmuch as he was faithful, neither was there any error or fault found in him. Then said these men, We shall not find any occasion against this Daniel, except we find it against him concerning the law of his God (Daniel 6:3-5).

I want you to notice that in all times, in all histories of the world, whenever there has been a divine rising, a new revelation, God coming forth with new dispensational orders of the Spirit, you will find there have been persecutions all over. Daniel experienced persecution because he reflected the power of the Holy Ghost. When the Spirit of the Lord moves mightily, trouble and difficulty arise. This is the result of three things that are very much against revelations of God and the Spirit of God.

Humanity, flesh, and natural things are against divine things. Evil powers work upon this position of the human life, and especially when the will is unyielded to God. Then the powers of darkness arise against the powers of divine order, but they never defeat them. Divine order is very often in minority, but it is always in majority. Yes, I said that right. Divine order is very often in the minority, but it is always in majority.

Wickedness may increase and abound, but when the Lord raises His flag over a saint, it is victory. Though it is in the minority, it always triumphs.

THE ELECT OF GOD

But of him are ye in Christ Jesus, who of God is made unto us wisdom, and righteousness, and sanctification, and redemption (First Corinthians 1:30).

The Holy Ghost wants us to understand our privileges—we are the elect of God, according to the foreknowledge of God through sanctification of the Spirit. Now sanctification of the Spirit is not on the lines of sin cleansing. It is a higher order than the redemption work. The blood of Jesus is rich for all-powerful cleansing, and it also takes away other powers and transforms us by the mighty power of God. But when sin is gone, yes, when we are clean and when we know we have the Word of God right in us and the power of the Spirit is bringing everything to a place where we triumph, then comes revelation by the power of the Spirit. The Spirit lifts us into higher ground, into all the fullness of God, which unveils Christ. It is called our sanctification of the Spirit.

I don't want you to stumble at the word *elect*—it is a most blessed word. You might say you are all elect; everyone in this place could say you are elected. God has designed that all men should be saved. This is the election, but whether you accept and come into your election, whether you prove yourself worthy of your election, whether you have so allowed the Spirit to fortify you, I don't know. But this is your election, your sanctification, so you can be seated at the right hand of God. This word *election* is a very precious word. Foreordained, predestinated—these are words that God designed before the world was, to bring us into triumph and victory in Christ.

YIELDING TO THE SPIRIT

Blessed be the God and Father of our Lord Jesus Christ, which according to his abundant mercy hath begotten us again unto a lively hope by the resurrection of Jesus Christ from the dead (First Peter 1:3).

Beloved, if there are any buts in your attitude toward the Word of truth, you have not yielded something to the Spirit. I do pray to God the Holy Ghost that we may be willing to yield ourselves to the sanctification of the Spirit, that we may be in the mind of God in the election, that we may have the mind of God in the possession of it.

Through sanctification of the Spirit, according to the election, you will get to a place where you are not disturbed. There is peace in sanctification of the Spirit, because it is a place of revelation and it takes you into heavenly places. It has a place where God comes and speaks and makes Himself known to you; and when you are face to face with God, you get a peace that passes all understanding and lifts you from state to state of inexpressible wonderment. It is really wonderful!

This sanctification of the Spirit brings us into definite line with this wonderful position of the glory of God. I want to keep the glory before us, the joy of a lively hope. Now a lively hope is exactly opposite to dead, exactly opposite to normal.

Lively hope is movement. Lively hope is looking into. Lively hope is pressing into. Lively hope is leaving everything behind you. Lively hope is keeping the vision. Beloved, lively hope sees Him coming!

GLORIES OF THE NEW CREATION

To an inheritance incorruptible, and undefiled, and that fadeth not away, reserved in heaven for you (First Peter 1:4).

Glory to God! I tell you it is great; it is very great. May the Lord help you to thirst after this glorious life of Jesus. Oh, brother, the Holy Ghost is more than new wine. The Holy Ghost is the manifestation of the glories of the new creation. This is our incorruptible inheritance. *Incorruptible* is one of those delightful words that God wants all the saints to grasp—everything corruptible fades away, everything seen cannot remain. Jesus said, "...where neither moth nor rust doth corrupt, and where thieves do not break through nor steal" (Matt. 6:20). None of these things are joined up with incorruptible. Incorruptible is that which is eternal, everlasting, divine, and therefore everything spiritual reaches a place where God is truly—what shall I say?—where God is truly in the midst of it. He is in existence from everlasting to everlasting. He is holy, pure, divine, and incorruptible.

This is one part of our inheritance in the Spirit—one part only. Hallelujah! Oh, how beautiful and forever perfect is our inheritance. It has no spot and wrinkle. It is holy, absolutely pure, and all traces of sin have withered. Everything that is mortal has been scattered and come into a place of purity and God is in the midst. Hallelujah!

Our Heavenly Destination

And I John saw the holy city, new Jerusalem, coming down from God out of heaven, prepared as a bride adorned for her husband (Revelation 21:2).

It is so lovely to think of the great and wonderful city we read about in Revelation.

Think about the marriage. Oh, it is glorious. I saw the holy city as a bride adorned for her husband, undefiled, pure, glorious, all white, completely pure. Who were they? They were once in the world, once corruptible, once defiled, now made spiritual and holy by the blood, lifted from corruptible to incorruptible, and now living as undefiled believers in the presence of God. Hallelujah!

Oh, beloved. God means it for us. Every soul must reach out to this ideal perfection. God has ten thousand more thoughts for you than you have for yourself. The grace of God is going to move us on. You will never sorrow anymore as long as you live. You will never weep anymore, but you will weep for joy. Glory! What a heaven of bliss, what a joy of delight, what a foretaste of heaven on earth.

But you say, "My burden is more than I can bear." Cheerfully bear the burden, for tomorrow you will be there. No sin would entice you; no evil spirit would be able to trip you—no, no, *no*, because of tomorrow with the Lord. We will be with the Lord forever and receive an inheritance that fades not away.

SANCTIFICATION AND PURIFICATION

Who are kept by the power of God through faith unto salvation ready to be revealed in the last time (First Peter 1:5).

Salvation is like sanctification of the Spirit. It is only a goal as you limit yourself. There is no limitation as we see the great preservation of the Master. We should never stand still for a moment but mightily move on in God. Ah, what a blessing. You have no idea what God will mean to you in trials and temptations—it is purification of the Spirit. Gold perishes, but faith never perishes—it is more precious than gold, though it be tried with fire. I went into a place one day and a gentleman said to me, "Would you like to see purification of gold this morning?"

I replied, "Yes."

He got some gold and put it in a crucible and put a blast of heat on it. First, it became blood red, and then changed and changed. Then I found this man took an instrument, passed it over the gold, which drew something off, something that was foreign to the gold. He did this several times until every part was taken away, and then at last he showed it to me again and said, "Look," and there we both saw our faces in the gold. It was wonderful.

My brother, the trial of your faith is much more precious than gold that perishes. When God so purifies you through trials, misunderstandings, persecutions, and sufferings, Jesus has given you the keynote: *rejoice* in that day.

Tried with Fire

That the trial of your faith, being much more precious than of gold that perisheth, though it be tried with fire, might be found unto praise and honour and glory at the appearing of Jesus Christ (First Peter 1:7).

Beloved, as you are tested in the fire, the Master is cleaning away all that cannot bring out the image of His face, cleaning away all the dross from your life, and every evil power, till He sees His face right in your life. Your flesh and all your human powers have to be perfectly submitted to the mighty power of God inwardly to express and manifest His glory outwardly, but you must be willing for the process, and say "Amen" to God—it may be very hard but God will help you.

It is lovely to know that in the chastening times, in the times of misunderstanding, and in hard tests when you are in the right and you are treated as though you were in the wrong, God is meeting and blessing you.

People say it is the devil. Never mind. Let the fire burn; it will do you good. Don't get raspy, but endure it joyfully. It is so sweet to understand this: love suffers long and is kind. How lovely to get to a place where you think no evil, are not easily provoked, and where you can bear all things, endure all things. Praise the Lord. Oh, the glory of it, the joy of it.

ARISE AND GET NEAR HIM

Whom having not seen, ye love; in whom, though now ye see him not, yet believing, ye rejoice with joy unspeakable and full of glory (First Peter 1:8).

Oh, how sweet it is to love our God whom we have not seen. There is no voice so gentle, so soft, so full of tenderness to me; there is no voice like His and no touch. Is that possible? God will make it possible to all. Though now we see Him not, yet we rejoice and believe with unspeakable and glorious joy.

Rejoice? Oh, what a salvation God has procured for us. I entreat you from the Lord to be so reconciled to Him that there will be no division between you and Him. When He would laugh, you would laugh. When He sees you in tears, His compassion would be all you need forever. Will you give Him preference? Will you give Him preeminence in all things? Shall He not have His right place and decide for you the way and plan of your life?

Brother, when you allow Him to decide for you, when you want nothing but His blessed will, when He has to be Lord and Governor over all, heaven will be there all the time. The Lord bless you with grace this morning to leave all and say, "I will follow You, Lord Jesus."

All you people who are longing to get nearer Jesus, I ask you in the name of Jesus to surrender yourself to Him. But you say, "Wigglesworth, I did it yesterday." I know, but today you want to do it more. I know I want to get nearer my Lord. Let us rise and get near to Him for a few minutes.

EMBRACING THE PROMISES

For all the promises of God in him are yea, and in him Amen, unto the glory of God by us (Second Corinthians 1:20).

God has never changed His mind concerning His promises. They are yea and amen to those that believe. God is the same yesterday and forever. To doubt Him is sin. All unbelief is sin. So we have to believe He can heal, save, fill with the Holy Ghost, and transform us altogether. Are you ready? What for? That you might be so chastened by the Lord, so corrected by Him, that as you pass through the fire, as you pass through all temptations, you may come out as Jesus came out of the wilderness, filled with the Spirit.

Are you ready? What for? That you may be so brought in touch with the Father's will that you may know that whatsoever you ask in faith, you will receive. This is the promise; this is the reality God brings to us. Are you ready? What for? That you might know yourself no more after the flesh, not yield to the flesh, but be quickened by the Spirit and live in the Spirit without condemnation, so that your testimony is bright, cheerful, and full of life. This is the inheritance for you today.

When we get unbelief out of the way, the baptism of fire, revelation, the gifts of the Spirit, the harmony, the comfort, the blessed unction will abound in us so we will never be dry. Every moment will be filled with life and power and joy in the Holy Ghost.

JUDGE YOURSELF BY GOD'S WORD

Examine yourselves, whether ye be in the faith; prove your own selves. Know ye not your own selves, how that Jesus Christ is in you, except ye be reprobates? (Second Corinthians 13:5)

There are two ways to enter into the presence of God. The first is through obedience. The next is that you examine yourself to see that you are in the faith. If you do not judge yourself, you will be judged. But if you judge yourself by the Word of God, you will not be condemned by the present evil world. The Spirit will teach you, bring all things to your remembrance, and you do not need any man to teach you. You do not need teachers, but you need *the* Teacher, which is the Holy Ghost, to bring all things to your remembrance. This is the office of the Holy Ghost. This is the power of His communication. This is what Paul means when he says, "God is love." Jesus, who is grace, is with you. But the Holy Ghost is the speaker, and He speaks everything concerning Jesus.

When the Word of God becomes the life and nature of you, you will find that the minute you open it, it becomes life to you—you have to be joined up with the Word. You are to be the epistles of Christ. He is the life and the nature of you. It is a new nature—new life, new breath, new spiritual atmosphere, and there is no limitation in this standard, but in everything else you are limited. "Greater is he that is in you, than he that is in the world" (1 John 4:4). The Word of God has to abide in you, for the Word is life, and it brings forth life, and this is the life that makes you free from the law of sin and death.

Kept in Perfect Peace

Thou wilt keep him in perfect peace, whose mind is stayed on thee: because he trusteth in thee (Isaiah 26:3).

If I find my peace is disturbed on any line, I know it is the enemy who is trying to work. How do I know this? Because the Lord has promised to keep your mind in perfect peace when it is stayed on Him.

Paul tells us to present our bodies as a living sacrifice, which is holy and acceptable unto God and our reasonable service. The Holy Spirit breathed through Paul as he wrote instructions on how to live a holy life.

And be not conformed to this world: but be ye transformed by the renewing of your mind, that ye may prove what is that good, and acceptable, and perfect, will of God (Romans 12:2).

Beloved, we are to live as holy sacrifices unto God, set apart from the world's influence, so that no impure thing defiles us.

Finally, brethren, whatsoever things are true, whatsoever things are honest, whatsoever things are just, whatsoever things are pure, whatsoever things are lovely, whatsoever things are of good report; if there be any virtue, and if there be any praise, think on these things (Philippians 4:8).

As we think about what is pure, we become pure. As we think about what is holy, we become holy. And as we think about our Lord Jesus Christ, we become like Him. We are changed into the likeness of the object on which our gaze is fixed.

A CHOSEN GENERATION

But ye are a chosen generation, a royal priesthood, an holy nation, a pecu-liar people; that ye should shew forth the praises of him who hath called you out of darkness into his marvellous light (First Peter 2:9).

All thoughts of holiness are God's. All manner of loving kindness and tender mercies are His. All weaknesses are made for us that we might be in that place of absolute helplessness, for when we are strong we are weak. Our divine acquaintance with Him will allow us to be broken, empty vessels, ready for Christ's use.

> *Whom have I in heaven beside Thee?*
> *And there is none on earth but Thee.*
> *Oh!* (Psalm 73:25)

That is a wonderful place, where all your springs are in Him, all your desires are after Him, and you long only for Him. Get ready that you may be touched by His inward earnestness this morning, that you may see the power of possibility in an impossible place, and that you may see that God can change you.

Are you ready? What for? That God shall be your all in all so you lose your identity in the perfection of His glorified purity. You will be lost to everything else except Him.

Are you ready? What for? That you may come to the banquet house with great faith and believe all things are possible. That you may come unhindered and lay hold of all things. That you may have a time of great refreshing as you come expressing yourself to God.

EPISTLES OF CHRIST

Ye are our epistle written in our hearts, known and read of all men: forasmuch as ye are manifestly declared to be the epistle of Christ ministered by us, written not with ink, but with the Spirit of the living God... (Second Corinthians 3:2-3).

Here we have a very remarkable word that the Spirit wants to enlarge for us. It is true that we must be the epistles of Christ. The epistle of Christ is a living power in the mortal flesh that quickens and divides everything that is not of the Spirit until you realize that you now live in a new order. The Spirit has manifested Himself in your mortal body. The Word has become life. It has quickened you all through, and you are not in any way subject to anything around you. You are above everything. You reign above everything.

The Word of God evidently sends you forth as the epistles of Christ, meaning to say that all human ideals, plans, and wishes for the future are past. In order to live, you must have Christ. In order for you to live, you must be emblematic, divinely sustained by another power greater than you, and His holy epistle. You do not seek your own any more. You are living in a place where God is on the throne, superintending your human life, changing everything, and making you understand this wonderful truth.

LIVE NOT UNDER THE LAW

For sin shall not have dominion over you: for ye are not under the law, but under grace (Romans 6:14).

If you go into the law at any time and under any circumstances, you miss the divine order of the Spirit. You cannot go back to the law. You are in a new order. Law can only deal out one thing. It is always, "Thou shalt not." There is no law to the Spirit. There never has been. You cannot find a law to Truth. The law has never had a place in a human body that has been filled with the power and the unction of the Holy Ghost. Law is done away, is past. Life has begun; the new creation is formed, and you are now living after the new order. Christ became the very principle of your human life and you are above the law. How many people are missing the greatest plan of the earth because they are continually trying to do something?

Many years ago, my wife and I were strongly convinced we should strictly observe the Sabbath Day in holiness. We got so far that we thought it was wrong to have the milkman call, and it was a very fearful thing to ride in anything on a Sunday. We were so tightened up by the law that we were bound hand and foot. There are thousands of people like that today.

God would have you in a new order. It is the law of the Spirit. It is a law of life. It is not a law of death and bondage. As sure as you are in law, you are in judgment, and you judge everybody. Law is always judgment, and no one is right but those people who are keeping the law. They are full of judgment. We have passed from death, from judgment, from criticism, from harshness, and from hardness of heart into pure, divine life.

BELIEF VERSUS ACTION

And after six days Jesus taketh Peter, James, and John his brother, and brin-geth them up into an high mountain apart, and was transfigured before them: and his face did shine as the sun, and his raiment was white as the light (Matthew 17:1-2).

When the glory appeared on the mount—as soon as it appeared and the disciples saw the whiteness, the brilliancy, the glory, the expression of the Master, and the very robes He wore becoming white and glistening—they began at once to think what they could do. Law will do that. What can we *do*?

And they began doing, and they wanted to make three tabernacles, one for Moses, one for Elijah, and one for Jesus. And then the cloud came. No person in the world should be worshiped but the Lord. When the cloud lifted, there was no one visible but Jesus.

If you turn to anybody but Jesus, you will be under the law, you will be under the rules of nature, and you will be human. It has always been so; people are always forming out things to do. But the man that believes God, it is counted to him for righteousness—not doing but believing. So God wants you to see that you have to cease from your doing, to get away from it. Believe there is a spiritual vitality that shall transform your very nature into a new creation.

In this new order, Jesus has one great plan for us—to fill us with the Holy Ghost so that we would focus perfectly on Him in our human life. And as we come into the light of this revelation by the Son, by the quickening of the Spirit, we will find our whole body regenerated with a new touch of divine favor, and we will think about spiritual things, and we will talk about spiritual things, and we will not touch anything that pertains to the flesh.

THE SPIRIT OR THE LETTER?

...The letter killeth, but the spirit giveth life (Second Corinthians 3:6).

After you have come into the fullness of the refreshing of God, you can get the letter instead of the life of the Word, and the letter will turn you to yourself, but the Spirit will turn you to Christ. People turn away from the Spirit and take the letter, and when they get in the letter they are full of condemnation. Just as you live in the Spirit, there will be no condemnation in you. There is something wrong when you are the only one that is right. As the Church rises into the glory of the Lord and the vision of the Lord, will she be full of the love of the Lord?

The Holy Ghost wants you to sweep through darkness. The Holy Ghost wants to fill you with truth. The Holy Ghost wants to stimulate you in liberty. The Holy Ghost wants you to rise higher and higher.

If you turn away from the Word of God, the Word of God will judge you and you will be brought into leanness. The man that is living in the Spirit will not turn aside to please anybody. The man that is filled with the Spirit is going on with God all the time, and he will cease from his own works. I want to stir your holy fidelity to know there is a place in the Holy Ghost that can keep you so that you do not get hard in the law, in judgment, in criticism, in hardness of heart. Get to a place where the Spirit has such a place with you that you will love to go God's way.

The judgment of God will begin at the house of God. You have the best when you have the Spirit, and the Spirit brings life and revelation. Don't turn to the law. Don't turn to the natural realm. See to it that you are free from the law. The law of the Spirit is life and it will keep you out of death, keep you out of judgment, keep you out of bondage.

Quick and Powerful

But if the ministration of death, written and engraven in stones, was glorious, so that the children of Israel could not stedfastly behold the face of Moses for the glory of his countenance; which glory was to be done away: how shall not the ministration of the spirit be rather glorious? (Second Corinthians 3:7-8)

When Moses knew that he was bringing the tables of stone with the commandments down to the Israelite people, his heart was so full of joy, his whole body was so full, his whole countenance was so full that the people could not look upon him because of the glory that was expressed in his face. What was it? He was bringing liberty to the people, and it was the law.

If the law, which had with it life and revelation and blessing for Israel, could bring that wonderful exhibition of beauty and glory, what is it that we are freed from? We have the Spirit living and moving in us, without harshness, and without "Thou shalt not." The Spirit of the Lord is breathing through us and making us free from the law of sin and death.

You will never get free in the flesh. You will never get free in the letter. You will only get free as the Spirit of the Lord breathes upon the Word and you receive it as life from the Lord, for the Word of the Lord is life. When you receive the Word of the Lord just as it is and believe it, you will find it quickens your whole body. You have to take the Word of God as the life of the Spirit, and you have to allow it to breathe through you, quickening your whole body, for the Spirit quickens, but the flesh profits nothing.

The Word may be quick and powerful, or it may be deathlike. God wants us to be through with death. The moment you turn from the spiritual health of this revelation of Christ is the moment you cease to go forward.

All for God

He hath shewed thee, O man, what is good; and what doeth the LORD *require of thee, but to do justly, and to love mercy, and to walk humbly with thy God?* (Micah 6:8)

I pray for you this morning, you mighty of the Lord, you children of the Most High God, you people whom the Lord is looking upon with great favor. Believe that as the Holy Ghost moved upon Paul and the apostles, He can bring you forth as tested and purified gold. Will you believe? May the blessing of God the Father, the Son, and the Holy Ghost fill you so that all the powers of hell shall not be able to prevail against you.

Was it ever thought possible that law could be done away? Yes, by something that is far more glorious. In the law they had no mercy, and God brought mercy right into the midst of the law, a thing that they did not know how to do.

The person who keeps the law never walks humbly but is always filled with self-righteousness. But now let the Spirit speak to us in the last days. What is it the Lord your God desires of you? "Thou shalt love the Lord thy God with all thine heart, and with all thy soul, and with all thy might" (Deut. 6:5). Isn't that a new spiritual vision? That isn't the law; that is a boundless position. The law could never do it.

There is no reserve. We are to love the Lord with our entire pure mind. The law had to be done away because, though it was glorious, it had to be exceeded by a pure heart, by all strength for God. Just fancy knowing you are so created after the fashion of God that you want all the strength out of your food for God, all the strength. Just think of people who have wonderful capabilities and wonderful minds, that your minds have to be all for God. Glorious, more glorious! It is exceeding glory.

THE SPIRIT EXCEEDS THE LAW

For if the ministration of condemnation be glory, much more doth the ministration of righteousness exceed in glory (Second Corinthians 3:9).

If you are in this love, you will be swallowed up with holy desire. You will have no desire, only the Lord. Your mind will be filled with divine reflection. Your whole heart will be taken up with the things that pertain to the Kingdom of God, and you will live in the secret place of the Most High, and you will abide there. Remember, it is abiding where He covers you with His feathers. It is an inner, inner, inner, inner place where the Lord now has the treasures. There is an exceeding glory. There is a glory where you forget your poverties, where you forget your weaknesses, where you forget your human-nature history and you go on to divine opportunity.

You see, the Law is a ministry of condemnation, and the Spirit is a ministry of righteousness. The difference is this: instead of preaching to the people, "Thou shalt not" any more, you now preach that there is a superabundant position in the Holy One. He has come in and transformed the whole situation till every judged thing is past, life flows through, and you preach righteousness. You will never get free by keeping the law, but if you believe in the blood, that will put you to death. And you will have divine life, and you can bypass the thing that binds you, because righteousness will abound where the law is of the Spirit.

POWER IN THE HOLY GHOST

If ye abide in me, and my words abide in you, ye shall ask what ye will, and it shall be done unto you (John 15:7).

The Holy Ghost people have a ministry. All the people who have received the Holy Ghost might be so filled with Him that the Holy Ghost within them brings forth healing power.

I believe the Holy Ghost whom you have received has power to bring you into concentration so that you dare believe God can heal even if you do not have a gift of healing. The gift of the Holy Ghost, when He has breathed in you, will make you alive so that it is wonderful. It seems almost then as though you have never been born. The jealousy God has over us, the interest He has in us, the purpose He has for us, and the grandeur of His glory are so marvelous God has called us into this place to receive gifts.

Claim your right. Claim your position. The man will never get a gift under any circumstances if he asks for it twice. I am not moved by what you think about it. I believe this is sovereignty from God's altar. You never get a gift if you ask for it twice. But God will have mercy upon you if you stop asking and believe.

When we get unbelief out of the way, the baptism of fire, the revelation, the gifts of the Spirit, the harmony, the comfort, and the blessed unction will abound till there will never be a dry meeting. Every meeting will be filled with life and power and joy in the Holy Ghost. May we indeed be alive with refreshing of the presence of the Most High God!

ABIDING IN POWER

Abide in me, and I in you. As the branch cannot bear fruit of itself, except it abide in the vine; no more can ye, except ye abide in me (John 15:4).

Abide in the presence of power where victory is assured. If we keep in the right place with God, God can do anything with us. There is a power and majesty on Jesus. He received the mighty anointing power of God. And He realized submission, and as He submitted He was more and more covered with power and led by the Spirit.

He came out of the wilderness full of God, clothed with the Spirit, and ready for the fight. The power had such an effect upon Him that other people saw it and flocked to hear Him, and great blessing came to the land.

The Holy Ghost coming upon an individual changes him and fertilizes his spiritual life. What is possible if we reach this place and abide in it? Only one thing is going to accomplish the purpose of God. To be filled with the Spirit, we must yield and submit until our bodies are saturated with God, so that at any moment God's will can be revealed. We want a great hunger and thirst for God. Thousands must be brought to knowledge of the truth; that will only be brought about by human instrumentality, when the instrument is at a place where he will say all the Holy Ghost directs him to. Be still and know that I am God—the place of tranquility, where we know He is in control, and where He moves us by the mighty power of His Spirit. Ezekiel said, "I prophesied as I was commanded." He did what he was told to do. It takes more to live in that place than any other I know of. To live in the place where you hear God's voice. Only by the power of the Spirit can you do as you are told quickly. We must keep at the place where we see God and hear His voice—where He sends us with messages that bring life and power and victory.

BURNING HEARTS

And they said one to another, Did not our heart burn within us, while he talked with us by the way, and while he opened to us the scriptures? (Luke 24:32)

It is a great thing to know that God is loosing you from the world, loosing you from a thousand things. You must seek to have the mind of God on all things. If you don't, you will stop His working.

I see that all revelation, all illumination, everything that God had in Christ was to be brought forth into perfect light that we might be able to live the same, produce the same, and be sons of God with power in every activity. It must be so. We must not limit the Holy One. And we must clearly see that God brought us forth to make us supernatural, that we might be changed all the time so that we may live every day in the Spirit. All of the revelations of God are just like a canvas thrown before our eyes, on which we see clearly step by step the entire divine will of God.

If the saints only knew how precious they are in the sight of God they would scarcely be able to sleep for thinking of His watchful, loving care. Oh, He is a precious Jesus! He is a lovely Savior! He is divine in His attitude toward us, and He makes our hearts burn. There is nothing like it. "Oh," they said on the road to Emmaus, "did not our heart burn within us, as He walked with us and talked with us?" Oh beloved, it must be so today. Always keep in mind that the Holy Ghost must bring manifestation. We must understand that the Holy Ghost is breath, the Holy Ghost is Person, and it is a most marvelous thing to me to know that this Holy Ghost power can be in every part of your body. You can feel it from the crown of your head to the soles of your feet. Oh, it is lovely to be burning all over with the Holy Ghost! And when that takes place, there is nothing but the operation of the tongue that must give forth glory and the praise.

IN THE SPIRIT

But Peter, standing up with the eleven, lifted up his voice, and said unto them, Ye men of Judaea, and all ye that dwell at Jerusalem, be this known unto you, and hearken to my words...Repent, and be baptized every one of you in the name of Jesus Christ for the remission of sins, and ye shall receive the gift of the Holy Ghost (Acts 2:14,38).

You must be in the place of magnifying the Lord. The Holy Ghost is the great Magnifier of Jesus, the great Illuminator of Jesus. And so after the Holy Ghost comes in, it is impossible to keep your tongue still. Why, you would burst if you didn't give Him utterance. Talk about a dumb baptized soul? Such a person is not to be found in the Scriptures. You will find that when you speak unto God in the new tongue He gives you, you enter into a close communion with Him hitherto never experienced.

We are in a strange place when the Holy Ghost comes in. If the incoming of the Spirit is lovely, what must be the outflow? The man who is filled with the Holy Ghost is always acting. Beloved, we must see that the baptism with the Holy Ghost is an activity with an outward manifestation.

Ah, brothers and sisters, we have no idea what God has for us if we will only begin! But, oh, the grace we need! We may make a mishap. If you do it outside of Him, if you do it for yourself, and if you want to be someone, it will be a failure. We shall only be able to do well as we do it in the name of Jesus. "What things soever ye desire, when ye pray, believe that ye receive them, and ye shall have them" (Mark 11:24). Live in the Spirit, walk in the Spirit, walk in communion with the Spirit, and talk with God. All leadings of the divine order are for you. I pray that if there are any who have turned to their own way and have made God second, they will come to repentance on all lines. Begin with God this moment.

A Child of Glory

For it became him, for whom are all things, and by whom are all things, in bringing many sons unto glory, to make the captain of their salvation perfect through sufferings (Hebrews 2:10).

We need to live very near God, so that we are daily nearing the goal. The terrestrial body will be beautiful in every way, to take in the glories and expression of heaven. I want you all to have a share; God says He will bring many sons to glory. Oh, take no rest and press forward for the mark of the prize of the high calling in Jesus Christ, earnestly contending for the faith once delivered to the saints.

People miss the greatest plan because they move from one thing to another. Become restful, believe God, and have an inward cry. Be so lost in God that He can grant you the desire of your heart. We need new bread, fresh every day, the Bread that comes down from heaven (see John 6:32-58). The law of the spirit of life in Christ Jesus has made me free from the law of sin and death. When sin is dethroned, disease cannot hold its seat, death has lost its sting, and victory is in Jesus Christ! To reign in life means that you are over every human weakness; all is under our feet. In Christ, we are over the devil, destroying his incoming, moving him away. Resist the devil and he will flee from you. Be indignant at every pain, every weakness. People today are going down because they fail to rise in Jesus's Name and put to flight the enemy. So stand firm against the devil, and He will flee from you.

Remembering Your Baptism

For Paul had determined to sail by Ephesus, because he would not spend the time in Asia: for he hasted, if it were possible for him, to be at Jerusalem the day of Pentecost (Acts 20:16).

The day of Pentecost is near at hand. Oh, what memories it had for Paul! We all look forward to Easter when the Holy Ghost fell as at the beginning, where the cross of Calvary made an open door for all hearts to be saved. The wonderful Holy Ghost descended to enlarge the hearts of all the people to live so in the Spirit that there should be new vision, new revelation, new equipment, and new men. The baptism of the Holy Ghost means a new creation after the order of the Spirit.

Paul was stirred as he remembered his mighty baptism in the Spirit, the victory that it had brought him into, the unlimited power to preach the Gospel, and the unhindered work of the Holy Spirit in him. The mighty unction of the Holy Spirit resided upon him.

There is a wonderful unction force when all the people of God who are baptized with the Holy Ghost come together. Oh, this longing cry in the hearts of the people that cannot be satisfied but with more of God. On that memorable journey from Jerusalem to Damascus, Paul had seen the risen Christ and, by the anointing of the Spirit, became the greatest missionary enterpriser the world has ever seen. Oh, yes! There is something in unity; there is something in fellowship; there is something in being of one accord! He has promised to fill the hungry with good things.

KEEPING THE VISION CLEAR

Blessed are the pure in heart: for they shall see God (Matthew 5:8).

The baptism of the Holy Ghost is not only the great essential power for victorious life and service—it is a separating force. Jesus said a man's foes would oftentimes be those of his own household (see Matt. 10:36). It means separation as sure as you live, if you follow the narrow way that leads unto life. It means persecution, but if you follow holiness, you will have no room for any but Jesus.

Let us keep the vision clear—pure in heart, upward, onward, heavenward, until the daybreak and the shadows flee away (see Song of Sol. 2:17). Jesus is the loveliest on earth. The Holy Ghost clothes Him. He meets the needs of all. You belong to the Church of the firstborn, the establishment of that wonderful place in the glory. Will you promise God nothing shall come between you and the throne—the heart of God and the mind of the Spirit? God has a choice for everyone who swears to his own hurt and changes not.

Is Jesus not beautiful? Could anything cloud that brow? He has the joy of heaven for us, so we can go from victory unto victory. Your faces display the glory—let us be jealous. Set your house in order. You must go your way. Follow Him. The building is going up. The top stone must be put on. Grace, grace unto it.

FLAMES OF FIRE

And of the angels he saith, Who maketh his angels spirits, and his ministers a flame of fire (Hebrews 1:7).

His ministers are to be flames of fire! It seems to me that no man with a vision, especially a vision by the Spirit's power, can read that wonderful verse without being kindled to such a flame of fire for his Lord that it seems as if it would burn up everything that would interfere with his progress. A flame of fire: a perpetual fire; a constant fire; a continual burning; a holy, inward flame, which is exactly what God's Son was in the world. I can see this. God has nothing less for us than to be flames!

It seems to me that if Pentecost is to rise and be effective, it must have a living faith, so that His great might and power flows through us until the life becomes energized, moved, and aflame for God. The import of our message is that the Holy Ghost has come to make Jesus king. I see a new creation rising with a kingly position, and I see that when the Holy Ghost comes, He is to crown Jesus King.

Not only is the King to be within, but all the glories of the kingly manifestations are to be brought forth. I see that we can come into the order of God where the vision becomes so much brighter, and where the Lord is manifesting His glory with all His virtues and gifts, and all His glory seems to fill the soul who is absolutely dead. He makes us alive to Him. There is much talk about death, but there is a death that is so deep in God that out of that death God brings the splendor of His life and all His glory.

LIVING FAITH IN GOD

Ye shall receive power, after that the Holy Ghost is come upon you: and ye shall be witnesses unto me... (Acts 1:8).

On the day of Pentecost He sent the power, and the remainder of the Acts of the Apostles tells of the witnessing of these Spirit-filled disciples, the Lord working with them, and how He confirmed the Word with signs following. The Lord Jesus is just the same today. The anointing is just the same. The Pentecostal experience is just the same, and we are to look for similar results as set forth in Luke's record of what happened in the days of the early Church.

John the Baptist said concerning Jesus, "...he shall baptize you with the Holy Ghost, and with fire" (Matt. 3:11). God's ministers are to be a flame of fire—a perpetual flame, a constant fire, a continual burning, and a shining light. God has nothing less for us than to be flames. We must have a living faith in God, a faith that God's great might and power may flame through us until our whole life is energized by the power of God. I realize that when the Holy Ghost comes, He comes to enable us to show forth Jesus Christ in all His glory, to make Him known as the One who heals today as in the days of old. The baptism in the Spirit enables us to preach as they did at the beginning, through the power of the Holy Ghost sent down from heaven, and with the manifestation of the gifts of the Spirit. Oh, if we would only let the Lord work in us, melting us until a new order arises, until we are moved with His compassion!

Holy Spirit Empowerment

Therefore I say unto you, What things soever ye desire, when ye pray, believe that ye receive them, and ye shall have them (Mark 11:24).

God has given us authority over all the power of the devil. Oh, that we may live in the place where we realize this always! Christ, who is the express image of God, has come to our human weaknesses to change them and us into divine likeness, to be partakers of the divine nature, so that by the power of His might we may not only overcome but rejoice in the fact that we are more than conquerors. God wants you to know by experience what it means to be more than a conqueror. The baptism in the Holy Spirit has come for nothing less than to empower us, to give the very power that Christ Himself had, so that you, a yielded vessel, may continue the same type of ministry that He had when He walked this earth in the days of His flesh.

He purposes that we should come behind in no gift. There are gifts of healing and the working of miracles, but we must apprehend these. There is the gift of faith by the same Spirit that we are to receive. The need in the world today is that we should be burning and shining lights to reflect the glory of Christ. We cannot do it with a cold, indifferent experience, and we never shall. His servants are to be flames of fire. Christ came that we might have life and life more abundantly. And we are to give that life to others, to be ministers of the life and power and healing virtue of Jesus Christ wherever we go.

You can receive something in three minutes that you can carry with you into glory. What do you want? Is anything too hard for God? God can meet you now. God sees inwardly. He knows all about you. Nothing is hidden from Him, and He can satisfy the soul and give you a spring of eternal blessing that will carry you right through.

THE POWER OF THE WORD

All scripture is given by inspiration of God, and is profitable for doctrine, for reproof, for correction, for instruction in righteousness (Second Timothy 3:16).

The Word of God is wonderful, and I believe that God wants to fill us with His Word. He wants us to be so filled with it that no matter where we are, the Word will be lived out in us. The Word is power, the Word is Life, the Word of God is faith, the Word is Jesus, and the Word of God is everlasting life to him who believes. "He that heareth My Word, and believeth on Him that sent Me, hath everlasting life" (John 5:24).

And we need to be careful in reading the Word; I believe it is too precious to rush over; we need to "rightly divide the Word of Truth" (see 2 Tim. 2:15). I want to speak to you tonight of the power given by God. Oh the power of the Holy Ghost, the power that quickens, the revealing power, the travailing power! The power that lives and moves, the power that brings about exactly what Jesus said, "When you receive, you will have power" (see Acts 1:8). I love to think that Jesus wanted all His people to have power, that He wanted all people to be overcomers.

How God fascinates me with His Word. I read and read and read, and there is always something new, and as I get deeper into the knowledge of the Bridegroom, I hear the voice of Jesus saying, "The bride rejoices to hear the Bridegroom's voice." The Word is His voice, and the nearer we are to Jesus, the more we understand the principles of His mission. He came to make a bride of His people; He came to find a body. God's message to us tonight is that Jesus is going to take a bride for Himself. So while we are here to talk about salvation, there are deeper truths God wants to show us. It is not only to be saved, but there is an eternal destiny in the plan of God for us.

OVERCOMING IN THE SPIRIT

Ye are of God, little children, and have overcome them: because greater is he that is in you, than he that is in the world (First John 4:4).

Why have we power when the Holy Ghost comes? It is because the Holy Ghost reveals Jesus. In order to understand what it means to have all power, two things are necessary: one is to have ears to hear and the other is to have hearts to receive. Every saint of God filled with the Spirit has a real revelation of truth: Greater is He that is in you than he that is in the world.

Jesus was so filled with the Holy Ghost that He stood in the place where He was always ready. He was always in the attitude where He brought victory out of every opportunity. The power of the Holy Spirit is within us, but it can be manifested only as we go in obedience to that opportunity that we have before us. If you wait until you think you have power after you have received the Holy Ghost, you will never know you have it.

Don't you know that the child of God who is in possession of the baptism is inhabited by the power of the Spirit? Remember when they tried to throw Jesus from the brow of a hill? He pressed through the midst of them and He healed the man with the blind eyes. Pressing through the crowd that was trying to kill Him, He showed forth His power. Some people might think that Jesus should have run away altogether, but He stopped to heal.

Jesus paid the full price and the full redemption for every need. Where sin abounds, grace can come in and abound much more and dispel all sickness.

WORKING THROUGH US

Likewise the Spirit also helpeth our infirmities: for we know not what we should pray for as we ought: but the Spirit itself maketh intercession for us... (Romans 8:26).

We are God's own children, quickened by His Spirit, and He has given us power over all the powers of darkness. Christ in us is the open evidence of eternal glory. Christ in us is the Life, the Truth, and the Way. We have a wonderful salvation that fits everybody.

I believe that a baptized person has no conception of the power God has given him until he uses it. I maintain that Peter and John had no idea of the greatness of the power they had, but they began to speculate. They said, "Well, as far as money goes, we have none of that, but we do have something; we don't exactly know what it is, but we will try it on you. In the Name of Jesus of Nazareth, rise up and walk," and it worked. In order to make yourself realize what you have in your possession you will have to try it, and I can assure you it will work all right.

The Acts of the Apostles would never have been written if the Apostles had not acted, and the Holy Spirit is still continuing His acts through us. May God help us to have some acts. There is nothing like Pentecost, and if you have never been baptized with the Holy Spirit, you are making a big mistake by waiting. Don't you know that the only purpose for which God saved you was that you might be a savior of others? For you to think that you have to remain stationary and just get to heaven is a great mistake.

TRIALS AS PREPARATION

My brethren, count it all joy when ye fall into divers temptations; Knowing this, that the trying of your faith worketh patience (James 1:2-3).

The Baptism is to make you a witness for Jesus. Thank God the hardest way is the best way; you never hear anything about the person who is always having an easy time. The preachers always tell of how Moses crossed the Red Sea when he was at wits' end. I cannot find the record of anyone in the Scriptures whom God used who was not first tried. So if you never have any trials, it is because you are not worth them.

Jesus was the *first fruits* and God has chosen us in Christ and has revealed His Son in us that we might manifest Him in power. God gives us power over the devil, and when we say the devil, we mean every thing that is wicked and not of God. Some people say we can afford to do without the Baptism of the Spirit, but I say we cannot. I believe any person who thinks there is a stop between Calvary and the glory has made a big mistake.

Beloved, we are bound for glory. God has predestined us for citizenship in His glorious Kingdom. And the Baptism of the Holy Spirit is a foretaste of glory divine. It is the breath of God that brings life and resurrection power into our lives, so that we can work the same miracles as the Apostles. Trials are inevitable, but our victory is assured. Stand confident in that victory. It will not fail you.

Faith Formed in You

...to them that have obtained like precious faith with us through the righteousness of God and our Saviour Jesus Christ (Second Peter 1:1).

Let God fulfill His great desire in us for heart purity, that Christ may dwell in our hearts by faith, that the might of God's Spirit may accompany our ministry.

It is good to have the Holy Spirit, but the sun inside must give brilliancy outside. Faith! For faith is substance and evidence. You were not saved by feelings or experiences. You were saved by the power of God the moment you believed the Word of God. God came in by His Word and laid the foundation. Faith bursts up the old life and nature by the power of God, until the Word of God replaces the old life.

You must come to God's Book. His Word is our foundation. When we speak of the Word, we speak of almighty power, a substance of rich dynamite diffusing through a person, displaying its might, and bringing all else into insignificance. We speak of the Word of God formed within the temple, a living principle laid down of rock. We speak of the Word of the Living God formed in us—mighty in thought, language, activity, movement, and unction, a fire mightier than dynamite and able to resist the mightiest pressure the devil can bring against it.

Be a man of desire, hunger and thirst. Don't be satisfied. I cannot move on faith unless it is better than my mind, greater than me. None are made on trailing clouds of glory; we are made in hard places; at Wit's End Corner, with no way out. A man is made in adversity. David said, "In distress, God brought me to a large place, and I was enlarged, and He helped me" (see Ps. 4:1; 18:36).

LOVING OUR NEIGHBORS

If a man say, I love God, and hateth his brother, he is a liar: for he that loveth not his brother whom he hath seen, how can he love God whom he hath not seen? (First John 4:20)

We must clearly understand whether we are of the right spirit or not, for no man can be of the Spirit of Christ and persecute another; no man can have the true Spirit of Jesus and slay his brother, and no man can follow the Lord Jesus and have enmity in his heart. You cannot have Jesus and have bitterness and hatred and persecute believers.

It is possible for us, if we are not careful, to have within us an evil spirit of unbelief, and even in our best state it is possible for us to have enmity unless we are perfectly dead and let the life of the Lord lead us. You remember Jesus wanted to pass through a certain place as He was going to Jerusalem. Because He would not stop and preach to them concerning the Kingdom, they refused to allow Him to go through their section of the country. And the disciples that were with Jesus said to Him, "Shall we call down fire from heaven upon them as Elijah did?" (see Luke 9:54).

But Jesus turned and said, "Ye know not what manner of spirit ye are of" (Luke 9:55).

There they were, following Jesus and with Him all the time, but Jesus rebuked that spirit. I pray God that we may know that our knowledge of Jesus is pure love, and pure love to Jesus is death to self on all lines, body, soul, and spirit. I believe if we are in the will of God, we will be perfectly directed at all times, and if we would know anything about the mighty works of Christ, we shall have to follow what Jesus said. Whatever He said came to pass.

RIGHTEOUS ON ALL LINES

Notwithstanding, lest we should offend them, go thou to the sea, and cast an hook, and take up the fish that first cometh up; and when thou hast opened his mouth, thou shalt find a piece of money: that take, and give unto them for me and thee (Matthew 17:27).

Many things happened in the lives of the apostles to show Jesus's power over all flesh. In regard to paying tribute, Jesus said to Peter, "We are free, we can enter into the city without paying tribute; nevertheless, we will pay." I like that thought, that Jesus was so righteous on all lines. It helps me a great deal. Then Jesus told Peter to do a very hard thing. He said, "Take that hook and cast it into the sea. Draw out a fish and take from its gills a piece of silver for thee and Me." This was one of the hardest things Peter had to do. He had been fishing all his life, but never had he taken silver out of a fish's mouth.

There were thousands and millions of fish in the sea, but one fish had to have a piece of silver in it. He went down to the sea as any natural man would, speculating and thinking, "How can it be?" But how could it not be, if Jesus said it would be? Then the perplexity would arise, "But how many fish are there, and which fish has the money?" No doubt many things were in Peter's mind that day, but thank God there was one fish, and Peter obeyed. Sometimes to obey in blindness brings the victory.

Brother, if God speaks, it will be as He says. What you need is to know the mind of God and the Word of God, and you will be so free you will never find a frown on your face or a tear in your eye. The more you know of the mightiness of revelation, the more that fearfulness will pass away. To know God is to be in the place of triumph. To know God is to be in the place of rest. To know God is to be in the place of victory.

REVELATION IN THE HOLY GHOST

When he, the Spirit of truth, is come, he will guide you into all truth...
(John 16:13).

When Jesus, our Mediator and Advocate, was so filled with the Holy Ghost, He gave a commandment through the Holy Ghost concerning these days we are in. I can see that if we are going to accomplish anything, it will be because we are under the power of the Holy Ghost.

Jesus said the Holy Ghost should take of the things of His Word and reveal them unto us. The Holy Ghost would live out in us all the life of Jesus. And if we could only think what this really means! It is one of the ideals. Talk about graduation! My word! Come into the graduation of the Holy Ghost by the Spirit, and you will simply strip out everything they have in any college there ever was. You would leave them all behind, just as I see the sun leave the mist behind in San Francisco. You would leave that which is as cold as ice and go into the sunshine. God the Holy Ghost wants us to have such an ideal of this fullness of the Spirit that we would neither be ignorant, nor would we have mystic conceptions, but we would have a clear, unmistakable revelation of all the mind of God for these days.

Glory! Oh, it is grand! Thank God for that interpretation. I beseech you, beloved, in the Name of Jesus, that you should see that you come right into all the mind of God. Jesus truly said, "But ye shall receive power after the Holy Ghost is come upon you" (see Acts 1:8). And I want you to know that "He shewed Himself alive after His passion by many infallible proofs, being seen of them forty days" (Acts 1:3). He is continually unfolding the power of resurrection to every one of us.

THE BAPTISM IS ESSENTIAL

And suddenly there came a sound from heaven as of a rushing mighty wind, and it filled all the house where they were sitting. And there appeared unto them cloven tongues like as of fire, and it sat upon each of them. And they were all filled with the Holy Ghost, and began to speak with other tongues, as the Spirit gave them utterance (Acts 2:2-4).

Remember the baptism of the Holy Ghost is resurrection. If you can touch this ideal of God, with its resurrection power, you will see that nothing earthly can remain. You will see that all disease will clear out. If you get so full of the Holy Ghost, all satanic forces and diseases will go. Resurrection is the word for it.

Resurrection shakes away death and breathes life in you, to let you know that you are from the dead, quickened by the Spirit, made like unto Jesus. Glory to God! Oh, the word resurrection! I wish I could say it just on parallel lines with the word Jesus. They very harmoniously go together. Jesus is resurrection, and to know Jesus in this resurrection power is simply to see that you are no longer dead but alive unto God by the Spirit.

There is a necessity of being baptized in the Holy Ghost for a businessman. For any kind of business you need to know the power of the Holy Ghost, because if you are not baptized with the Holy Ghost, satan has a tremendous power to interfere with the power of your life. If you come into the baptism of the Holy Ghost, there is a new plane for your business.

Beloved, we must see that this baptism of the Spirit is greater than all. You can talk as you like, say what you like, do as you like, but until you have the Holy Ghost, you won't know what the resurrection touch is. Resurrection is by the power of the Spirit. Resurrection is evidence that we have woken up with a new line of truth that cannot cease to be but will always go on with a greater force of God's increasing power.

An Unlimited Source of Power

This Jesus hath God raised up, whereof we all are witnesses. Therefore being by the right hand of God exalted, and having received of the Father the promise of the Holy Ghost, he hath shed forth this, which ye now see and hear (Acts 2:32-33).

Oh, this is a new day for a person that is baptized. The Spirit is an unlimited source of power. He is in no way stationary. There is nothing stationary in God. God has no place with a man who is stationary. The man who is going to catch the fire, hold forth the truth, always be on the watchtower, is the man who is going to be the beacon for all saints, having a light greater than his natural order. He must see that God's grace, God's life, and God's Spirit are mightier than he is.

The man who is baptized in the Holy Ghost is baptized in a new order altogether. It cannot be that you shall ever be ordinary after that. You are on an extraordinary plane; you are brought into line with the mind of God. You have come into touch with ideals on every line. If you want oratory, there it is in the baptism of the Spirit. If you want the touch of quickened sense that moves your body till you know that you are fully renewed, it is the Holy Ghost. And while I say so much about the Holy Ghost today, I withdraw everything that doesn't put Jesus in the ordered place He belongs, for when I speak about the Holy Ghost it is always with reference to revelations of Jesus.

The Holy Ghost is only the revealer of the mighty Christ, who has made it so that we may never know any weakness; all limitations are gone! And you are now in a place where God has taken the ideal and moved you on with His own velocity, which has a speed beyond all human mind and thought. Glory to God!

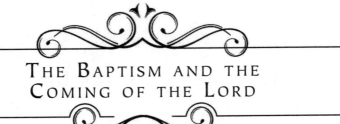

The Baptism and the Coming of the Lord

Be patient therefore, brethren, unto the coming of the Lord. Behold, the husbandman waiteth for the precious fruit of the earth... (James 5:7).

The Holy Ghost could not come till the apostles and those who were in the upper room were all of one mind, heart, and all in one accord with themselves and with God. What is the precious fruit of the earth? Is it cabbages? Is it grapes? The precious fruit of the earth is the Church, the Body of Christ. And God has no thought for other things. He causes the others to grow, like the glory of the flower. He looks into the beauty of it, because He knows it will please us. But when speaking about the precious fruit of the earth, our Lord has His mind upon you today.

So if you want the coming of the Lord, you must certainly advocate every believer being filled with the Holy Ghost. The more a man is filled with the Holy Ghost, the more he will be ready to forecast and send forth this glorious truth.

What will be the manifestation of the coming of the Lord? If we were ready, and if the power of God was pressing that truth today, we should be rushing up against one another saying, "He is coming; I know He is coming." "He is coming!" "Yes, I know He is." Every person round about would be saying, "He is coming," and you would know He is coming. Praise God, He is coming!

THE SPIRIT COMES LIKE RAIN

He shall come down like rain upon the mown grass: as showers that water the earth. In his days shall the righteous flourish; and abundance of peace so long as the moon endureth (Psalm 72:6-7).

What a wonderful divine position God means us all to have, to be filled with the Holy Ghost. There is something so remarkable and so divine about this great open door into all the treasury of the Most High. As the Spirit comes like rain upon the mown grass, He turns the barrenness into greenness and freshness and life. Oh, hallelujah!

God would have you know that there is a place where you are dispensed with and where God spiritually comes to be your assurance and sustaining power, till your dryness is turned into springs, till your barrenness begins to be floods, till your whole life becomes vitalized by heaven, till heaven sweeps through you and dwells within and turns everything inside out, and till you are absolutely so filled with divine possibilities that you begin to live in a new creation. The Spirit of the Living God sweeps through all weaknesses.

Beloved, God the Holy Ghost wants to bring us to a great revelation of life. He wants us to be filled with all the fullness of God. One of the most beautiful pictures we have in the Scriptures is of the Trinity. I want you to see how God unfolded heaven, and heaven and earth became the habitation of Trinity. Right on the banks of Jordan, Trinity was made manifest: the voice of God in the heavens looking at His well-beloved Son coming out of the waters, and there the Spirit was manifested in the shape of a dove.

The dove is the only bird without gall, so timid a creature that at the least thing it moves and is afraid. No person can be baptized with the Holy Spirit and have bitterness or gall. When the Holy Ghost gets possession, there is a new man entirely—the whole being becomes saturated with divine power. We become a habitation of Him who is all light, all revelation, all power, and all love. Yea, God the Holy Ghost is so manifested within us that it is glorious.

THE BLESSED BEATITUDES

Blessed are the meek: for they shall inherit the earth (Matthew 5:5).

Oh, give us that blessed state where we are perfectly and wholly made meek. Glory to God! I pray God it shall never be said any more about us that we have lost our temper. Can it be possible God is going to so help us today that we shall be new men and new women in Christ Jesus? The beatitudes of the Spirit are truly lovely.

> *Blessed are they which do hunger and thirst after righteousness: for they shall be filled* (Matthew 5:6).

Oh, hallelujah! Glory to God! Don't you see how God works on these lines? How could you thirst after righteousness without God getting you through? If you go right to the end of the chapter you will see the last verse says: "Be ye therefore perfect, even as your Father which is in heaven is perfect" (Matt. 5:48). So don't fail when you are halfway through or a quarter of the way through. You have to go right through this chapter, and then you have to be perfected even as He is perfect. And the Lord has never told anything to us that cannot be. God is the maker of all things, and He is remolding us. God wants every one of us so blessed that we shall know that we have been in the presence of Jesus.

Brothers, sisters, we must become like the living epistles of Christ. We must display the works of Almighty God in every facet of our day, to every person we know. God wants every one of us to display the beatitudes to the world, not in the spirit of the law, but in the freedom of the Spirit.

THE RIGHTEOUSNESS OF GOD

And my tongue shall speak of thy righteousness and of thy praise all the day long (Psalm 35:28).

We have to be the mouthpiece of God. We have to be God in the world. The Son of God is not here. God is not here, but the Spirit of the Living God has come to fill our bodies, so that we may speak as the oracles of God and teach men the principles of God, in order that men shall hear the voice of God. For truly prophetic utterances shall come forth, and we should listen to them.

"Blessed are they which do hunger and thirst after righteousness: for they shall be filled" (Matt. 5:6). It is grand, "They shall be filled." Oh yes, praise the Lord! Did you notice that this has a grand close? "For they shall be filled." We must emphasize the fact that God will not fail to fill us. You must not miss the plan. In the twenty-fourth Psalm there is a wonderful word:

He that hath clean hands, and a pure heart; who hath not lifted up his soul unto vanity, nor sworn deceitfully. He shall receive the blessing from the Lord, and righteousness from the God of his salvation (Psalm 24:4-5).

No man can hunger and thirst after righteousness if God had not put the thirst in. And I want you to notice what kind of righteousness this is. This righteousness is the righteousness of Jesus. Righteousness is more than paying our way. We hear someone say, "Oh, I never do anything wrong to anybody. I always pay my way." It is a natural law that men should pay their way, but there is a higher law than the natural, and the higher is the law of the Spirit of life. I must see that Jesus is the ideal righteousness, and He is such a perfect righteousness. Believe in Him as the righteousness of God, look at Him as the principle of righteousness, and see the plan of God through Him.

OVERFLOWING WITH MERCY

Blessed are the merciful: for they shall obtain mercy (Matthew 5:7).

You cannot belong to the Lord and not be merciful. You cannot have the baptism of power without also having supernatural mercy. It is a divine touch of heaven. This power of heaven sweeps through disease, stops satanic forces, sweeps through the soul, and stops the devil in his onslaughts. Mercy frees the captives, looses the oppressed, and sets the helpless going. This spirit of mercy is what God wants to give us every morning. Oh, for heaven to bend down upon us with this deep inward cry of a touch of Him—His majesty, His glory, His might, and His power.

Beloved, it is a very remarkable thing that the merciful always obtain mercy. Oh, the spiritual qualities of Jesus have been brought into a life that is quickening us from the dead! Oh that spiritual and natural measure. Look at it—first full, then pressed down, then shaken together, and then running over. That is the measure God wants to give, a spiritual measure, a high tide that never knows anything less than a flowing of life. Oh brother, it is lovely; sister, it is the most charming thing on earth. This divine touch of heaven is sweeter than all; it is better than all. And so it brings us this morning into a place where we say, "Glory to God, it lasts." Has it touched you, beloved?

God wants us to have this new wine. Oh, how it thrills the human heart! How it mighty sweeps you right into heaven!

A CHOSEN PEOPLE

But ye are a chosen generation, a royal priesthood, an holy nation, a peculiar people; that ye should shew forth the praises of him who hath called you out of darkness into his marvellous light (First Peter 2:9).

Sons of God, partakers of all the inheritance, God has chosen us! We are chosen for an order higher than any natural plan. God undertakes to bring you into sonship, into a new birth, into a new inheritance. God's design is far greater than human conception. Do we dare believe we are sons and daughters of God? What manner of love is this? It is far beyond all human comprehension.

God wants me to claim the position of a son—a greater position than I have ever thought. We are called! There need not be any wavering in this truth, but rather we should embrace the substance of a living faith to believe! Believe! The grace of God changes our inheritance forever. It changes our hopes and plans from darkness to light and from the power of satan unto God. Behold what manner of love the Father has bestowed upon us that we should be called the Sons of God.

God has called you to a great place—if you dare believe. God says it shall be so. God makes it so if I believe. It is a great position! It is the greatest position of eternal interest to man. From today God honors you as a son. We shall be like Him. God lives in man to manifest His great plan. The world has lost its charm; I now live in a new order. This is no building on sand. You cannot move this inheritance with the wind. We have a joy and peace the world cannot understand. Children of God—He is in us!

Every Sin Must Go

Now the God of hope fill you with all joy and peace in believing, that ye may abound in hope, through the power of the Holy Ghost (Romans 15:13).

We are filled with the hope of the Glory of God. Our citizenship is in heaven; we belong to the King. Oh, it is so real! We can be entirely possessed by Him, always being changed by the regeneration of the Spirit. We are not looking forward to the things of time. Instead, we are being transformed. The Lord is our life, and where the Spirit of the Lord is there is liberty (see Col. 3:17).

Your life is hid with Christ in God, and He wants to manifest Himself so no darkness can come near you. Children of the Light, love the Light, live in the Light.

Every sin must go
In the cleansing flow
Rolled away, rolled away
The burden of my heart rolled away.

Faith is the living principle of the Word of God, an operation of the Spirit of life, and every man that has this hope purifies himself. Be holy and live in the principle of holiness. It is accomplished if you believe. He that believes has the righteousness of God through Jesus Christ by faith. Beloved, now we are the sons of God, and we know that when He shall appear we shall be like Him, for we shall see Him as He is. God grant it to us all. Amen!

FAITH COMES BY HEARING

He that hath an ear, let him hear what the Spirit saith unto the churches...
(Revelation 2:7).

Jesus said, "Be not afraid, only believe" (Mark 5:36). This is one of those marvelous truths of the Scriptures that is written for our benefit, that we may believe as we see the almightiness of God. It is also our privilege, not only to enter in by faith, but to become partakers of the blessing He wants to give us. My message is on the lines of faith, because some do not hear in faith, and it profits them nothing.

There is a hearing of faith and also a hearing that means nothing more than listening to words. I beseech you to see to it that everything done may bring not only blessing to you but strength and character, so that you may be able to see the goodness of God. I want to impress upon you the importance of believing what the Scripture says. This is a wonderful Word. In fact, all of the Word of God is wonderful. It is an everlasting Word, a Word of power, a Word of health, a Word of substance, a Word of life. It gives life into the very nature of a man, to everyone that lays hold of it, if he believes. I want you to understand that there is a need for the Word of God.

You must catch this truth. Apart from the Holy Ghost and the Word, you will never convince anybody of sin. When the Holy Ghost comes into us, then we shall convince the world of sin. We come into the fullness of God by the Spirit and by the Word.

ENCOUNTERING THE HEALER

And, behold, a woman, which was diseased with an issue of blood twelve years, came behind him, and touched the hem of his garment: For she said within herself, If I may but touch his garment, I shall be whole. But Jesus turned him about, and when he saw her, he said, Daughter, be of good comfort; thy faith hath made thee whole. And the woman was made whole from that hour (Matthew 9:20-22).

Now listen! Some people put the touch of the Lord in the place of faith. The Lord would not have that woman believe that the touch had done it. As soon as she touched Him, she felt the virtue go through her, which is true. When fiery serpents bit the Israelites in the wilderness, God's Word said through Moses, "He that looketh shall be healed" (see Num. 21:8).

The look made it possible for God to do it. Did the touch heal the woman? No. The touch meant something more—it was a living faith. Jesus said, "'thy faith hath made thee whole...'" (Mark 5:34). If God would just move on us to believe, there wouldn't be a sick person who could not receive healing.

This poor, helpless woman, who had been growing weaker and weaker for twelve years, pushed into the crowded thoroughfare when she knew Jesus was in the midst. She was stirred to the depths, and she pushed through and touched Him. If you will believe God and touch Him, you will be healed at once. Jesus is the Healer! Just believe and receive the healing virtue of Jesus.

But he was wounded for our transgressions, he was bruised for our iniquities: the chastisement of our peace was upon him; and with his stripes we are healed (Isaiah 53:5).

WITH FAITH COMES VICTORY

For we through the Spirit wait for the hope of righteousness by faith...faith which worketh by love (Galatians 5:5-6).

The greatest weakness in the world is unbelief; the greatest power is the faith that works by love. Love, mercy, and grace are bound eternally to faith. Fear is the opposite to faith, but there is no fear in love, and those whose hearts are filled with a divine faith and love have no question in their hearts as to being caught up when the Lord Jesus comes.

The world is filled with fear, remorse, and brokenness, but faith and love are sure to overcome. "Who is he that overcometh the world, but he that believes that Jesus is the Son of God?" God has established the earth and humanity on the lines of faith; as you come into line, fear is cast out, the Word of God comes into operation, and you find bedrock.

All the promises of God in Christ are yea and amen to those who believe. When you have faith in Christ, the love of God is so real you feel you could do anything for Jesus. Believers love. "We love Him, because He first loved us" (1 John 4:19). When did He love us? When we were in the mire. What did He say? "Thy sins be forgiven thee" (Matt. 9:5). Why did He say it? Because He loved us. What for? "That He might bring many sons to glory" (Heb. 2:10). His object? That we might be with Him forever.

Beloved, come into line with faith and abide in Christ. God the Holy Ghost will surely help you overcome the trials and temptations you face.

Heir to the Promises of God

For whatsoever is born of God overcometh the world: and this is the victory that overcometh the world, even our faith (First John 5:4).

Our entire pathway is an education for this high vocation and calling. How glorious is this hidden mystery of love to us, the undeserving. I am heir to all the promises of God because I believe. What a great heritage! I overcome because I believe the truth, and the truth makes me free. Christ is the root and source of our faith, and because He is in what we believe for, it will come to pass.

There can be no wavering—he who believes is definite. A definite faith brings a definite experience and a definite utterance. There is no limit to the power of God, for God is rich to all who will call upon Him. Lay in your claim for your children, your families, and your co-workers, that many sons may be brought to glory. As your prayer rests upon the simple principle of faith, nothing shall be impossible to you.

The root principle of all this divine overcoming faith in the human heart is Christ, and when you are grafted deeply into Him you may win many lives to the faith. Jesus is the Way, the Truth, the Life, and the secret to every hard problem in your heart. God confirms this faith in us that we may be refined in the world having neither spot nor blemish nor any such thing. It is the Lord who purifies and brings to the place where the fire burns up the dross, and there anoints us with fresh oil, so that at all times we may be ready for Him. God is separating us for Himself, just as He separated Enoch for a walk with Himself. Because of a definitely implanted faith, Enoch had the testimony that he pleased God before his translation. As the Day of the Lord hastens on, we too need to walk by faith until we overcome all things by our simple belief in the Lord Jesus Christ and we walk right into glory.

THE KINGDOM WITHIN

...the kingdom of heaven suffereth violence, and the violent take it by force (Matthew 11:12).

The Kingdom of Heaven is within us, the Christ, the Word of God. The Kingdom of Heaven suffers violence. How? Every suffering one, every paralyzed condition, if you feel distress in any way, it means that the Kingdom is suffering violence at the hands of the adversary. Could the Kingdom of Heaven bring weakness, disease, consumption, cancers, or tumors? The Kingdom of God is within you. It is the life of Jesus, the power of the Highest, pure, and holy. It has no disease or imperfection. But satan comes to steal and kill and destroy.

Oh! Be not asleep concerning the deep things of God. Have a flaming indignation against the power of satan. Lot had a righteous indignation, but it was too late; he should have had it when he went into Sodom. Be thankful you are alive to hear and that God can change the situation. Fools are afflicted because of their iniquity; they draw near to death, then they cry to the Lord in their trouble, and He heals them out of their distresses. Catch faith by the grace of God and be delivered. Anything that takes me from an attitude of worship, peace, joy, and of consciousness of God's presence has a satanic source. Greater is He that is in you.

By the grace of God we are to see tonight we are to keep authority over the body, making the body subject to the higher power—God's mighty provision for sinful humanity.

> *Jesus paid it all,*
> *All to Him I owe;*
> *Sin had left a crimson stain,*
> *He washed it white as snow.*

THE SPIRIT BRINGS LIFE

Behold, I send the promise of my Father upon you: but tarry ye in the city of Jerusalem, until ye be endued with power from on high (Luke 24:49).

Jesus told His disciples to wait for the Holy Ghost. God also promised through the prophet Joel, "...I will pour out my spirit upon all flesh...upon the servants and upon the handmaids in those days will I pour out my spirit" (Joel 2:28-29).

That is beautiful! The Spirit moving, the Spirit giving, the Spirit speaking, the Spirit making life! Can't you hear the Master say, "My Word is spirit and life?" Only by the Spirit can we understand that which is spiritual. We cannot understand it. We have to be spiritual to understand it. No man can understand the Word of God without being quickened by the new nature. The Word of God is for the new nature. The Word of God is for the new life, to quicken mortal flesh in this order.

What a thought God had when He was forming creation and making it so that we could bring forth sons and daughters in the natural, quickened by the Spirit in the supernatural, received up to glory, and then made ready for a marriage! May God reveal to us our position in this Holy Ghost order that we may see how wonderful the Lord has His mind upon us. Salvation is glory. The Spirit of the Lord is with us, revealing the Word, bringing to us—not eternal life, for we have that—but bringing to us a process of this eternal life, showing us that it puts to death everything else. Eternal life came to us when we believed, but the process of eternal life can begin today, making us know that now we are sons of God.

Do not let fear in any way come in. Let the harmonizing, spiritual life of God breathe through you that oneness, and when we get into oneness today, oh the lift, oh the difference! When our hearts are all blended in one thought, how the Spirit lifts us, how revelation can come! God is ready to take us far beyond anything we have had before.

BAPTISM OF FIRE

...He shall baptize you with the Holy Ghost, and with fire (Matthew 3:11).

Breathe upon us, breathe upon us,
With Thy love our hearts inspire:
Breathe upon us, breathe upon us
Lord, baptize us now with fire.

Thank God for the breath of the Spirit, the new creation dawning. Thank God for spiritual revelation. Fire, holy fire, burning fire, purging fire, taking the dross out, making us pure gold. Fire! "He shall baptize you with the Holy Ghost, and with fire." It is a different burning to anything else. It is a burning without consuming. It is illumining. It is a different illumination to anything else. It so illumines the very nature of the man till within the inner recesses of his human nature there is a burning, holy, divine purging through till every part of dross is consumed.

The fire destroys carnality, in all its darkness, and the human mind, with all its blotches. We shall be burned by fire till the very purity of the Christ of God shall be through and through and through till the body shall be consumed. It seems to me the whole of the flesh of Jesus was finished up, was consumed in the Garden, on the cross, in His tragic moments, in the twelfth chapter of John's gospel as He speaks about seed falling and as He says in the great agony with sweat upon His brow, "If it be possible." There is a consuming of the flesh till the invisible shall become so mighty that that which is visible shall only hold its own for the invisible to come forth into the glorious blessed position of God's sonship.

CHRIST LIVETH IN ME

For whether we live, we live unto the Lord; and whether we die, we die unto the Lord: whether we live therefore, or die, we are the Lord's (Romans 14:8).

Oh, to live! If I live, I live unto Christ. If I die, I die unto Christ. Living or dying, I am the Lord's. What a wonderful word comes to us by this saintly, holy, divine person, who was full of holy richness! I want to say a word more about this holy man, Paul, so filled with the power of the Holy Ghost that when his flesh was torn to pieces with the rocks, the Spirit moved in his mortal life, and though his fleshly body was all the time under great privation, the Spirit moved in his life. By the mercy of God he lived; he moved, energized, and was filled with a power a million times larger than himself. In death oft, in prisons, in infirmities, in weaknesses, in all kinds of trials, but the Spirit filled his human body, and he came to us in a climax, as it were, of soul and body mingled, with the words, "I am ready to be offered. There is the guillotine. I am ready to be offered."

Already he had been on the altar of living sacrifice and taught us how to be, but here he comes to another sacrifice, "I am ready to be offered." It is said Paul was sawn asunder. I do not know how it was, but I thank God he was ready to be offered. What a life! What a consummation! What a holy invocation! What an entire separation! What a prospect of glorification! Can it be? Yes, as surely as you are in the flesh, the same power of the quickening of the Spirit can come to you till whether in your body or out of your body you can only say, "I am not particular, just so I know:

Christ liveth in me!
Christ liveth in me!
Oh! what a salvation this,
That Christ liveth in me.

DWELLING IN DIVINE GLORY

Therefore said I unto you, that no man can come unto me, except it were given unto him of my Father (John 6:65).

Jesus knew from the beginning who would betray Him. Every person that has eternal life, it is the purpose of the Father, it is the loyalty of God's Son, it is the assembly of the firstborn, it is the new begotten of God, it is the new creation, it is a heaven-designed race that is going to equip and get you through everything. You are in the glory. There is a bridge of eternal security for you if you dare believe in the Word of God. There is not a drop between you and the glory. It is divine, it is eternal, it is holy, it is the life of God, and He gives it, and no man can take the life that God gives to you from you.

Wonderful! It is His nature from heaven. It is a divine nature. It is an eternal power. It is an eternal life. It belongs to heaven. I am dwelling upon the sovereignty, the mercy, and the boundless love of God. I am dwelling upon the wonderful power of God's order. The heavens, the earth, and under the earth are submissive to the Most High God. All demon power has to give place to the royal kinship of God's eternal throne. Every knee shall bow, every devil shall be submitted, and God will bring us some day right in the fullness of the blaze of eternal bliss, and the brightness of His presence will cast every unclean spirit and every power of devils into the pit forever and ever and ever.

SAVED THROUGH FAITH

For by grace are ye saved through faith; and that not of yourselves: it is the gift of God (Ephesians 2:8).

We read in the Word that *by faith* Abel offered unto God a more excellent sacrifice than Cain; *by faith* Enoch was translated that he should not see death; *by faith* Noah prepared an ark to the saving of his house; *by faith* Abraham, when he was called to go out into a place which he should after receive for an inheritance, obeyed (see Heb. 11). There is only one way to all the treasures of God, and that is *the way of faith.* All things are possible, the fulfilling of all promises, *to him that believes.*

Read the twelfth chapter of Acts, and you will find that people were praying all night that Peter might come out of prison. But there seemed to be one thing missing despite all their praying—faith. Rhoda had more faith than all the rest of them. When the knock came at the door, she ran to it for she was expecting an answer to her prayers; and the moment she heard Peter's voice, she ran back and announced to them that Peter was standing at the door. They had no faith and did not believe her. When she insisted that he was there, they said, "Well, perhaps God has sent his angel." But Rhoda insisted, "It is Peter." And Peter continued knocking. And they went out and found it so. What Rhoda had believed for had become a glorious fact.

Beloved, there is a lot in an "Amen." You never get any place until you have the Amen inside of you. That was the difference between Zacharias and Mary. When the Word came to Zacharias he was filled with unbelief until the angel said, "thou shalt be dumb...because thou believest not my words" (Luke 1:20). Mary said, "...be it unto me according to thy Word" (Luke 1:38). And the Lord was pleased that she believed that there would be a performance. When we believe what God has said, *there shall be a performance.*

In Constant Communion

For we walk by faith, not by sight (Second Corinthians 5:7).

I find the Bible food for my soul. It is strength to the believer. It builds up our character in God. And as we receive with meekness the Word of God, the Spirit is changing us from glory to glory. And by this Book comes faith, for faith comes by hearing and hearing by the Word of God (see Rom. 10:17). And we know that "...without faith it is impossible to please him..." (Heb. 11:6).

I believe that all our failures come because of an imperfect understanding of God's Word. I see that it is impossible to please God on any other line but by faith, and everything that is not of faith is sin. You say, "How can I obtain this faith?" You see the secret in Hebrews 12:2, "Looking unto Jesus the author and finisher of our faith...." He is the author of faith. Oh, the might of our Christ who created the universe and upholds it all by the might of His power! God has chosen Him and ordained Him and clothed Him, and He who made this vast universe will make us a new creation. He spoke the Word and the stars came into being, can He not speak the Word that will produce a mighty faith in us?

Ah, this One who is the author and finisher of our faith comes and dwells within us, quickens us by His Spirit, and molds us by His will. He comes to live His life of faith within us and to be to us all that we need. And He who has begun a good work within us will complete it and perfect it; for He not only is the author but the finisher and perfecter of our faith.

THE POWER OF THE WORD

All scripture is given by inspiration of God, and is profitable for doctrine, for reproof, for correction, for instruction in righteousness: that the man of God may be perfect, thoroughly furnished unto all good works (Second Timothy 3:16-17).

Never compare the Bible with other books. Comparisons are dangerous. They speak from earth; the Bible speaks from heaven. Never think or say that this Book contains the Word of God. It *is* the Word of God—supernatural in origin, eternal in duration, inexpressible in value, infinite in scope, divine in authorship, regenerative in power, infallible in authority, universal in interest, personal in application, *inspired in totality*. Read it through. Write it down. Pray it in. Work it out. Pass it on. *It is the Word of God.*

The Word of God comes in to separate us from everything that is not of God. It destroys. It also gives life. He must bring to death all that is carnal in us. It was after the death of Christ that God raised Him up on high, and as we are dead with Him we are raised up and made to sit in heavenly places in the new life that the Spirit gives. God has come to lead us out of ourselves into Himself, and to take us from the ordinary into the extraordinary, from the human into the divine, and make us after the image of His Son.

Oh, what a Savior! What an ideal Savior! It is written, "Now are we the sons of God, and it doth not yet appear what we shall be: but we know that, when he shall appear, we shall be like him; for we shall see him as he is" (1 John 3:2). But even now, the Lord wants to transform us from glory to glory, by the Spirit of the Living God. Have faith in God, have faith in the Son, have faith in the Holy Spirit; and the triune God will work in you, working in you to will and to do all the good pleasure of His will.

In the Pursuit of Righteousness

He that followeth after righteousness and mercy findeth life, righteousness, and honour (Proverbs 21:21).

It is as easy as possible to be holy, but you can never be holy by your own efforts. When you lose your heart and He takes your heart, and you lose your desires and He takes your desires, then you live in that sunshine of bliss that no mortal can ever touch. God wants us to be entirely eaten up by this holy zeal of God, so that every day we shall walk in the Spirit. It is lovely to walk in the Spirit, for He will cause you to dwell in safety, to rejoice inwardly, and to praise God reverently.

All excellent glory is in Him; all righteousness is in Him. Everything that pertains to holiness and godliness, everything that denounces and brings to death the natural, everything that makes you know that you have ceased to be forever, is always in an endless power in the risen Christ. What was the ministry of Christ? When you come to the very essence of His ministry it was the righteousness of His purpose. The excellence of His ministry was the glory that covered Him. His Word was convincing, inflexible, divine, with a personality of an eternal endurance. It never failed. He spoke and it stood fast. It was an immovable condition with Him, and His righteousness abides.

May the Holy Ghost show us that there must be a ministry of righteousness. Christ is righteousness through and through. He is lovely! Oh, truly, He is beautiful! God wants to fix it in our hearts that we are to be like Him, like Him in character. God wants righteousness in the inward parts, so that we may be pure through and through. The Bible is the plumb line of everything, and unless we are plumbed right up with the Word of God, we will fail in righteousness.

But we all, with open face beholding as in a glass the glory of the Lord, are changed into the same image from glory to glory, even as by the Spirit of the Lord (Second Corinthians 3:18).

So there is glory upon glory, and joy upon joy, and a measureless measure of joy and glory. Beloved, we get God's Word so wonderfully in our hearts that it absolutely changes us in everything. And as we so feast on the Word of the Lord, so eat and digest the truth and inwardly eat of Christ, we are changed every day from one state of glory to another. You will never find anything else but the Word that takes you there, so you cannot afford to put aside that Word.

These grand truths of the Word of God must be your testimony, must be your life, your pattern. "Ye are...the epistle of Christ" (2 Cor. 3:2-3). God says this to you by the Spirit. When there is a standard that has not yet been reached in your life, God, by His grace and mercy, and by your yieldedness, can fit you for that place. You can only prepare by offering a broken heart, a contrite spirit, and yielding to the will of God. But if you will come with a whole heart to the throne of grace, God will meet you and build you up on His spiritual plane.

The sacrifices of God are a broken spirit: a broken and a contrite heart, O God, thou wilt not despise (Psalm 51:17).

A LIVING REVELATION OF HIS WORD

Now then we are ambassadors for Christ, as though God did beseech you by us: we pray you in Christ's stead, be ye reconciled to God (Second Corinthians 5:20).

God wants to bring to us a living revelation of His Word, a living fact that shall by faith bring into action the principle within our own hearts, so that Christ can dethrone every power of satan. We need to be stirred up to understand the mightiness of God within us, so that we may put to proof the almighty power of God. God has not brought life into us by His Son to remain dormant, but He has brought within us a power, a revelation, a life that is great. God wants to reveal this greatness through us.

John the Baptist had God's revelation for his day. Jesus said there had been no greater among those born. John was filled with the Holy Ghost from his mother's womb, yet Jesus said he who is least in the Kingdom of Heaven is greater than John. John had a wonderful revelation and a mighty anointing; how mightily the power of God rested upon him—all Israel was moved through this mighty power of God through John. Yet satan came to John in prison and suggested a question to his mind: Is Jesus really the Christ? Jesus sent word to reassure John and said:

Go and shew John again those things which ye do hear and see. The blind receive their sight, and the lame walk, the lepers are cleansed, and the deaf hear, the dead are raised up, and the poor have the Gospel preached to them (Matthew 11:4-5).

God wants men to be flames of fire, strong in the Lord and in the power of His might. God has made provision for you to be strong, to be on fire as alive from the dead, as those who have seen the King and have a resurrection touch.

STIRRING UP GOD WITHIN

Wherefore I put thee in remembrance that thou stir up the gift of God, which is in thee by the putting on of my hands (Second Timothy 1:6).

I believe that God wants to bring to our eyes and ears a living realization of what the Word of God is, what the Lord God means, and what we may expect if we believe it. It is only this truth revealed to our hearts that can make us so much greater that we had ever any idea we were.

I believe there are volumes of truth right in the midst of our own hearts; only there is the need of revelation and of stirring ourselves up to understand the mightiness that God has within us. We may prove what He has accomplished in us if we will only be willing to agree with what He has accomplished in us. For God has not accomplished something in us that should lie dormant, but He has brought within us a power, a revelation, a life that is so great, that I believe God wants to reveal the greatness of it.

The possibilities of man in the hands of God! There isn't anything you can imagine greater than what the man may accomplish. But everything on a natural basis is very limited to what God has for us on a spiritual basis. If man can accomplish much in a short time, what may we accomplish if we take the revealed Word and as the truth that God has given us and that he wants to bring out in revelation and force?

Free from Sin

No man can serve two masters: for either he will hate the one, and love the other; or else he will hold to the one, and despise the other. Ye cannot serve God and mammon (Matthew 6:24).

If you love the world, you cannot love God, and the love of God cannot be in you; so God wants a straight cut, because if you are in Christ Jesus, you are of a new creation order; you are in Him and, therefore, you walk in the Spirit and are free from condemnation.

If you are without condemnation, you are in a place where you can pray through, where you have a revelation of Christ. You cannot, if you follow the definite leadings of the Spirit of Christ, have any fellowship with the world; and the Spirit of the Lord reveals this fact to us.

He wants you to live without condemnation. What will that mean? The law of the Spirit of life in Christ Jesus will make you free from the law of sin. Sin will have no dominion over you. You will have no desire to sin, and it will be as true of you as it was of Jesus when He said, "Satan cometh, but findeth nothing in Me" (see John 14:30). Satan cannot condemn; he cannot draw; he has no power.

To be filled with God means that you are free! Filled with joy, peace, blessing, endowment, strength of character in God, and transformed by His mighty power.

REDEMPTION IS GREATER

For what the law could not do, in that it was weak through the flesh, God sending his own Son in the likeness of sinful flesh, and for sin, condemned sin in the flesh (Romans 8:3).

God wants to show you that there is a place where we can live in the Spirit and not be subject to the flesh. Live in the Spirit till sin has no dominion, till we reign in life and see the clothing of God over us in the Spirit. Sin reigned unto death, but Christ reigned over sin and death, and so we reign with Him in life.

People say, "Could anything be greater than the fellowship which prevailed in the Garden of Eden, when God walked and talked and had fellowship with men?" Yes, redemption is greater. The moment a man is born again he is free from the world and lives in heavenly places. He has no destination, except "in the Glory." Redemption is, therefore, greater than the Garden, and God wants you to know that you may come into this glorious redemption not for salvation only, but also for your bodies; to know they are redeemed from the curse of the law; to know you have been made free, and to know that all praise and glory are due to the Son of God. Hallelujah!

No more Egypt places! No more sandy deserts! Praise the Lord! Free from the law of sin and death. *Righteousness was fulfilled in us!* Brother, sister, I tell you there is a redemption, there is an atonement in Christ. His personality dwells in you. You can attain His godlikeness and have a blessed resemblance of Christ, of "God in you" that shall not fail if you believe the Word of God.

FILLED WITH GOD

And to know the love of Christ, which passeth knowledge, that ye might be filled with all the fulness of God (Ephesians 3:19).

Jesus was manifested to destroy the works of the devil. God was manifested in Jesus; the fullness of God came into Jesus, and He walked about, filled with God. Is it to be mine? May I be filled with God? Yes.

How can I be so filled with God that all my movements, all my desires, my entire mind and my entire will is so moved upon by a new power that "I am not," for God has taken me? Praise the Lord! Certainly it can be so.

Did you ever examine the condition of your new birth unto righteousness? Did you ever investigate it? Did you ever try to see what there was in it? Were you ever able to fathom the fullness of that redemption plan that came to you through believing in Jesus?

You have to see that *before the foundation of the world* this *redemption was completed* and set in order before the fall; and then notice that this redemption had to be so mighty and had to redeem us all so perfectly, that there should be no lack in the whole of redemption!

You are born of an incorruptible power of God; born of the Word, who has the personality, the nature of God. You were begotten of God, and you are not your own. You have passed from death unto life, and have become an heir of God and a joint heir of Christ in the measure in which you believe His Word. The natural flesh, the first order, has been changed into a new order, for the first order was Adam, the natural, and the last order was Christ, the Heavenly; and now you become changed by a heavenly power existing in an earthly body. I want you to see that you are born of a power, and have existing in you a power, of which God took and made the world that you are in. It is this law of the Spirit of life in Christ Jesus that makes you free from the law of sin and death.

Thirsty for More

Thou hast loved righteousness, and hated iniquity; therefore God, even thy God, hath anointed thee with the oil of gladness above thy fellows (Hebrews 1:9).

Wherever Jesus went, the multitudes followed Him because He lived, moved, breathed, was penetrated, clothed, and filled with God. As a Son of Man, the Spirit of God rested upon Jesus, the Spirit of creative holiness. It is lovely to be holy. Jesus came to impart to us the Spirit of holiness, a flame of holy, intense desire after God's likeness.

We are only at the edge of things; the Almighty plan is marvelous for the future—a revival to revive all we touch within and without, a floodtide with a cloudburst behind it. Jesus left 120 men to turn the world upside down. The Spirit is upon us to change the situation. We must move on to let God increase in us for the deliverance of others. We must travail through until souls are born and quickened into new relationship with heaven. Jesus had divine authority with power, and He left it for us. We must preach truth, holiness and purity in the inward parts.

I am thirsty for more of God. He was not only holy, but He loved holiness. Hallelujah! Let us live holiness, and revival will come down. God will enable us to do the work to which we are appointed. All Jesus said came to pass including signs and wonders. Amen. Only believe, and yield and yield, until all the vision is fulfilled. God has a design, a purpose, a rest of faith. We are saved by faith, kept by faith. Faith is substance; it is also evidence. God is! He is! And He is a rewarder of those who diligently seek Him. I am sure of this. We have to testify, to bear witness to what we know. To know that we know is a wonderful position.

THE POWER OF THE WORD

In the beginning was the Word, and the Word was with God, and the Word was God (John 1:1).

We are living in the inheritance of faith because of the grace of God, saved for eternity by the operation of the Spirit who brings forth purity unto God. This is to be a new epoch, a new vision, and new power. Christ in us is a thousand times greater than we know. All things are possible if you dare believe. The treasure is in earthen vessels that Jesus may be glorified through. Let us go forth ringing glory to God.

Faith is a substance, a mightiness of reality, a deposit of divine nature, God's creativity within. The moment you believe, you are mantled with a new power to lay hold of possibility and to make it reality. Have the faith of God. The man who comes into great association with God needs a heavenly measure. Faith is the greatest of all. We are saved by a new life, the Word of God, an association with the living Christ. We are a new creation and God is continually taking us into new revelation.

The Word made all. His Word begets me, and within me there is a substance that has almighty power in it if I dare believe. Faith going on to be an act, a reality, a deposit of God, an almighty flame to move you to act, so that signs and wonders are done.

Jesus said, "Are ye able to drink of the cup that I drink of and be baptized with the baptism I am baptized with?" (See Matt. 20:22.) The cup and the baptism are a joined position. You cannot live if you want to bring everything into life. His life is manifested power overflowing. Humanity must decrease if the life of God is to be manifested. There is not room for two kinds of life in one body. Death for life: this is the price to pay for the manifested power of God through you.

WALKING IN THE SPIRIT

If we live in the Spirit, let us also walk in the Spirit (Galatians 5:25).

As the Holy Ghost reveals Jesus, He is so real. He is the living Word—effective, acting, speaking, thinking, praying, and singing. Oh, it is a wonderful life, this substance of the Word of God. It includes possibility and opportunity; it confronts you, bringing you to a place undaunted. Greater is He that is in you. Paul said, "When I am weak, then am I strong." Jesus walked in supremacy. He lived in the Kingdom, and God will take us through because of Calvary. He has given us power over all the power of the enemy. He won it for us at Calvary.

Beloved, there is not one who cannot be helped. God has opened the doors for us to let Him manifest signs and wonders. The authority is inside, not outside. We must keep a strong resolve by resting on the authority of God's Word. Our great desire and purpose is to do what He says.

We are called to walk together with God through the Spirit. It is delightful to know that we can talk with God and hold communion with Him. Through this wonderful baptism in the Spirit that the Lord gives us, He enables us to talk to Himself in a language that no man understands, a language of love. Oh, how wonderful it is to speak to Him in the Spirit, to let the Spirit lift, and lift, and lift us until He takes us into the very presence of God!

I always say that you cannot sing victory in a minor key. If your life is not in constant pitch, you will never ring the bells of heaven. You must always be in tune with God, and then the music will come out as sweet as possible.

SPIRITUAL LIBERTY

For which cause we faint not; but though our outward man perish, yet the inward man is renewed day by day (Second Corinthians 4:16).

There will nothing please the Lord so much as for us to come into our fullness of redemption, because I believe, "the Lord is that Spirit: and where the Spirit of the Lord is, there is liberty" (2 Cor. 3:17). Liberty is beautiful when we satisfy ourselves in the Lord. We must never transgress because of liberty. What I mean is this: to take opportunities because the Spirit of the Lord is upon me would be wrong. But it would be perfectly justifiable if I clearly allow the Spirit of the Lord to have His liberty with me. The Spirit's extravagant positions are always to edify, to strengthen character, and to bring us all the more into conformity with the life of Christ.

I believe we have come to such liberty of the Spirit that it shall be so pure it shall never bring a frown of distraction over another person's mind. When the Holy Ghost gets full concentration of the operation of the human life, He always works out divine wisdom. And when He gets perfect control of a life, His vitality flows through that divine source so that all the people may receive edification in the Spirit.

He shall lift us up into a higher state of grace than ever we have been. You will be in the place where God is absolutely the exchanger of thought, and the exchanger of act, and the exchanger of your inward purity. He will be purifying you all the time, and lifting you higher, and you will know you are not of this world.

The Riches of Salvation

For we know that if our earthly house of this tabernacle were dissolved, we have a building of God, an house not made with hands, eternal in the heavens (Second Corinthians 5:1).

I maintain that, by the grace of God, we are so rich and so abounding. We have such a treasure house, such a storehouse of God. We are the precious fruit of the earth. God has told us that all things shall work together for good to us. God has said that we should be the children of the Highest. God has declared these things in His Word, and you will never reach those beatitudes if you lay hold of the bulrush; it will keep you down.

How am I to have all the treasures of heaven and all the treasures of God? It is not by focusing my eyes on the things that are seen, for they will fade away. I must get my eyes upon the things that are not seen, for they will remain as long as God reigns. Where are we? Are our eyes on the earth? You once had your eyes on the earth. All your members were in the earth, working out the plan of the earth. But now a change is taking place. I read in the Scriptures: "...that ye should be married to another, even to him who is raised from the dead, that we should bring forth fruit unto God" (Rom. 7:4).

You are joined unto another, you belong to another, you have a new life, and you have a new place. God has changed you. Is it a living fact? If it is only a word, it will finish up there, but if it is a spiritual fact, and you reign in it, you will face your day and say, "Thank God, I never knew I was so rich!"

LOSING YOUR LIFE IN CHRIST

For we know that if our earthly house of this tabernacle were dissolved, we have a building of God, an house not made with hands, eternal in the heavens (Second Corinthians 5:1).

That is a perfect condition of a heavenly atmosphere and dwelling place. If I live on the earth, I fail everything. If I continue on the earth, everything I do will be mortal and will die. If I live in the heavenly things, in the heavenly place, everything I touch will become spiritual, vital, purified, and eternal.

Beloved, Christ can bring every one of us, if we will, into an activity of a wholehearted dependency where God will never fail us but we shall reign in life, we shall travail and bring forth fruit. For Zion, when she travails, shall make the house of hell shake. Shall we reach it? Our blessed Lord reached it. Every night He went alone and reached ideals and walked the world in white. He was clothed with the Holy Spirit from heaven.

You cannot get into life but out of death, and you cannot get into death but by life. The only way to go into fullness with God is for His life to swallow up your life. In order for your life to be swallowed up, you must become helpless so that His life strengthens yours. Instead of the natural life being strengthened the supernatural life comes forth with abounding conditions.

People want holiness. People want righteousness. People want purity. People have an inward longing to be clothed upon. May the Lord lead you this morning to the supply of every need far more than you can ask or think. May the Lord bless you as you are led to dedicate yourself afresh to God this very day. Amen.

THROUGH THE BLOOD

...Your life is hid with Christ in God. When Christ, who is our life, shall appear, then shall ye also appear with him in glory (Colossians 3:3-4).

God has a plan for us in this life of the Spirit, this abundant life. Jesus came that we might have life. Satan comes to steal and kill and destroy, but God has for us a full measure of abundance, pressed down, shaken together, and overflowing. God fills us with His own personality and presence, making us salt and light and giving us revelation of Himself. God is with us in all circumstances, afflictions, persecutions, and in every trial, girding us with truth.

God's Word is a tremendous Word, a productive Word, and it produces power. It produces God-likeness. We get to heaven through the Word of God, and we have peace through the blood of His cross. Redemption is ours through the knowledge of the Word. I am saved because God's Word says so.

If thou shalt confess with thy mouth the Lord Jesus, and shalt believe in thine heart that God hath raised him from the dead, thou shalt be saved (Romans 10:9).

If I am baptized with the Holy Spirit it is because Jesus said, "Ye shall receive power, the Holy Ghost coming upon you." We must all have one idea—to be filled with the Holy Ghost, to be filled with God.

The Holy Ghost has a royal plan, a heavenly plan. He came to unveil the King, to show the character of God, to unveil the precious blood. As I have the Holy Spirit within me, I see Jesus clothed for humanity; the Spirit moved Jesus, led Jesus. We read of some who heard the Word of God but were not profited, because faith was lacking in them. We must have a living faith in God's Word, quickened by the Spirit.

Walking in a Royal Way

Verily, verily, I say unto you, He that heareth my word, and believeth on him that sent me, hath everlasting life, and shall not come into condemnation; but is passed from death unto life (John 5:24).

Only believe! Only believe! God will not fail you, beloved. It is impossible for God to fail. Believe God and rest in Him. God's rest is an undisturbed place, a place where heaven bends to meet you. The Bible is the most important Book. But some people have to be pressed in before they can be pressed on. Oh! This glorious inheritance of joy and holy faith, this glorious baptism in the Holy Ghost. It is a perfected place! All things are new, for you are Christ's and Christ is God.

God means us to be in this royal way. When God opens a door, no man can shut it. John made a royal way, and Jesus also walked in this royal way. Jesus left this way for us to follow Him so He could bring forth the greater works through us. Jesus left His disciples with a revelation that meant much to them, and He adds much more to that revelation through His Spirit. God will supply all our needs, so that a great indwelling force of power may meet the needs of the poor through us. If we do not step into our privileges, it is a tragedy.

There is no standing still in this blessed life. It is a fearful thing to fall into the hands of the Living God. Oh, that blessed concession of God to fill us with the Holy Ghost. He will lead us into all truth and show us things to come.

THE PURE IN HEART SEE GOD

Blessed are the pure in heart: for they shall see God (Matthew 5:8).

As He is, so are we in this world. We are the offspring of God with impulse divine. We must get into line. The life of the Son of God to make the whole body a flame of fire. After you have received you shall have power. God has given me a blessed ministry to help to stir others up—our gatherings must be for increase. I am jealous to come into the divine plan. If I wait further for power I have mistaken the position. If I could only feel the power! Ah! We have been too much on that line. When the Holy Ghost came He came to abide. What are you waiting for? God is waiting for you to act. Jesus was perfect activity. He began to do and to teach. He lived in the realm of divine appointment making the act come forth. God never separates power from holiness—the pure in heart see God. The Holy Ghost reveals Him. He who believes that Jesus is the Christ overcomes the world. He is the source of revelation. The fullness of God dwells in Him.

> *Christ liveth in me,*
> *Christ liveth in me.*
> *Oh, what a salvation this,*
> *That Christ dwelleth in me.*

After the Holy Ghost came, with the revelation of the purity of Jesus, we saw things that were unseen before. The Holy Ghost came in as the breath of the moving of the mighty wind. Is the Holy Spirit a person? Yes! Wind! Breath! Fire! Our God is a consuming fire. You never know what you have until you begin. We are baptized into one Spirit. We are tomorrow what we design to be today. This is a rising tide, a transformation.

THE POWER OF TESTIMONY

Who is he that overcometh the world, but he that believeth that Jesus is the Son of God? This is he that came by water and blood, even Jesus Christ; not by water only, but by water and blood. And it is the Spirit that beareth witness, because the Spirit is truth. For there are three that bear record in heaven, the Father, the Word, and the Holy Ghost: and these three are one. And there are three that bear witness in earth, the Spirit, and the water, and the blood: and these three agree in one (First John 5:5-8).

This is the confidence we have in Him. If we ask anything according to His will, He hears us, and we have the petition we have desired of Him. When the Holy Ghost comes in, it is to crown Jesus King. We must dare and press on to that place where God will come forth with mighty power. Men of faith always have a good report. God has given us a large open door and will bless people as we dare to believe His Word.

The opportunity is all around—the needy are everywhere, so begin! You shall receive power, the Holy Ghost coming upon you. The stones will cry out against us if we do not press on. May God give us the hearing of faith that the power may come down like a cloud. Press on until Jesus is glorified and multitudes are gathered in. Let us all stand and offer ourselves unto God.

Receive! Receive! Receive! You shall receive power.

We must be the mouthpieces of God, not by letter but by the Spirit, and we must be so in the will of God that He will rejoice over us with singing. If we are in the Spirit, the Lord of life is the same Spirit. "Now the Lord is that Spirit: and where the Spirit of the Lord is, there is liberty" (2 Cor. 3:17). There is no liberty that is going to help the people so much as your testimony of faith.

Continually Filled with the Spirit of God

And the disciples were filled with joy, and with the Holy Ghost (Acts 13:52).

It is a serious thing to have the baptism and yet be stationary; to live two days in succession on the same spiritual plane is a tragedy. We must be willing to deny ourselves everything to receive the revelation of God's truth and to receive the fullness of the Spirit. Only that will satisfy God, and nothing less must satisfy us.

Yes, there is a power, a blessing, an assurance, a rest in the presence of the Holy Ghost. You can feel His presence and know that He is with you. You need not spend an hour without this inner knowledge of His holy presence. With His power upon you there can be no failure. You are above par all the time.

The most important thing is to make Jesus Lord. Men can grow lopsided by emphasizing the truth of divine healing. Man can get wrong by all the time preaching on water baptism. But we never go wrong in exalting the Lord Jesus Christ, giving Him the preeminent place and magnifying Him as both Lord and Christ, yes, as God of all gods. As we are filled with the Holy Ghost, our one desire is to magnify Him. We need to be filled with the Spirit to get the full revelation of the Lord Jesus Christ. God's command is for us to be filled with the Spirit. We are no good if we only have a full cup. We need to have an overflowing cup all the time. It is a tragedy not to live in the fullness of overflowing. See that you never live below the overflowing tide.

INWARD POWER

...Be filled with the Spirit (Ephesians 5:18).

While it is right to covet earnestly the best gifts, you must recognize that the most important thing is to be filled with the power of the Holy Ghost Himself. You will never have trouble with people who are filled with the power of the Holy Ghost, but you will have a lot of trouble with people who have the gifts and have no power. The Lord wants us to come behind in no gift, but at the same time He wants us to be so filled with the Holy Ghost that it will be the Holy Spirit manifesting Himself through the gifts.

Where the glory of God alone is desired, you can look for every needed gift to be made manifest. To glorify God is better than to idolize gifts. We prefer the Spirit of God to any gift, but we can look for the Trinity in manifestation, different gifts by the same Spirit: there are different administrations, but the same Lord, and diversities of operation, but the same God working all in all. Can you conceive of what it will mean for our Triune God to be fully manifesting Himself through us?

Watch that great locomotive boiler as it is filled with steam. You can see the engine letting off some of the steam, as it remains stationary. It looks as though the whole thing might burst. You can see saints like that. They start to scream, but that is not to edification. But when the locomotive moves on, it serves the purpose for which it was built, and pulls along much traffic with it. It is wonderful to be filled with the power of the Holy Ghost, and for Him to serve His own purposes through us.

Through our lips divine utterances flow, our hearts rejoice, and our tongue is glad. It is an inward power within which is manifested in outward expression. Jesus Christ is glorified. As your faith in Him is quickened, from within you there will flow rivers of living water. The Holy Spirit will pour through you like a great river of life and thousands will be blessed because you are a yielded channel through whom the Spirit may flow.

THE NAKED WORD OF GOD

And this is the confidence that we have in him, that, if we ask any thing according to his will, he heareth us: and if we know that he hear us, whatsoever we ask, we know that we have the petitions that we desired of him (First John 5:14-15).

It is necessary that we find our bearings in this Word. There is nothing that will bring to you such confidence as a life that is pleasing to Him. When Daniel's life pleased God, he could ask to be kept in the lions' den. But you cannot ask with confidence until there is a perfect union between you and God, as there was always perfect union between God and Jesus. The foundation is confidence in and fidelity to God. Some people think that Jesus wept because of the love that He had for Lazarus, but that could not be. Jesus knew that these people who were around the grave, and even Martha, had not come to the realization that whatever He would ask of the Father He would give Him. Their unbelief brought brokenness and sadness to the heart of Jesus; and He wept because of this.

The moment you pray you find that the heavens are opened. If you have to wait for the heavens to be opened something is wrong. I tell you disobedience to God and His laws makes us lose the confidence. Jesus said He prayed for the benefit of those who stood around, but He knew that the Father always heard Him. And because He knew that His Father always heard Him, He knew that the dead could come forth.

There are times when there seems to be a stone wall in front of us, as black as midnight, and there is nothing left but confidence in God. There is no feeling. What you must do is have a fidelity and confidence to believe that He will not fail, and cannot fail. We shall never get anywhere if we depend upon our feelings. There is something a thousand times better than feelings, and it is the naked Word of God.

FAITH

So then faith cometh by hearing, and hearing by the Word of God (Romans 10:17).

There is a divine revelation within you that came in when you were born from above, and this is a real faith. To be born into the new kingdom is to be born into a new faith. Paul speaks of two classes of brethren, one of whom are obedient, and the other of whom are disobedient. The obedient always obey God when He first speaks. God will use obedient believers to make the world know that there is a God. The just shall live by faith. You cannot talk about things that you have never experienced.

It seems to me that God has a process of training us. You cannot take people into the depths of God unless you have been broken yourself. I have been broken and broken and broken. Praise God that He is near to them that are of a broken heart. You must have a brokenness to get into the depths of God. There is a rest of faith; there is a faith that rests in confidence on God. God's promises never fail.

The Word of God can create a faith that is never daunted, a faith that never gives up and never fails. We fail to realize the largeness of our Father's measure, and we forget that He has a measure which cannot be exhausted. It pleases Him when we ask for most. "How much more." It is the much more that God shows me. I see that God has a plan of healing. It is on the line of perfect confidence in Him. The confidence comes not from our much speaking, but it comes because of our fellowship with Him. There is a wonderful fellowship with Jesus. The chief thing is to be sure that we take time for communion with Him. There is a communion with Jesus that is life, and that is better than preaching. If God tells you definitely to do anything, do it, but be sure it is God who tells you.

Count It All Joy

My brethren, count it all joy when ye fall into divers temptations (James 1:2).

James addressed this letter "...to the twelve tribes which are scattered abroad" (James 1:1). Only one like the Master could stand and say to the people, "Count it all joy" when they were scattered everywhere, driven to their wits' end, and persecuted. The Scriptures say that "...they wandered in deserts, and in mountains, and in dens and caves of the earth" (Heb. 11:38). These people were scattered abroad, but God was with them.

It does not matter where you are if God is with you. He that is for you is a million times more than all who can be against you. Oh, if we could by the grace of God see that the beatitudes of God's divine power come to us with such sweetness, whispering to us, "Be still, My child. All is well." Only be still and see the salvation of the Lord. Oh, what would happen if we learned the secret to only ask once and believe? What an advantage it would be if we could only come to a place where we know that everything is within reach of us.

God wants us to see that every obstacle can be moved away. God brings us into a place where the difficulties are, where the pressure is, where the hard corner is, where everything is so difficult that you know there are no possibilities on the human side so that God must do it. All these places are of God's ordering. God allows trials, difficulties, temptations, and perplexities to come right along our path, but there is not a temptation or trial that can come to man that God has not given a way out. You have not the way out; it is God who can bring you through.

PERFECT LOVE

And we have known and believed the love that God hath to us. God is love; and he that dwelleth in love dwelleth in God, and God in him. Herein is our love made perfect, that we may have boldness in the day of judgment: because as he is, so are we in this world. There is no fear in love; but perfect love casteth out fear: because fear hath torment. He that feareth is not made perfect in love (First John 4:16-18).

Let me tell you what perfect love is. He who believes that Jesus is the Son of God will overcome the world. What is the evidence and assurance of salvation? You must believe on the Lord Jesus in your heart. Every expression of love is in the heart. When you begin to breathe out your heart to God in affection, the very being of you, the whole self of you, desires Him. Perfect love means that Jesus has gotten a grip of your intentions, desires, and thoughts and has purified everything. Perfect love cannot fear.

What God wants is to impregnate us with His Word. His Word is a living truth. I would pity one who has gone a whole week without temptation. Why? God only tries the worthy people. If you are passing through difficulties, and trials are rising, and darkness is appearing, and everything becomes so dense you cannot see through—hallelujah! God is seeing through. He is a God of deliverance, a God of power. Oh, He is close to you if you will only believe. He can anoint you with fresh oil; He can make your cup run over. Jesus is the balm of Gilead, yes, the Rose of Sharon.

WAITING FOR OUR AFFECTION

And the Lord direct your hearts into the love of God, and into the patient waiting for Christ (Second Thessalonians 3:5).

I believe that God, the Holy Ghost, wants to bring us into line with such perfection of beatitude, of beauty, that we shall say, "Lord, Lord, though Thou slay me, yet will I trust Thee" (see Job 13:15). When the hand of God is upon you, and the clay is afresh in the Potter's hands, the vessel will be made perfect, as you are pliable in the almightiness of God. Only melted gold is minted; only moistened clay is molded; only softened wax receives the seal; only broken, contrite hearts receive the mark as the Potter turns us on His wheel. We are shaped and burnt to take and keep the mark, the mold, and the stamp of God's pure gold. He can put the stamp on this morning. He can mold you afresh. He can change the vision. He can move the difficulty.

The Lord of Hosts is in the midst of you and is waiting for your affection. Remember His question, "...Simon, son of Jonas, lovest thou me more than these?" (John 21:15). He never lets the chastening rod fall upon anything except what is marring the vessel. If there is anything in you that is not yielded and bent to the plan of the Almighty, you cannot preserve that which is spiritual only in part. When the Spirit of the Lord gets perfect control, then we begin to be changed from glory to glory by the expression of God's light in our human frame, and the whole of the body begins to have the fullness of His life manifested until God so has us that we believe all things.

Brother, Sister, if God brings you into oneness and the fellowship with the most High God, your nature will quiver in His presence, but God can chase away all the defects, all the unrest, all the unfaithfulness, all the wavering and He can establish you with such strong consolation of almightiness that you just rest there in the Holy Ghost by the power of God ready to be revealed. God invites us to higher heights and deeper depths.

IF CHRIST BE IN YOU

And if Christ be in you, the body is dead because of sin; but the Spirit is life because of righteousness (Romans 8:10).

I am realizing very truly these days that there is a sanctification of the Spirit where the thoughts are holy, where the life is beautiful, with no blemish. As you come closer into the presence of God, the Spirit wafts revelations of His holiness till He shows us a new plan for the present and the future. The heights and depths, the breadth, the lengths of God's inheritance for us are truly wonderful.

> *Make me better, make me purer,*
> *By the fire which refines,*
> *Where the breath of God is sweeter,*
> *Where the brightest glory shines.*
> *Bring me higher up the mountain*
> *Into fellowship with Thee,*
> *In Thy light I'll see the fountain,*
> *And the blood that cleanseth me.*

Oh, what a vision, beloved! The body is dead because sin is being judged, is being destroyed. The whole body is absolutely put to death, and because of that position there is His righteousness, His beauty; and in the Spirit is life, freedom, and joy. The Spirit lifts the soul into the presence of heaven. Ah, this is glorious. "Count it all joy when ye fall into divers temptations" (James 1:2). Perhaps you have been counting it all sadness until now. Never mind. Turn the scale and you will get a lot out of it, more than ever you had before. Tell it to Jesus now. Express yours inward heart throbbings to Him.

> *He knows it all, He knows it all,*
> *My Father knows, He knows it all,*
> *The bitter tears, how fast they fall,*
> *He knows, my Father knows it all.*

THAT RESURRECTION TOUCH

That I may know him, and the power of his resurrection...(Philippians 3:10).

Beloved, God wants us to have some resurrection touch about us. We may enter into things that will bring us sorrow and trouble, but through them God will bring us to a deeper knowledge of Himself. Never use your human plan when God speaks His Word. You have your cue from an Almighty source that has all the resources, which never fades away. His coffers are beyond measure, overflowing with extravagant abundance, waiting to be poured out upon us.

Hear what the Scripture says: "...God...giveth to all men liberally, and upbraideth not..." (James 1:5). The almighty hand of God comes to our weakness and says, "If thou dare to trust Me and will not waver, I will abundantly satisfy thee out of the treasure house of the Most High." "And upbraideth not." What does it mean? He forgives, He supplies, He opens the door into His fullness, and He makes us know that He has done it all. When you come to Him again, He gives you another overflow without measure, an expression of a Father's love.

Who wants anything from God? He can satisfy every need. He satisfies the hungry with good things. I believe a real weeping would be good for us. You are in a poor way if you cannot weep. I do thank God for my tears. They help me so that I do like to weep in the presence of God. I ask you in the name of Jesus, will you cast all your care upon Him? "For he careth for you" (1 Pet. 5:7). I am in great need this morning; I do want an overflow. Come on, beloved. Let us weep together. God will help us. Glory to God. How He meets the need of the hungry.

WORKING WITHIN IN THE WILDERNESS

As it is written in the book of the words of Esaias the prophet, saying, The voice of one crying in the wilderness, Prepare ye the way of the Lord, make his paths straight (Luke 3:4).

The Word of God came to John the Baptist in the wilderness. There was nothing ordinary about John—all was extraordinary. John was filled with the Holy Ghost from his mother's womb. He had the burden. John was stern, but the land was opening to Jesus. John left his father and mother behind, his heart bleeding at the altar. He bore the burden, the cry, and the need of the people. John came neither eating nor drinking—John came crying in the desert. The only place he could breathe and be free was in the wilderness—the atmosphere of heaven—until he turned with a message to declare the preparation needed—repentance.

God spoke to John in the wilderness about water baptism. It was a clean-cut, new way. He had been with circumcision, but this new message of repentance and water baptism made him an outcast. It was the breaking down of the old plan. God put John through an individual purging and repurposing in his life. God pressed through his life. God moved multitudes through John and changed the situation. All were startled! Awakened! Thinking the Messiah had come. The searching was tremendous! Is this He? Who can it be? John preached the mighty Gospel of Jesus to the crowd. The people, the multitude, cried out and were baptized by John in the Jordan as they confessed their sins.

As with John, the Spirit first works in you, then God works through you for others. He searches us deeply, purging and pressing us into His likeness. Then He pours His mighty Spirit through us to touch the world. But we must first let Him work in us.

THE LIKENESS OF GOD

Verily, verily, I say unto you, He that believeth on me, the works that I do shall he do also; and greater works than these shall he do; because I go unto my Father. And whatsoever ye shall ask in my name, that will I do, that the Father may be glorified in the Son. If ye shall ask any thing in my name, I will do it (John 14:12-14).

Jesus is speaking here, and the Spirit of God can take these words of His and make them real to us. "He that believeth on Me...greater works than these shall he do." What a word! Is it true? If you want the truth, where will you get it? "Thy word is truth," Christ said to the Father. When you take up God's Word, you get the truth.

God is not the author of confusion or error, but He sends forth His light and truth to lead us into His holy habitation, where we receive a revelation of the truth like the noonday in all its clearness. The Word of God works effectually in us, as we believe it. It changes us and brings us into new fellowship with the Father, with the Son, and with the Holy Spirit, into a holy communion, into unwavering faith, into a mighty assurance, and it will make us partakers of the very nature and likeness of God, as we receive His exceedingly great and precious promises and believe them. Faith comes by hearing, and hearing by the Word of God. Faith is the operative power.

We read that Christ opened the understanding of His disciples, and He will open up our understanding and our hearts and will show us wonderful things that we should never know but for the mighty revelation and enlightenment of the Spirit that He gives to us.

POWER TO OVERCOME

He that believeth on me, the works that I do shall he do also; and greater works than these shall he do; because I go unto my Father (John 14:12).

Did any one ever work as He did? I do not mean His carpentering. I refer to His work in the hearts of the people. He drew them to Him. They came with their needs, with their sicknesses, with their oppression, and He relieved them all. This royal Visitor, who came from the Father to express His love, talked to men, spent time with them in their homes, found out their every need. He went about doing good and healing all who were oppressed of the devil, and He said to them and He says to us, "You see what I have been doing, healing the sick, relieving the oppressed, casting out demons. The works that I do shall ye do also." Dare you believe? Will you take up the work that He left and carry it on? "He that believeth on Me!" What is this? What does it mean? How can just believing bring these things to pass? What virtue is there in it?

There is virtue in these words because He declares them. If we will receive this word and declare it, the greater works shall be accomplished. This is a positive declaration of His, "He that believeth on Me, greater works than these shall he do," but unbelief has hindered our progress in the realm of the spiritual.

Put away unbelief. Open your heart to God's grace. Then God will come in and place in you a definite faith. He wants to remove every obstruction that is in the world before you. By His grace He will enable you to be so established in His truth, so strong in the Lord and in the power of His might, that whatever comes across your path to obstruct you, you can arise in divine power and rebuke and destroy it.

FAITH FOR VICTORY

Therefore I say unto you, What things soever ye desire, when ye pray, believe that ye receive them, and ye shall have them (Mark 11:24).

He that believes that Jesus is the Christ overcomes the world. Because we believe that Jesus is the Christ, the essence of divine life is in us by faith and causes a perfect separation between the world and us. We have no room for sin. It is a joyful thing for us to be doing what is right. He will cause that abundance of grace to so flow into our hearts that sin shall not have dominion over us. Sin shall not have dominion, or sickness, or affliction. He that dares to believe, dares to trust, will see victory over every oppression of the enemy.

These are the words of our Lord Jesus. It is not our word but the word of the Lord, and as this word is in us; He can make it like a burning passion in us. We make the Word of God our own as we believe it. We receive the Word and we have the very life of Christ in us. We become supernatural by the power of God. We find this power working through every part of our being. Now Christ gives us something besides faith. He gives us something to make faith effectual. Dare to say in faith and it shall be done. Christ has promised these things, and He does not lie.

Grace is God's benediction coming right down to you, and when you open the door to Him—that is an act of faith—He does all you want and will fulfill all your desires. You open the way for God to work as you believe His Word, and God will come and supply your every need all along the way.

LIKE A DOVE

The Spirit of the Lord is upon me, because he hath anointed me to preach the gospel to the poor; he hath sent me to heal the brokenhearted, to preach deliverance to the captives, and recovering of sight to the blind, to set at liberty them that are bruised, to preach the acceptable year of the Lord (Luke 4:18-19).

John baptized Jesus in the Jordan, and the Holy Spirit descended in a bodily shape like a dove upon Him. Being full of the Holy Ghost, the Spirit led Jesus into the wilderness to be more than conqueror over the archenemy. Then He returned in the power of the Spirit to Galilee and preached in the synagogues, and at last He came to His old hometown, Nazareth, where He announced His mission in the words I have just quoted. For a brief while He ministered on the earth, and then gave His life a ransom for all. But God raised Him from the dead. And before He went to the glory, He told His disciples that they should receive the power of the Holy Ghost upon them, too. Thus, through them, His gracious ministry would continue.

This power of the Holy Ghost was not only for a few apostles, but even for them that are afar off, even as many as the Lord our God should call (see Acts 2:39), even for us today. Some ask, "But was not this power just for the privileged few in the first century?" No. Read the Master's great commission as recorded by Mark, and you will see it is for them who believe.

And he said unto them, Go ye into all the world, and preach the gospel to every creature. He that believeth and is baptized shall be saved; but he that believeth not shall be damned (Mark 16:15-16).

THE MIND OF CHRIST

Nicodemus...came to Jesus by night, and said unto him, Rabbi, we know that thou art a teacher come from God: for no man can do these miracles that thou doest, except God be with him. Jesus answered and said unto him, Verily, verily, I say unto thee, Except a man be born again, he cannot see the Kingdom of God (John 3:1-3).

Nicodemus was struck by the miracles performed, and Jesus pointed out the necessity of a miracle happening every time a man would see the kingdom. When a man is born of God, is brought from darkness to light, a mighty miracle is performed. Jesus saw every touch by God as a miracle, and so we may expect to see miracles today. It is wonderful to have the Spirit of the Lord upon us. I would rather have the Spirit of God on me for five minutes than to receive a million dollars.

There is a place where God, through the power of the Holy Ghost, reigns supreme in our lives. The Spirit reveals, unfolds, takes of the things of Christ and shows them to us, and prepares us to be more than a match for satanic forces.

Do you see how Jesus mastered the devil in the wilderness? Jesus knew He was the Son of God and satan came along with an "if." How many times has satan come along to you this way? He says, "After all, you may be deceived. You know you really are not a child of God." If the devil comes along and says that you are not saved, it is a pretty sure sign that you are. When he comes and tells you that you are not healed, it may be taken as good evidence that the Lord has sent His Word and healed you (see Ps. 107:20). The devil knows that if he can capture your thought life, he has won a mighty victory over you. His great business is injecting thoughts, but if you are pure and holy you will instantly shrink from them. God wants us to let the mind that was in Christ Jesus—that pure, holy, humble mind of Christ—be in us.

SEEK THE LORD

...Wait for the promise of the Father, which, saith he, ye have heard of me. For John truly baptized with water; but ye shall be baptized with the Holy Ghost not many days hence (Acts 1:4-5).

In the first chapter of Acts, we see that Jesus gave commandment to the disciples that they should wait for the promise of the Father, and He told them that not many days hence they would be baptized with the Holy Ghost. Luke tells us that he had written his former treatise concerning all that Jesus began both to do and teach. The ministry of Christ did not end at the cross, but the Acts and the epistles give us accounts of what He continued to do and teach through those whom He indwelt. And our blessed Lord Jesus is still alive and continues His ministry through those who are filled with His Spirit. He is still healing the brokenhearted and delivering the captives through those on whom He places His Spirit.

Are you oppressed? Cry out to God. It is always good for people to cry out. You may have to cry out. The Holy Ghost and the Word of God will bring to light every hidden, unclean thing that must be revealed. There is always a place of deliverance when you let God search out what is spoiling and marring your life. He is just the same Jesus—exposing the powers of evil, delivering the captives, letting the oppressed go free, purifying them, and cleansing their hearts.

Those evil spirits that inhabited the man who had the legion did not want to be sent to the pit to be tormented before their time, and so they cried out to be sent into the swine. Hell is such an awful place that even the demons hate the thought of going there. How much more should men seek to be saved from the pit? God is compassionate and says, "Seek ye the Lord while he may be found..." (Isa. 55:6). And He has further stated, "For whosoever shall call upon the name of the Lord shall be saved" (Rom. 10:13). Seek Him now, call on His name right now, and there is forgiveness, healing, redemption, deliverance, and everything you need for right here and now and that will satisfy you throughout eternity.

RECEIVE THE HOLY GHOST

But ye shall receive power, after that the Holy Ghost is come upon you...
(Acts 1:8).

When I see people seeking the Holy Ghost, do you know, beloved, I believe it is wrong to wait for the Holy Ghost; the Holy Ghost is waiting for us. The Holy Ghost has come and He will not return until the Church goes to be with her Lord forevermore. So when I see people waiting, I know something is wrong. The Holy Ghost begins to reveal uncleanness, judgments, hardness of heart, all impurity, and until the process of cleansing is complete, the Holy Ghost cannot come. When the body is clean and sanctified, however, Jesus delights to fill us with His Holy Spirit. I know it will never stop, for we are wholly God's in the process of cleansing, as the Holy Ghost prepares our bodies to be a temple for the Spirit to be made like Him.

If you will believe, you shall see the salvation of God. Only believe. The baptism of the Holy Ghost brings us into the Kingdom of God, out of a natural order, and into a divine order with divine power for promotion until we are charged by the power of God. A man is in a great place when he has no one to turn to but God. With only God to help, we are in a great place. God shall change the situation. Not I, but Christ. We have come into a divine place where God works the miracle. We are baptized into the same Spirit and have become partakers of the divine nature, living in a divine transformation, with our whole body aflame with the same passion Jesus had.

THE ABIDING HOLY GHOST

And ye shall be witnesses unto me... (Acts 1:8).

Here is the hallmark of the mystery of divine ability, which must come in its fullness in our day. Jesus went about doing good. It is a tremendous thing to be born into by God. It is a serious thing, once engrafted, to grieve the Holy Ghost. The baptism of the Holy Ghost is a fearful place if we are not going on with God. Great is our conviction of sin. The Holy Ghost comes to abide. God must awaken us to our responsibility, an inbreathed life of power. We can never be the same after the Holy Ghost has come upon us. We must be instant in season and out of season, full of the Spirit, always abounding, always full of the life of God, and ready for every emergency.

The baptism of the Holy Ghost is to prepare us for when two ways meet where only God can give decision and bring off the victory, so you can stand still and see the salvation of God. It's a great place to reach such a place of dignity, to be able to shout when the walls are up, when it looks as if all would fail. Shout! Shout! The victory is yours! The victory is yours! Not to come at some future time. The victory is yours. Just as you shout, the ensign will arise and the walls will fall and you will walk in and possess the city. It's a designed position. It is not of our making; it's a rising position, honoring the cry of the Master. "It is finished," not, "to be finished." "It is finished."

God can make manifest that position as I am in loyalty with His divine purposes. It is no little thing to be baptized with the Holy Ghost and to be saved from the power of satan unto God. God has declared it: we must be living epistles of Christ, known and read by all men.

THE BREATH OF THE ALMIGHTY

In the last day, that great day of the feast, Jesus stood and cried, saying, If any man thirst, let him come unto me, and drink (John 7:37).

God will not allow those who trust in Him to become failures in the straightened place. God does the work. Yes. He can. This Word is a living Word of divine activity with momentum. It has the power to change the nature by the power of the Spirit. All disease and weakness must go at the rebuke of the Master. God enables us to bind the enemy and set free the captive. Beloved, arise, for the glory of the Lord is risen upon you, pouring life into your weakness. God makes you the head, not the tail.

This is a wonderful day, filled with the Spirit. The breath of the Almighty, God the Holy Ghost, can take the Word of Jesus and inbreathe into the hearers a quickened Spirit. Jesus began to do, then to teach. You are in a divine process with revelation and divine power in the place of manifestation.

We have an almighty God. He imparts power to a needy world, for you have renewed power, the power of changing. The Holy Ghost is coming upon you. Then God is glorified and the needs of the poor are met. You receive power, the unction goes forth, and God is glorified.

I am pursuing a course—how to enter the Kingdom of the Master so that I am full of compassion for others, a compassion that fails not, that sees when no other sees, that feels when no other feels. It's a divine compassion. It comes by the Word, for He is the Word of God. Beloved, enter into this compassion with me. Receive the Holy Ghost, and go forth in power.

Holy Victory and Boldness

If we confess our sins, he is faithful and just to forgive us our sins, and to cleanse us from all unrighteousness (First John 1:9).

You must give God your life. You must see that sickness has to go and God has to come in; that your lives have to be clean, and God will keep you holy; that you have to walk before God, and He will make you perfect. I want to say to you believers that there is a very blessed place for you to attain to, and the place where God wants you is a place of victory. When the Spirit of the Lord comes into your life, it must be victory.

The disciples, before they received the Holy Ghost, were always in bondage. Jesus said to them one day, just before the Crucifixion, "One of you shall betray Me," and they were so conscious of their inability and their human depravity and their helplessness that they said one to another, "Is it I?" And then Peter was ashamed that he had taken that stand, and he rose up and said, "Though all men deny Thee, yet will not I." And likewise the others rose and declared that neither would they; but they—every one—did leave Him.

But, beloved, after they received the power of the endowment of the Holy Ghost upon them, if you remember, they were made like lions to meet any difficulty. They were made to stand any test. After the power of God fell upon them in the upper room, those men who failed before the Crucifixion came out in front of all those people who were gathered together and accused them of crucifying the Lord of Glory. They were bold. What had made them so? I will tell you. Purity is bold. Take, for instance, a little child. It will gaze straight into your eyes for as long as you like, without winking once. The purer the bolder, and I tell you God wants to bring us into that divine purity of heart and life—that holy boldness. Not officiousness; not swelled-headedness; not self-righteousness; but a pure, holy, divine appointment by One who will come in and live with you, defying the powers of satan, and standing you in a place of victory—overcoming the world.

CHANGED INTO THE POWER OF GOD

These things I have spoken unto you, that in me ye might have peace. In the world ye shall have tribulation: but be of good cheer; I have overcome the world (John 16:33).

Brother, God can make *you* an overcomer. When the Spirit of God comes into your body, He will transform you; He will quicken you. Oh, there is a life in the Spirit that makes you free from the law of sin and death, and there is an audacity about it—also there is a personality about it. It is the personality of the Deity. *It is God in you.* I tell you that God is able to so transform and change and bring you into order by the Spirit that you can become a new creation after God's order. There is no such thing as defeat for the believer. Without the Cross, without Christ's righteousness, without the new birth, without the indwelling Christ, without this divine incoming of God, I see myself a failure. But God the Holy Ghost can come in and take our place till we are renewed in righteousness and made the children of God.

Do you think that God would make you to be a failure? God has never made man to be a failure. He made man to be a son, to walk about the earth in power. When I look at you, I know that there is a capability that can be put into you that can control and bring everything into subjection. Yes, there is the capacity of the power of Christ to dwell in you, to bring every evil thing under you till you can put your feet upon it and be master over the flesh and the devil; till within you nothing rises except that which will magnify and glorify the Lord. Peter was frail, helpless, and, at every turn of the tide, a failure. And God filled that man with the Spirit of His righteousness, till he went up and down, bold as a lion, and when he came to death—even crucifixion—he counted himself unworthy of being crucified like his Lord, and asked that his murderers would hang him upside down on the tree. There was a deep submissiveness in Peter, a power that was greater than all flesh. Peter had changed into the power of God.

Truth in Scripture

He that believeth on me, as the scripture hath said, out of his belly shall flow rivers of living water (John 7:38).

The Scriptures do not tell two stories. They tell the truth. I want you to know the truth, and the truth will set you free. What is truth? Jesus said, "I am the way, the truth, and the Life" (John 14:6). I do not find anything in the Bible but holiness and nothing in the world but worldliness. If I live in the world, therefore, I shall become worldly; but, on the other hand, if I live in the Bible, I shall become holy. This is the truth, and the truth will set you free. The power of God can remodel you. He can make you hate sin and love righteousness. He can take away bitterness and hatred and covetousness and malice and can so consecrate you by His power, through His blood, that you are made pure—every bit holy. God has given me the way of life, and I want to give it to you, as though this were the last day I had to live. Jesus is the best there is for you, and you can take Him with you.

God gave His Son to be the propitiation for your sins, and not only so, but also for the sins of the whole world. Jesus came to make us free from sin—free from disease and pain. When I see any who are diseased and in pain, I have great compassion for them. When I lay my hands upon them, I know God means men to be so filled with Him that the power of sin shall have no effect upon them, and they shall go forth, as I am doing, to help the needy, sick, and afflicted.

But what is the main thing? To preach the Kingdom of God and His righteousness; Jesus came to do this. John came preaching repentance. The disciples began by preaching repentance toward God and faith in the Lord Jesus Christ, and I tell you, beloved, if God has really changed you, there is repentance in your heart.

THE SUBSTANCE OF FAITH

Now faith is the substance of things hoped for, the evidence of things not seen. For by it the elders obtained a good report. Through faith we understand that the worlds were framed by the word of God, so that things which are seen were not made of things which do appear (Hebrews 11:1-3).

Faith is the substance and it is a reality, and God wants to bring us to the fact of it. He wants us to know that we have something greater than we can see, because everything you can see and handle is going to pass away. The heavens are going to be wrapped up, and the earth will melt with fervent heat, but the Word of the Lord shall abide forever.

God spoke the Word and made the world, and I want to impress upon you this wonderful Word, which made the world. I am saved by the incorruptible Word, the Word that made the world, and so my position by faith is to lay hold of the things that cannot be seen and believe the things that cannot be understood.

Live in the Acts of the Apostles and you will see every day some miracle worked by the power of the Living God. It comes right to the threshold, and God brings everything along to you. Do not fail to claim your holy position so that you will overcome the power of the devil. The best time you have is when you have the most difficult position. Ask God to give you the grace to use the faith you have. Peter had precious, wonderful faith. Beloved, only believe!

Without Sin

For we have not an high priest which cannot be touched with the feeling of our infirmities; but was in all points tempted like as we are, yet without sin (Hebrews 4:15).

The very thought of Jesus will confirm truth and righteousness and power in your mortal bodies. There is something very remarkable about Him. When John saw Him, the impression that he had was that He was as a Lamb without blemish and without spot. When God speaks about Him, He says, "He came forth in the brightness of the expression of the countenance of God." When revelation comes it says, "In Him is all fullness."

I want you, as Paul describes it wonderfully in Hebrews, to consider Him when you are weary and tempted and tried and all men are against you. Consider Him who has passed through it all, that He might be able to succor you in the trial as you are passing through, and He will sustain you in the strife. When all things seem as though you have failed, the Lord of hosts, the God of Jacob, the salvation of our Christ, will so reinforce you that you will be stronger than any concrete building that was ever made.

The greatest plan that ever Jesus showed forth in His ministry was the ministry of service. He said, "I am amongst you as one that serveth" (see Luke 22:27). And when we come to a place where we serve for our love's sake, because it is the divine hand of the Master upon us, we shall find out that we shall never fail. Love never fails when it is divinely appointed in us.

CLIMBING JACOB'S LADDER

...I am among you as he that serveth (Luke 22:27).

The greatest plan that Jesus ever showed forth in His ministry was the ministry of service. He said, "I am amongst you as one that serveth." And when we come to a place where we serve for our love's sake, because it is the divine hand of the Master upon us, we shall find out that we shall never fail. Love never fails when it is divinely appointed in us, but this is not so in our human nature and has not been from the beginning.

I speak to you precisely on resurrection touches. We have come into divine resurrection touches in Christ. God had to use His operation power for the greatest work on earth. Christ rose from the dead by the operation of the power of God. And the operation of the resurrection of Christ in our hearts will dethrone, and at the same time as it dethrones, it will build. Callousness will have to change; hardness will have to disappear; all evil thoughts must be gone, and instead of that, lowliness of mind.

What beautiful cooperation with God in thought and power and holiness! This is a wonderful plan for us. But how will it come to pass? It comes by transformation, resurrection, thoughts of holiness, intense zeal, desire with God for all of God, till we live and move in the atmosphere of holiness.

Don't forget the ladder that Jacob saw. When I was going over the hill and saw Jerusalem for the first time, a person said to me, "See that place there? That is where the ladder was seen from earth to heaven." Brother, if you have not reached all, the ladder is from heaven to earth to take you from earth to heaven. Do not be afraid of taking the steps. You will not slip back. Have faith in God. Resurrection life is divine. It is more divine in thought, more wonderful in revelation. You are living in the Spirit, wakened into all likeness, quickened by the same Spirit!

His Divine Life

Thus saith the LORD, thy Redeemer, the Holy One of Israel; I am the LORD thy God which teacheth thee to profit, which leadeth thee by the way that thou shouldest go (Isaiah 48:17).

Beloved, God would have us see that no man is perfect on any line, only as the living Word abides in Him. Jesus Christ is the express image of God, and the Word is the only factor that works in you and brings forth these glories of identification between you and Christ.

When we have entered in with God into the mind of the Spirit, we have found that God reaches our hearts. Nothing is so sweet as to know the heart yearns with compassion. Eyes may see, ears may hear, but you may be immovable on the lines of love and compassion unless you have an inward cry—where deep calls unto deep. When God gets into the depth of our heart, He purifies every intention and fills us with His own joy. When Moses received the tablets of stone, God made his face to shine. How much deeper and more wonderful are His commandments written in our hearts. They are the deep movements of eternity. Oh, beloved, let God the Holy Ghost have His way in unfolding to us the grandeur of Christ's glory. When we have no confidence in ourselves, our whole trust rests upon the authority of the mighty God who has promised to be with us at all times.

The Baptism of the Holy Ghost infuses us into an intensity of zeal—into the likeness of Jesus. This divine life will let us see God has begun His work in us. There is no other plan for a baptized soul, except to be dead indeed. We must live in the Spirit, growing in the ideal as our Master, always beholding the face of Jesus. His righteousness will be revealed within when we cry out of the depths for God's righteousness. May God lead our every step in His divine life. Amen.

ABOVE ALL WE CAN ASK

To the intent that now unto the principalities and powers in heavenly places might be known by the church the manifold wisdom of God (Ephesians 3:10).

This wisdom of God is only revealed in the depths of humiliation where the Holy Ghost has full charge. There alone the vision comes to all His saints. We are now in the process of revelation.

The Holy Ghost is the ideal and brings out the very essence of heaven through the human soul. Oh, the need of the baptism of the Holy Ghost.

What is the glory? All the glory that ever comes is from Him. You have the glory in the measure that you have the Son of glory in you. If you are filled with Jesus, you are filled with the glory. When we have the spirit of wisdom and revelation in the knowledge of Him, there is nothing to hinder the Holy Ghost having the control of the whole being.

"That Christ may dwell in your hearts by faith..." (Eph. 3:17). Faith is the production of all things. Are we children of circumstances or children of faith? If we are on natural lines, we are troubled at the wind blowing. As it blows it whispers fearfulness; but if you are rooted and grounded you can stand the tests, and it is only then that you prove what is the breadth and length and depth and weight of the love of Christ (see Eph. 3:18-19).

He is the light of life. He promised to give us exceedingly abundantly above all we can ask or think. How can this be, you say? It is fulfilled in the glory. It's a tremendous thing. God will do something! Beloved, it is not according to your mind at all, but according to the mind of God, according to the revelation of the Spirit. The blood has been poured out. The Holy Ghost has been sent down. It's above all you can ask! But God can do it.

A HOLY CALLING, A HOLY VISION

Humble yourselves therefore under the mighty hand of God, that he may exalt you in due time (First Peter 5:6).

What a holy calling! We each have our own work and we must do it, so that boldness may be ours in the day of the Master's appearing. What a privilege to care for the flock of God, to be used by God to encourage people, to help stand against the manifold trials that affect the needy. As the Lord is always encouraging us, we can encourage others. There must be willingness, a ready mind, a yielding to the mind of the Spirit. There is no place for the child of God in God's great plan except in humility.

God can never do all He wants to do, all that He came to do through the Word, until He gets us to the place where He can trust us, and we are in *abiding fellowship with Him* in His great plan for the world's redemption. We have this illustrated in the life of Jacob. It took God twenty-one years to bring Jacob to the place of contrition of heart, humility, and brokenness of spirit. God even gave him power to wrestle with strength, and he said, "I think I can manage after all," until God touched his thigh, making him know that he was mortal and that he was dealing with immortality. As long as we can save ourselves, we will do it.

Look at the Master at Jordan, submitting Himself to the baptism of John, then again submitting Himself to the cruel cross. Truly, angels desire to look into these things, and all heaven is waiting for the man who will burn all the bridges behind him and allow God to begin a plan in righteousness, so full, so sublime, beyond all human thought, but according to the revelation of the Spirit.

LIVING FOR GLORY

Make you perfect in every good work to do his will, working in you that which is wellpleasing in his sight, through Jesus Christ; to whom be glory for ever and ever. Amen (Hebrews 13:21).

When perfection is spoken of in the Word, it is always through a joining up with eternal things. Perfection is a working in us of the will of God. There are some of us here that would be faint-hearted if we thought we had to be perfect to get in the blessing with God. How is it going to be?

The blood of Jesus covers our actions and our mind. As we yield and yield, we find ourselves in possession of another mind, the mind of Christ, and this allows us to understand the perfection of His will. Someone says, "I can never be perfect! It is beyond my furthest thought." Just so! It is! But as we press on, the Holy Ghost enlightens and we enter in, as Paul says, according to the revelation of the Spirit. I am perfected as I launch out into God by faith, His blood covering my sin, His righteousness covering my unrighteousness, His perfection covering my imperfection. *I am holy and perfect in Him.*

You must be established in the fact that it is His life, not yours. Your faith is in His Word, in His life. You are disconnected from the earth and insulated by faith. Be strengthened by the fact that God is doing the business, not you. You are in the plan, and God is working it out. You can be settled in your knowledge that you are in a union with His will. It is a daily work, an eternal work of righteousness that perfects you in the Spirit. Live for His glory, let there be no withdrawal, no relinquishing, no looking back, but going on for His glory now and forever.

THE WIND OF LIFE

The spirit of God hath made me, and the breath of the Almighty hath given me life (Job 33:4).

I believe that God, the Holy Ghost, wants to reveal the fullness of redemption through the power of Christ's atonement on Calvary until every soul shall get a new sight of Jesus, the Lamb of God.

He is lovely. He is altogether lovely. Oh, He is so beautiful! You talk about being decked with the rarest garments, but oh, brother, He could weep with those who weep. He could have compassion on all. There were none who missed His eye. Do you know that love and compassion are stronger than death? If we touch God, the Holy Spirit, He is the ideal principle of divine life for weaknesses; He is health; He is joy.

He is waiting to impart life. Oh, if only you would believe! Oh, you need not wait another moment. Receive the impartation of life by the power of the Word. Do you now know that the Holy Ghost is the breath of heaven, the breath of God, the divine impartation of power that moves in us and raises us from the dead and quickens all things? One of the things that happened on the day of Pentecost in the manifestation of the Spirit was a mighty, rushing wind. The Third Person of the Trinity manifested as the wind; He gave power, mighty revelation, glory, and emancipation. Glory to God! His power moves us, transforms us, and sends us. This wind was the life of God coming and filling the whole place where they were sitting. And when I say to you, "Breathe in," I do not mean merely breathe; I mean breathe in God's life, God's power, and the personality of God. Hallelujah!

FAITH FOR HEALING

And a certain woman, which had an issue of blood twelve years, and had suffered many things of many physicians, and had spent all that she had, and was nothing bettered, but rather grew worse, when she had heard of Jesus, came in the press behind, and touched his garment. For she said, If I may touch but his clothes, I shall be whole (Mark 5:25-28).

This poor woman was in an awful state. She had spent all her money on physicians and was "...nothing bettered, but rather grew worse." No doubt she thought of her weakness, but faith is never weak. She may have been very weary, but faith is never weary. The opportunity had come for her to touch Him, "And straightway the fountain of her blood was dried up; and she felt in her body that she was healed of that plague" (Mark 5:29).

The opportunity comes to you now to be healed. Will you believe? Will you touch Him? There is something in a living faith that is different from anything else. I have seen marvelous things accomplished just because people said, "Lord, I believe." Jesus knew that virtue had gone out of Him and He said, "Who touched me?" The woman was fearful and trembling, but she fell down before the Lord and told Him all the truth. "And he said unto her, Daughter, thy faith hath made thee whole; go in peace, and be whole of thy plague" (Mark 5:34).

The power of the Spirit is in our midst. How many of you dare claim your healing? Who will dare claim your rights of perfect health? All things are possible to him who believes. Jesus is the living substance of faith. You can be perfectly adjusted by the blood of Jesus. We must believe in the revelation of the Spirit's power and see our blessed position in the risen Christ. Only believe! Only believe! All things are possible, only believe! "For as the lightning cometh out of the east, and shineth even unto the west; so shall also the coming of the Son of man be" (Matt. 24:27).

OUR GLORIOUS INHERITANCE

*[I] cease not to give thanks for you, making mention of you in my prayers...
that ye may know what is the hope of his calling, and what the riches of the
glory of his inheritance in the saints (Ephesians 1:16,18).*

This is the plan of God for us, our inheritance, that the world should receive a blessing through us. God has come in us, living in us with a divine life. The Word of the Lord will reveal that all things are possible, if you dare believe, and signs and wonders are within reach of all of us.

The Lord has this treasure within us. We have become partakers of the divine nature: the moment you believe, you are begotten with a new power, a lively hope, the power to lay hold of impossibilities and make them actual. I have seen the possibilities of every man in Christ. I must show you that by the grace of God, it is impossible under all circumstances to fail.

There is nothing made without the Word of God. Peter says, "I am begotten with this Word." There is something within me that has Almighty power within it, if I dare believe it; it is heavenly treasure and is called the substance of faith.

When you have nothing, you can possess all things. If you rely upon anything else, you cannot possess the greater things. Our infinite God is behind the man who has no trust in earthly things; you are in a place where you are trusting in nothing but God. I have never yet condemned anyone of taking means, or using means, but I see the difference between having a whole Bible, a rich inheritance in God, and a part. I see the plan of God is so much greater than all else; if I have Him, I have life in me; I have an abundance of this life. The living Word of Christ saves me, which is the substance of my faith.

THE NECESSITY OF THE ROCK

Through faith we understand that the worlds were framed by the Word of God, so that things which are seen were not made of things which do appear (Hebrews 11:3).

Now beloved, you will clearly see that God wants to bring us to a foundation. If we are ever going to make any progress in divine life, we shall have to have a real foundation. And there is no foundation, only the foundation of faith for us. All our movements, and all that ever will come to us which is of any importance, will be because we have *a Rock*. And if you are on the Rock, no powers can move you. Today we need to firmly stand on the Rock.

On any line of principle of your faith, you must have something established in you to bring that forth. And there is no establishment outside God's Word for you. Everything else is sand. Everything else shall split apart. If you build upon anything else but the Word of God, on imaginations, sentimentality, any feelings, or any special joy, it will mean nothing without a foundation in the Word of God.

We must not measure ourselves by ourselves; if we do we shall always be small. Measure yourself by the Word of God, the great measurement that God brings to you. Don't be fearful; He wants to make us strong, powerful, stalwart, resolute, resting upon the authority of God. It is on this line that I can only speak, and shall we not equip ourselves like men? We have seen the King; we have been quickened from death. God has worked special miracles in us all; we are made with one great design and purpose. Let us fashion our life on the Rock, on the plan He has for us.

We must have something better than sand, and everything is sand except the Word. There isn't anything that will remain—we are told the heaven and earth will be melted up. But we are told the Word of God shall be forever, and not one jot or tittle of the Word of God shall fail. And if there is anything that is satisfying me today more than another, it is, "...thy word is settled in heaven" (Ps. 119:89).

THE WORD BECAME FLESH

In the beginning was the Word, and the Word was with God, and the Word was God. The same was in the beginning with God. All things were made by him; and without him was not any thing made that was made (John 1:1-3).

There we have the foundation of all things, which is the Word. It is a substance. It is a power. It is more than relationship. It is personality. It is a divine injunction to every soul who enters into this privilege, to be born of this Word, to be created by this Word, to have knowledge of this Word. It is a substance; it is an evidence of things not seen. It brings about what you cannot see. It brings forth what is not there and takes away what is there. God took the Word and made the world of things that did not exist. And we live in the world that was made by the Word of God, and it is inhabited by millions of people. It is a substance.

And Jesus is the Word. The Word became flesh and dwelt among us. And we beheld and saw the glory of God. Oh, beloved, He is the Word! He is the principle of God. He is the revelation sent forth from God. All fullness dwells in Him. God does nothing small. He is grand, possesses all manner of wisdom, and is unfolding the mysteries and the grandeur of His design for humanity. Oh, this wonderful salvation.

God is a reality and proving His mightiness in the midst of us. And as we open ourselves to divine revelation, and get rid of all things that are not of the Spirit, then we shall understand how mightily God can take us on in the Spirit, and move the things that exist, and bring the things that do not into prominence. Oh, the riches, the depths of the wisdom of the Most High God! It took nine months to bring us forth into the world after we were conceived, but it only takes one moment to beget us as sons. As He was conceived in the womb by the Holy Ghost, so we were conceived the moment we believed and became sons of God with promise. And oh how the whole creation groans for sonship!

THE REVELATION OF GOD

Concerning his Son Jesus Christ our Lord, which was made of the seed of David according to the flesh; and declared to be the Son of God with power, according to the spirit of holiness, by the resurrection from the dead (Romans 1:3-4).

Sons must have power. We must have power with God, power with man. We must be above all the world. We must have power over satan, power over the evils. I want you just this moment to think with me because it will help you with this concept. You can never make evil pure. Anything that is evil never becomes pure in that sense. There is no such thing as ever changing impurity into purity. The carnal mind is never subject to the will of God and cannot be. There is only one thing that can be done—it must be destroyed.

I want you to go with me to when God cast out satan who was impure. Satan lived in the glory, but his pride spoiled him. And pride is an awful thing. Pride in the heart, thinking we are something when we are nothing. Building up a human constitution out of our own. Oh, yes, it is true the devil is ever trying to make you think you are great. You never find God doing it. It is always satan who comes on and says, "What a wonderful address you gave! How wonderful you did that, and how wonderful you prayed and sung that song." That is all the devil. There is not an atom of God in it, not from beginning to end.

The people have always perished when there has been no vision. God wants us to have visions, and revelations, and manifestations. You cannot have the Holy Ghost without having manifestations. You cannot have the Holy Ghost without having revelations. You cannot have the Holy Ghost without your nature being transformed. It was the only credential that Joshua and Caleb could enter the land because they were of another spirit. And we must live in a power, in a transformation, and in a divine attainment where we cease to be, where God becomes enthroned so richly.

In Pursuit of God

But without faith it is impossible to please him: for he that cometh to God must believe that he is, and that he is a rewarder of them that diligently seek him (Hebrews 11:6).

I believe that there is only one way to all the treasures of God, and it is the way of faith. All the promises are yea and amen to those who believe. You get to know God by an open door of grace. He has made a way. It is a beautiful way; all His saints can enter in by that way and find rest. The way is the way of faith; there isn't any other way. If you climb up any other way, you cannot work it out.

There is a big difference between saying that you have faith and having it. God wants to impart to us a faith that can laugh at impossibilities and rest in peace. There is no other faith that appropriates what God has for us to us. The greatest sin in the entire world is unbelief. It will shut everything out from you; it will hinder your progress and blight the prospects of your life. It will shut heaven and open hell; but if you believe God your faith will shut hell and open heaven. Faith is the substance of things hoped for and the evidence of things not seen. God's work is a perfect plan. There is no such thing as reading the Word of God and remaining ordinary after it. It is impossible for you to have a refusal from God if you believe Him. God rewards those who diligently seek Him.

It is impossible to have faith without peace. There are nine gifts of the Spirit and nine fruits, and the third gift is the gift of faith, and the third fruit is peace. It is impossible to have faith without peace. Faith is not howling and screaming and rolling on the floor, it is not making a lot of to-do, it is simply God manifested in the flesh through a faith that rests upon the omnipotent Word of God. Oh, this blessed incarnation of the Spirit through the Word of God! Jesus wants us to know that by the power of the Spirit that you can be filled with the presence of God, and God wants you to know that His name never fails.

Lost in the Spirit

...Be filled with the Spirit (Ephesians 5:18).

Do you remember the day when the Lord laid His hand on you? You say, "I couldn't do anything but praise the Lord." Well, that was only the beginning. Where are you today? The divine plan is that you increase until you receive the measureless fullness of God. You do not have to say, "It was wonderful when I was baptized with the Holy Ghost!" If you have to look back to the past to make me know that you are baptized, then I fear you are backslidden. If the beginning was good, it ought to be better day by day, until everyone is fully convinced that you are filled with the fullness of God! I don't want anything less than being full, and to be fuller and fuller until I am overflowing day by day.

Do you realize that if you have been created anew and begotten again by the Word of God, there is within you the same word of power, the same light and life that the Son of God Himself had? God wants to flow through you in marvelous power and divine utterance and grace until your whole body is aflame of fire. God intends each soul in Pentecost to be a live wire. So many people who have been baptized with the Holy Ghost came in because there was a movement, but so many of them have become monuments, and you cannot move them. The baptism in the Spirit should be an ever-increasing enlargement of grace. Jump in, stop in, and never come out; for this is the baptism to be lost in, where you only know one thing, and that is the desire of God at all times.

Oh, Father, grant unto us a real look into the glorious liberty you have designed for the children of God who are delivered from this present evil world, separated, sanctified, and made meet for Your use, whom You have designed to be filled with all Your fullness!

THE EVERLASTING WORD

The grass withereth, the flower fadeth: but the word of our God shall stand for ever (Isaiah 40:8).

Suppose that all the people in the world did not believe; it would make no difference to God's Word. It would be the same. You cannot alter God's Word. It is from everlasting to everlasting, and they who believe in it shall be like Mount Zion, which cannot be moved.

God heals by the power of His Word. But the most important thing is this: Are you saved? Do you know the Lord? Are you prepared to meet God? You may be an invalid as long as you live, but you may be saved by the power of God. You may have a strong, healthy body, but may go straight to hell because you know nothing of the grace of God and salvation. Thank God, I was saved in a moment—the moment I believed. And God will do the same for you. The Spirit of God wants us to understand there is nothing that can interfere with our getting into perfect blessing except our unbelief. Unbelief is a terrible hindrance. As soon as we are willing to allow the Holy Ghost to have His way, we shall find great things will happen all the time.

But oh, how much of our own human reason we have to get rid of! How much human planning we have to become divorced from! What would happen right now if everyone believed God? I love the thought that God the Holy Ghost wants to emphasize truth. If we will only yield ourselves to the divine plan, He is right here to do great things, and to fulfill the promise in Joel 2:21, "Fear not, O land; be glad and rejoice: for the Lord will do great things."

Unclouded Faith

...Believe in the Lord your God, so shall ye be established; believe his prophets, so shall ye prosper (Second Chronicles 20:20).

How many of us believe the Word? It is easy to quote it, but it is more important to believe it than to quote it. It is very easy for me to quote, "Now are we the sons of God," but it is more important for me to know whether I am a son of God. When the Son of God was on the earth, He spoke with power, and His words came to pass.

Faith is the evidence, the assurance, that the word that God has said is true. It is the gift of God. Unclouded faith proves all things, believes all things. Those who have faith in God see the promise. God can so fill a man with His Spirit that he can laugh and believe in the face of a thousand difficulties. Keep His Word at all costs. God's will is worked in us until the substance of faith dwells within. We are so saved that all things are possible. The Word of God brought forth this entire world. Faith is creative.

Jesus is all we need. Faith is loyalty to Jesus, belief on the basis of the blood. The just shall hold constant communion with God and be so shaped by the Spirit through faith in the Word. Truly, beloved, God has prepared us for wonderful things.

But as it is written, Eye hath not seen, nor ear heard, neither have entered into the heart of man, the things which God hath prepared for them that love him. But God hath revealed them unto us by his Spirit: for the Spirit searcheth all things, yea, the deep things of God (1 Corinthians 2:9-10).

VICTORIOUS FAITH

For whatsoever is born of God overcometh the world: and this is the victory that overcometh the world, even our faith (First John 5:4).

Everything depends upon our being filled with the Holy Ghost. And there is nothing you can come short of if the Holy Ghost is the prime mover in your thoughts and life, for He has a plan greater than ours and if He can only get us in readiness for His plan to be worked out, it will be wonderful.

Everything depends upon our believing God. If we are saved, it is only because God's Word says so. We cannot rest upon our feelings. We cannot do anything without a living faith. It is surely God Himself who comes to us in the person of His beloved Son and so strengthens us that we realize that our body is surrounded by the power of God, lifting us into the almightiness of His power. All things are possible to us in God. The purpose of God for us is that we might be in the earth for a manifestation of His glory, that every time satanic power is confronted, God might be able to say of us as He did of Job, "What do you think about him?" God wants us so manifested in His divine plan in the earth that satan will have to hear God. The joy of the Lord can be so manifested in us that we shall be so filled with God that we shall be able to rebuke the power of the devil.

God greatly wants to bring us in harmony with His will. Every one of us can be filled to overflowing. God is here with His divine purpose to change our weakness into mighty strength and faith. The Word of God! Oh, brother, sister, have you got it? It is marrow to your bones. It is unction. It is resurrection from every weakness. It is life from the dead. God the Holy Ghost would give us such a revelation of Christ that we would go away as men who had seen the King. Let God have His way. Touch God today. Faith is victory.

WALKING IN FAITH

[Abraham]...believed in hope, that he might become the father of many nations, according to that which was spoken, So shall thy seed be. And being not weak in faith, he considered not his own body now dead, when he was about an hundred years old, neither yet the deadness of Sarah's womb: he staggered not at the promise of God through unbelief; but was strong in faith, giving glory to God (Romans 4:18-20).

Faith is our great inheritance, for the just shall live by faith. Abraham waited twenty-five years for God to fulfill His promise to give him a son. He looked to God, who never fails, and believed His word. As we live in the Spirit, we live in the process of God's mind and act according to His will.

Could a child be born? Yes—on the law of faith in God who had promised. Faith always brings joy! Faith makes us know who God is. Those who trust in God want not. The more Abraham was pressed, the more he rejoiced. He didn't look at his own body. Abraham was strong in faith, giving glory to God, believing God was able to perform what He had promised. The less there was to hope in, the more Abraham believed in hope.

If we knew the value of trial, we should praise God for it. It is in the furnace of affliction God gets us to the place where He can use us (see Isa. 48:10). Before God puts you in the furnace, He knows you will go through. It is never above what we are able to bear. If you know the baptism of the Holy Ghost is in the Scriptures, never rest until God gives it to you. If you know it is scriptural to be healed of every weakness—to be holy, pure, to overcome amid all conditions—never rest until you are an overcomer. If you have seen the face of God and have had vision and revelation, never rest until you attain it. We must be blameless amid the crooked positions of the world. Jesus was God's pattern for us, a first fruit clothed with power. We must walk in His name.

THE FAVORED PLACE

I am crucified with Christ: nevertheless I live; yet not I, but Christ liveth in me: and the life which I now live in the flesh I live by the faith of the Son of God, who loved me, and gave himself for me (Galatians 2:20).

A re you in? Oh, be *in!* Be in Christ in God. Be ready for action, moved by the very breath of the Spirit of God, to pray through, to preach through, to manifest the glory of the Lord. A double portion of the Spirit will bathe you in ecstasy, delight, and joy, so that each son will say, "Thy will be done."

To have union with God is worth all. God alone has the Word of eternal life, and He offers us direct communion with Him. It is a transmitting power, an ascent and descent of communication, charged by the divine operation of the Spirit. You are in a favored place, a priceless position. If you have no way out but God, you will gain the closest revelation of who He is.

He spoke of that spiritual bread at the Last Supper. The disciples were so fed from the depths; they knew they had never had that before. This was not an earthly conception; it had no earth roots. It was all divine, perfect. God wants such a people that He can feed with the finest wheat. For the harvest is fully ripe and ready to be gathered in.

I beseech you therefore, brethren, by the mercies of God, that ye present your bodies a living sacrifice, holy, acceptable unto God, which is your reasonable service. And be not conformed to this world: but be ye transformed by the renewing of your mind, that ye may prove what is that good, and acceptable, and perfect, will of God (Romans 12:1-2).

FLAMES OF FIRE

And of the angels he saith, Who maketh his angels spirits, and his ministers a flame of fire (Hebrews 1:7).

His ministers are to be flames of fire! This means so much for us. It seems to me that no man with a vision, especially a vision by the Spirit's power, can read that wonderful verse—that divine truth—without being kindled to such a flame of fire that burns up everything that interferes with his progress.

You must believe that God the Holy Ghost is touching you. For this is not your own human desire—it is a divine inclination, a heavenly call, that has caused you to begin to crave after God, and He will never cease until He has accomplished every purpose of His in your heart. It is His purpose to take you into the Promised Land. What an inward burning—what an inward craving God can give! It is a taste of the heavenlies! And we want more of these wonderful joys, until God has absolutely put His stamp upon everyone by the power of His presence.

Now, beloved, you can have something that you can carry with you into the glory. What do you want? Is anything too hard for God? God can meet you now. God sees you inwardly, He knows all about you, nothing is hidden from Him, and He can satisfy your soul and give you a spring of eternal blessing that will carry you right through. You are made a flame by the igniting of His power inside you.

Offer yourselves to Him and reach heaven.

WALKING IN THE POWER OF GOD

Finally, my brethren, be strong in the Lord, and in the power of his might (Ephesians 6:10).

One thing moves me—the truth that I must at all costs live by the power of the Spirit. You can never be the same again after you have received this wonderful baptism in the Holy Spirit. It is important that day by day we should be full of wisdom and faith and full of the Holy Ghost. God is longing for us to come into such a fruitful position as the sons and daughters of God, with the marks of heaven upon us, His divinity bursting through our humanity, so that He can express Himself through our lips of clay.

He can take clay lips, weak humanity, and make an oracle for Himself. He can take frail human nature and by His divine power make our bodies to be His holy temple, washing our hearts whiter than snow. Our Lord Jesus says, "...All power is given unto me in heaven and in earth" (Matt. 28:18). He longs that we should be filled with faith and with the Holy Ghost and declares to us, "...He that believeth on me, the works that I do shall he do also; and greater works than these shall he do; because I go unto my Father" (John 14:12). He has gone to the Father so that we might display greater works than He did on the earth.

The Holy Spirit has the divine commission from heaven to impart revelation to every son of God concerning the Lord Jesus, to unfold to us the gifts and the fruit of the Spirit. He will take of the things of Christ and show them to us. When we are filled with the Spirit of God, we will have wisdom. When we pray in the Holy Ghost, faith will be evident, and the power of God will be manifest in our midst. Oh, how wonderful to be sons and daughters of God!

A FIRM FOUNDATION

Therefore whosoever heareth these sayings of mine, and doeth them,
I will liken him unto a wise man, which built his house upon a rock
(Matthew 7:24).

It is quite easy to construct a building if the foundation is secure. It is not so easy to rise spiritually, unless you have a real spiritual power working within you. It will never do for us to be top heavy—the base must always be very firmly set. So I believe that while we might go on from here, we will have to consider the pit from whence we were dug. Except we rightly understand the spiritual leadings, according to the mind of God, we will never be able to stand when the winds blow, when the trials come, and when satan appears as an angel of light. We shall never be able to stand unless we are firmly fixed in the Word of God.

There must be three things in our lives if we wish to go right through with God in the fullness of Pentecost. First we must be grounded and settled in love. We must have a real knowledge of what love is, and then we must have a clear understanding of the Word, for love must manifest the Word. Then we must understand clearly our own ground, because it is our own ground that needs to be looked after the most.

The Lord speaks at least twice of the good ground into which seed is sown, which also bore fruit and brought forth some one hundred fold, and some sixty, and some thirty. It was in different portions of thirty, sixty, and one hundred fold even in the good ground. I maintain truly that there is no limitation to the abundance of a harvest when the ground is perfectly in the hand of the Lord. So we must clearly understand that the Word of God can never come forth with all its primary purposes unless our ground is right. But God will help us, I believe, to see that He can make the ground in perfect order as it is put into His hands.

PROPHETIC UTTERANCES

And it shall come to pass afterward, that I will pour out my spirit upon all flesh; and your sons and your daughters shall prophesy, your old men shall dream dreams, your young men shall see visions: and also upon the servants and upon the handmaids in those days will I pour out my spirit (Joel 2:28-29).

God wants you to be so balanced in spiritual unction that you will always be able to do what pleases Him, and not what shall please other people or yourself. The ideal must be that it shall all be to edification, and everything must go on to this end to please the Lord. "Follow after charity [love], and desire spiritual gifts, but rather that ye may prophesy" (1 Cor. 14:1). When they came to Moses and said that there were two others in the camp prophesying, Moses said, "…would God that all the Lord's people were prophets…" (Num. 11:29). That is a clear revelation that God would have us in such a spiritual, holy place that He could take our words and so fill them with divine power that we would speak only as the Spirit leads in prophetic utterances.

Beloved, there is spiritual language, and there is also human language, which always stays on the human plane. There is a divine incoming into our human language so it is changed by spiritual power, and brings life to those who hear you speak. But this divine touch of prophecy will never come except when we are filled with the Spirit. If you wish to be anything for God, do not miss His plan. God has no room for you on ordinary lines. You must realize that within you there is the power of the Holy Spirit, who is forming within you everything you require.

THE NEW ORDER OF THE SPIRIT

But the manifestation of the Spirit is given to every man to profit withal (First Corinthians 12:7).

The Holy Ghost is inspiration, the Holy Ghost is revelation, the Holy Ghost is manifestation, the Holy Ghost is operation, and when a man comes into the fullness of the Holy Ghost he is in perfect order and built up on scriptural foundations. I have failed to see any man who understood the twelfth, thirteenth, or fourteenth chapters of First Corinthians, unless he had been baptized with the Holy Ghost. He may talk about it, but it is all a surface condition. When he gets baptized with the Holy Ghost, he speaks about a deep inward conviction by the power of the Spirit working in him, a revelation of that Scripture. On the other side, there is so much that a man receives when he is born again. He receives his first love and has a revelation of Jesus.

But God wants a man to be on fire so that he will always speak as an oracle of God. He wants to so build that man on the foundations of God that everyone who sees and hears him will say, "That is a new man after the order of the Spirit."

When a man is filled with the Holy Ghost, he has a vital power that makes people know he has seen God. He ought to be in such a place that if he should go into a neighbor's house, or out amongst people, they will feel that God has come in their midst. What we want is more of the Holy Ghost. Oh, beloved. It is not merely a measure of the Holy Ghost, it is a pressed-down measure. It is not merely a pressed-down measure, it is shaken together and running over. Anybody can hold a full cup, but you cannot hold an overflowing cup, and the baptism of the Holy Ghost is an overflowing cup. Praise the Lord!

THE LIFE-GIVING WORD

In the beginning was the Word, and the Word was with God, and the Word was God (John 1:1).

We have here a wonderful subject. All God's Word is life-giving—it is life and light. If we are poor it is because we do not know the Word of God. God's Word is full of riches ever opening to us fresh avenues of divine life. It is the Spirit that quickens us. Jesus said, "...the words that I speak unto you, they are spirit, and they are life" (John 6:63). The Word has a mighty changing power effectively working in us. We need not remain in the same place two days. It is the Word of God, and He richly gives us all things to enjoy. This Bible is the copy of the Word—the original is in the glory.

You will find the moment you reach the glory you will have the principle of the Word. The Author is there—the Author of faith is there. He is our life and fills us with illumination—the Holy Ghost unveiling unto us the Christ. When we receive the baptism in the Holy Ghost, we receive a new ministry with divine power and glory. The Kingdom of God is not meat and drink, but righteousness, peace, and joy in the Holy Ghost. Jesus is coroneted when you receive the Holy Ghost, and the Holy Ghost reveals the Christ who reigns in every believer. Have you received the Holy Ghost since you believed? Jesus is king over your desires, and no man can call Jesus Lord but by the Holy Ghost.

GLORY AND VIRTUE

According as his divine power hath given unto us all things that pertain unto life and godliness, through the knowledge of him that hath called us to glory and virtue (Second Peter 1:3).

People have a great misunderstanding about glory, though they often use the word. There are three things that ought to take place in the baptism. It was a necessity that the moving by the mighty rushing wind should be made manifest in the upper room; also that they should be clothed with tongues as of fire. The body should receive not only the fire but also the rushing wind. The personality of the Spirit is in the wind, and the manifestation of the glory is in the wind, which is the breath of God.

The inward man receives the Holy Ghost instantly with great joy and blessedness he cannot express. Then the power of the Spirit, this breath of God, takes of the things of Jesus and sends forth as a river the utterances of the Spirit. When the body is filled with joy, it is sometimes so inexpressible. Joy is thrown on the canvas of the mind, and the canvas of the mind has great power to move the operation of the tongue to bring out the very depths of the inward heart's power, love, and joy. By the same process, the Spirit, which is the breath of God, brings forth the manifestation of the glory.

Sometimes people wonder why it is that the Holy Ghost is always expressing Himself in words. It cannot be otherwise. You could not understand it otherwise. You cannot understand God by shakings, and yet shakings may be in perfect order sometimes. But you can always tell when the Spirit moves and brings forth utterances. They always magnify God. The Holy Ghost has a perfect plan. He comes right through every man who is so filled and brings divine utterances so that we may understand what the mind of the Lord is.

EXPRESSING GLORY IN REJOICING

Therefore my heart is glad, and my glory rejoiceth...(Psalm 16:9).

Rejoicing brings forth glory. You see, when the body is filed with the power of God, then the only thing that can express the glory is the tongue. "Oh God, my heart is fixed; I will sing and give praise, even with my glory" (Ps. 108:1). Glory is the presence of God, and the presence of God always comes by the tongue, which brings forth the revelations of God. God first brings His power into us, and then He gives us verbal expression by the same Spirit. It is the outward manifestation of what exists within us: "out of the abundance of the heart the mouth speaketh" (Matt. 12:34).

Virtue has to be transmitted, and glory has to expressed. So God, by filling us with the Holy Ghost, has brought into us this glory, that out of us may come forth the glory. The Holy Ghost understands everything Christ has in the glory; He brings God's latest thought through the heart of man. So we must be in touch with God Almighty to bring out on the face of the earth all the things that God has in the heavens. This is an ideal for us, and God help us not to forsake the sense of holy communion we have with Him when we enter into the closet in privacy, so that publicly He may manifest His glory.

We must see the face of the Lord and understand His ways. There are things that God says to me that I know must take place. It does not matter what people say. I have been face to face with some of the most trying moments of men's lives, when it meant so much if I kept the vision and held fast to what God had said. A man must be in an immoveable condition, and the voice of God must mean to him more than what he sees, feels, or what people say. He must have a revelation born in heaven, transmitted or expressed in some way. We must bring heaven to earth.

NEVER IMPOVERISHED

According as his divine power hath given unto us all things that pertain unto life and godliness, through the knowledge of him that hath called us to glory and virtue (Second Peter 1:3).

Oh, this is a lovely verse. There is so much depth in it for us. Oh, what wonderful things He has given us, "through the knowledge of him that hath called us to glory and virtue." You cannot get away from Him. He is the center of all things. He moves the earth, transforms beings, can live in every mind, and can plan every thought. Oh, He is there all the time. You will find that Paul is full of the might of the Spirit breathing through him, and yet he comes to a place where he feels he must stop. For there are greater things than he can even utter by prayer, the Almighty breathing through the human soul.

In the last of Ephesians 3 are these words that no human man could ever think or plan with pen and ink. Paul's words are so mighty, so of God, when he speaks about God's ability to do all things, "…exceeding abundantly above all that we ask or think…" (Eph. 3:20). The mighty God of revelation! The Holy Ghost gave these words of grandeur to stir our hearts, to move our affections, to transform us altogether. This is ideal! This is God.

Shall we teach them? Shall we have them? Oh, they are ours. God has never put anything over on a pole where you could not reach it. He has brought His plan down to man, and if we are prepared this morning, oh, what there is for us! I feel sometimes we have just as much as we can digest, yet there are such divine nuggets of precious truth held before our hearts, it makes you understand that there are yet heights, and depths, and lengths, and breadths of the knowledge of God laid up for us. We might truly say, "My heavenly bank, my heavenly bank, the house of God's treasure and store. I have plenty in here; I'm a real millionaire."

Immersed in God

But covet earnestly the best gifts: and yet shew I unto you a more excellent way (First Corinthians 12:31).

I see a difference between having a gift and being filled with the Holy Ghost. God's Word says, "Covet earnestly the best gifts." I would rather see the Church filled with the Holy Ghost than seeking gifts. When you are filled with God any gift can come into operation. May God awaken us that signs and wonders may be worked among us again as in Acts 6. Here the whole Church had a revival; great grace was upon them all.

Many came to Peter because he was filled with the divine presence, and today it is latter rain and must be intensified. Don't miss the high tide of God's divine order. Believe, and the living flow begins; the divine tide arises. Stir up, be on fire, open wide the door, expect, for it's available now. After 2,000 years, God is again visiting the earth in a mighty way. That's the ideal—salvation, healing, and the baptism of the Holy Ghost for multitudes. God will bring them in, and He will baptize with the Holy Ghost.

Let us wake up and stay awake. We will be disappointed unless we see God's glory in manifestation. Receive the Holy Ghost and be filled with God so that the floods pour onto the dry ground and overflowing rivers of living water flow until multitudes are brought in and healed.

PERFECTLY FORMED

For we are his workmanship, created in Christ Jesus unto good works, which God hath before ordained that we should walk in them (Ephesians 2:10).

There are five senses in the world. When Christ has come into you, there are five senses of spiritual acquaintance—the hearing of faith, the feelings after God, the supernatural sight, the speaking after the mind of the operation of the Spirit, the tasting after God's plan. Yet God wants us to be so triune, perfectly joined, till the very Christ is formed in us, His very life manifested in humanity, till we know we have no questions. No matter what other people say, we know in whom we have believed and are persuaded. There are things that can be moved, and there are things that cannot be moved. There are things that can be changed, and there are things that cannot be changed.

We have within us an incorruptible nature that cannot be moved. It does not matter who is moved or what is moved; the things that God has given us remain. Some things can be wrapped up and folded like a garment. The heavens may be rolled up like a scroll and melt with fervent heat. The very earth we are standing on may be absolutely melted. But we are as endurable as He is, for we have the same life, the incorruptible life, the eternal power. We belong to a new company. We belong to the firstborn. We have the nature of the Son. We belong to eternity.

LIVING WITHOUT CONDEMNATION

There is therefore now no condemnation to them which are in Christ Jesus, who walk not after the flesh, but after the Spirit. For the law of the Spirit of life in Christ Jesus hath made me free from the law of sin and death (Romans 8:1-2).

God is on His throne and can take you a thousand miles in a moment. Have faith to jump into His supernatural plan. Are you ready? What for? To be so changed by the order of God that you will never have this human order of fear any more. Remember: "Perfect love casteth out fear" (1 John 4:18). Step into the full tide of the life of the manifestation of God. Your new nature has no corruption in it. Eternal life is not just during your lifetime; it is forever. You are regenerated by the power of the Word of God and it is in you as an incorruptible force, taking you on from victory to victory till death itself can be overcome, till sin has no authority, till disease could not be in the body. This is a living fact by the Word of God.

You say, "How can I come into it?" Read carefully the first two verses of Romans 8. Right in this present moment there is no condemnation. This law of the Spirit of life is a law in the body, a law of eternity, a law of God, a new law. It is not the law of the Ten Commandments but a law of life in the body changing you in the body till there is no sin power, no disease power, and no death power. Believe it!

ALIVE TO CHRIST

Set your affection on things above, not on things on the earth (Colossians 3:2).

Belief is a fact. Don't join the endeavor society, but come into the faith society, and you will leap into the promises of God, which are yea and amen to all that believe. Don't look down your nose and murmur any more. Have a rejoicing spirit, get the praise of God in your heart, go forth from victory to victory, rise in faith and believe it. You must not live in yourself. You must live in Christ. Set your mind upon things above. Keep your whole spirit alive in God. Let your inheritance be so full of life divine that you live above the world and all its thoughts and cares.

What does it mean for Him to be the Son of God to you and me? God is holy. God is light. God is love. Jesus was the fullness of God on earth. The same fullness, the same life, the same maturity has to be in you till you are dead to the world and alive to God in the Spirit.

O Lord, move away disease, move away blind eyes, move away imperfect vision. Give the Word, let us understand the blood, let us understand the spirit of prophecy, of testimony. Let us understand, oh God, that You are still building the foundation on the prophets and on the apostles and on all that work Your wonderful Word. So build us till every soul is filled with divine grace.

An Ambassador of Blessing

...I will bless thee, and...thou shalt be a blessing (Genesis 12:2).

God bless you! When He blesses, no one can curse. When God is with you it is impossible for anyone to be against you. When God has put His hand upon you every way will open with benediction to others. The greatest thing that God has allowed us to come into is the plan of distributing His blessing to others.

When we know the power of Almighty God, we need never be afraid of any weapon that is formed against us, believing that the Lord of Hosts will rise up and stand against the enemy. God's power and His wonderful benediction is upon us. What a wonderful Christ!

The Lord shall lead us forth, from factory to victory. Oh, what a blessing to know that we are the fruit of the Lord! His people are the precious fruit of the earth. I am not afraid to say these things to you because I know God means to bless you. Why should you go away without blessing when God has promised you a measure that cannot be measured? Why should you fear when God removes fear?

Are you ready? What for? Oh, for His blessing to fill your life, overflow you, change you. Are you ready? What for? To get a childlike simplicity and look into the face of the Father and believe that all His promises are yea and amen to you. Are you ready? What for? To be awakened into the Spirit of acquaintance that believes all things and dares to ask the Father.

THE TREASURE HOUSE OF GOD

And he shall bring forth thy righteousness as the light, and thy judgment as the noonday (Psalm 37:6).

How exhaustless is the treasure house of the Most High! How near God is to us when we are willing to draw nigh! And how He comes to us with refreshing when our hearts are attuned and desire Him only, for the desires of the righteous shall be granted. God has for us today a stimulation of divine acquaintance, a life divine to flow through our being that shall be sufficient for us in all times of need. When God is for you, who can be against you? What a blessed assurance this is to the hungry heart. How it thrills one to the very depths of their soul.

Oh, come to the banquet table, that wonderful reserve, that great and blessed day of appointment for us with the King, that we may believe that all the precious promises are yea and amen to us as we dare believe. Oh, to believe God! Oh, to rest upon what He says, for there is not one jot or tittle of the Word that shall fail till all is fulfilled! Has He not promised and will He not also perform? Our blessed Lord of life and glory impressed upon us before He left that He would send the Comforter, and the Lord would hear us when we pray.

The Spirit Himself brings forth light and truth to edify and build up the Church in the most holy faith, that we might be ready for all activity in God. For the Spirit of the Lord is upon us to bring forth what God has declared and ordained, that we should go forth bearing precious fruit and come forth rejoicing, singing, and harvesting together. Oh, to keep in the covenant place where you are hidden in Christ, where He alone is superseding, controlling, leading, directing, and causing you to live only for the glory of God.

WALK IN HOLINESS

...Be ye holy; for I am holy (First Peter 1:16).

Don't forget that you are entrusted with the Word of life, which speaks to you as the truth. Jesus was the Way, the Truth, and the Life, and He declared eternal life by the operation of the Gospel, for we receive immortality and life by the Gospel. You can understand that for those who receive the life of Christ, they pass out of condemnation into eternal life. What about those who do not? They are still under condemnation, without hope and without God in the world and in danger of eternal destruction. God save them!

It is a great purpose that God has for us that we can be changed, and you are in a great place when you are willing to have this change take place. You are in a greater place when you are willing to drop everything that has brought you to where you thought you could not be changed, and when you have dropped all things that have hindered you, you will leap forth and be tremendously changed.

If you have held onto anything on a human plane, no matter how it has come, if it is not according to the biblical standard of the Word of God, let it be weeded out. If you do not get it weeded out, there is a time coming that wood, hay, and stubble will be burned and the gold, the silver, and the precious stones will stand the fire. Lots of people would like to know what kind of crown they will have when they get to glory. Well, the Lord will take everything that could not be burnt by the fire and make your own crown, so everybody is forming his own crown. Now you be careful not to be all wood, hay, and stubble. Have something left for the crown. There is a crown of life that doesn't fade away that I am trying to help you build for today.

WHATSOEVER WE ASK

...He that believeth on me, the works that I do shall he do also; and greater works than these shall he do; because I go unto my Father. And whatsoever ye shall ask in my name, that will I do, that the Father may be glorified in the Son (John 14:12-13).

Listen to the words of Jesus. I know that we will see the rising tide of blessing and divine healing go forth with greater power, but satan will always try to hinder the real work of God. Whenever the power of God is being manifested, satan will be there trying to upset it. Satanic forces may be there, but God is greater.

We must see these greater works that the Lord promises we should see. What is it that you should want? "Whatsoever ye shall ask in my name, that I will do" (John 14:13). Is there any purpose in it? Yes, "that the Father may be glorified in the Son."

If you want God to be glorified in the Son, you must live in the position where these things are being done. Praise God. The power of God is available to deliver people. Have such a confidence in what the Lord said so that you take Him at His word because He said it. Glory to God.

Let us take a look at the last part of this verse; it is very important. It says, "And whatsoever ye shall ask in My name...." Tell me, what does *whatsoever* mean? It means everything. There is a difference between everything and anything. Whatsoever you ask, everything you ask, will be done if you believe. Redemption is so complete that the person who believes it is made complete. People are waiting for the manifestations of the sons of God.

LIVING BY FAITH

For verily I say unto you, That whosoever shall say unto this mountain, Be thou removed, and be thou cast into the sea; and shall not doubt in his heart, but shall believe that those things which he saith shall come to pass; he shall have whatsoever he saith. Therefore I say unto you, What things soever ye desire, when ye pray, believe that ye receive them, and ye shall have them (Mark 11:23-24).

These are days when we need to have our faith strengthened, when we need to know God. God has designed that the just shall live by faith, no matter how he may be fettered. I know that God's Word is sufficient. One word from Him can change a nation. His Word is from everlasting to everlasting. It is through the entrance of this everlasting Word, this incorruptible seed, that we are born again, and come into this wonderful salvation. Man cannot live by bread alone but must live by every word that proceeds out of the mouth of God (see Matt. 4:4). This is the food of faith, for "...faith cometh by hearing, and hearing by the Word of God" (Rom. 10:17).

Everywhere men are trying to discredit the Bible and take out the miraculous from it. One preacher says, "Well, you know, Jesus arranged beforehand to have that colt tied where it was, and for the men to say just what they did" (see Matt. 21:2). I tell you, God can arrange everything without going near. He can plan for you, and when He plans for you, all is peace. All things are possible if you will believe. Another preacher said, "It was an easy thing for Jesus to feed the people with five loaves. The loaves were so big in those days that it was a simple matter to cut them into a thousand pieces each" (see John 6:5-15). But he forgot that one little boy brought those five loaves all the way in his lunch basket. There is nothing impossible with God. All the impossibility is with us when we measure God by the limitations of our unbelief. We have a wonderful God, a God whose ways are past finding out and whose grace and power are limitless.

ALL THINGS THAT PERTAIN TO LIFE

According as his divine power hath given unto us all things that pertain unto life and godliness, through the knowledge of him that hath called us to glory and virtue (Second Peter 1:3).

God brings us into a place of perfect love and perfect faith. A man who is born of God is brought into an inward affection, a loyalty to the Lord Jesus that shrinks from anything impure. You see the purity of a man and woman when there is a deep natural affection between them; they disdain the very thought of either of them being untrue. I say that in the measure that a man has faith in Jesus, he is pure. He who believes that Jesus is the Christ overcomes the world. It is a faith that works by love. We cannot doubt in our hearts. Just as we have heart fellowship with our Lord, our faith cannot be daunted.

There comes, as we go on with God, a wonderful association, an impartation of His very life and nature within. As we read His Word and believe the promises that He has so graciously given to us, we are made partakers of His very essence and life. The Lord is our Bridegroom, and we are His bride. His words to us are spirit and life, transforming us and changing us, expelling that which is natural and bringing in that which is divine. It is impossible to comprehend the love of God as we think on natural lines. We must have the revelation from the Spirit of God. God gives liberally. He that asks will receive.

God is willing to bestow on us all things that pertain to life and godliness. Oh, it was the love of God that brought Jesus. And it is this same love that helps you and me to believe. In every weakness God will be your strength. You who need His touch, remember that He loves you. Look away to the God of all grace, whose very essence is love, who delights to give liberally all the inheritance of life and strength and power that you are in need of.

WALK IN THE LIGHT AND BE FILLED

But if we walk in the light, as he is in the light, we have fellowship one with another, and the blood of Jesus Christ his Son cleanseth us from all sin (First John 1:7).

We have a Jesus who heals the brokenhearted, who lets the captives go free, who saves the very worst. Dare you, dare you, spurn this glorious Gospel of God for spirit, soul, and body? Dare you spurn this grace? I realize that God can never bless us on the lines of being hard-hearted, critical, or unforgiving. This will hinder faith quicker than anything.

I remember being at a meeting where there were some people tarrying for the baptism—seeking for cleansing, for the moment a person is cleansed the Spirit will fall. There was one man with eyes red who was weeping bitterly. He said to me, "I shall have to leave. It is no good my staying if I don't I change things. I have written a letter to my brother-in-law, and filled it with hard words, and this thing must first be straightened out."

He went home and told his wife, "I'm going to write a letter to your brother and ask him to forgive me for writing to him the way I did." "You fool!" she said. "Never mind," he replied, "this thing is between God and me, and it has got to be cleared away." He wrote the letter and came again, and straightway God filled him with the Spirit.

I believe there are a great many people who would be healed, but they are harboring things in their hearts that are blight. Let these things go. Forgive, and the Lord will forgive you. Bring everything to the light. God will sweep it all away if you will let Him. Let the precious blood of Christ cleanse from all sin. If you will but believe, God will meet you and bring into your lives the sunshine of His love.

An Inward Working of Power

And when they had prayed, the place was shaken where they were assembled together; and they were all filled with the Holy Ghost, and they spake the Word of God with boldness (Acts 4:31).

Brothers and sisters, God anointed Jesus, who went about doing good, for God was with Him; and today we know for a fact, He is the risen Christ. There is something about this risen, royal, glorified Christ that God means to confirm in our hearts. The power of the risen Christ makes our hearts move and burn, and we know that there is within us that eternal working by the power of the Spirit. Oh, beloved, it is eternal life to know Jesus! Surely the kingdom of darkness is shaken when we come into touch with that loftiness, that holiness, that divine integrity of our Master who is so filled with power and grace. This blessed divine inheritance is for us.

Beloved, life cannot come out unless it is within. God transforms the heart and life, and there must be an inward working of the power of God, or it cannot come forth outwardly. We must understand that the power of Pentecost, as it came in the first order, was to free people. People are tired of smoke and deadness, tired of imitations. We want realities, people who have God within them, who are always filled with God. This is a more needy day than any, and we should be filled with the Holy Ghost.

We must be like our Master. We must have definiteness about all we say. We must have an inward confidence and knowledge that we are God's property, bought and paid for by the precious blood of Jesus, and now the inheritance is in us. People may know that Jesus died and that He rose again, and yet they may not have salvation. Beloved, you must have that witness. God wants you to know how to take the victory and shout in the face of the devil and say, "Lord, it is done."

HOLINESS AND TRANSFORMATION

...Be ye holy; for I am holy (First Peter 1:16).

God desires that we have an abundant life. On the day of Pentecost, people perceived something remarkable happened when the fishermen encountered the power of God. Brothers and sisters, it was the Holy Ghost. He is the personality and power and presence of the third Person of the Trinity. Many of us have been longing for years for God to come forth and now He is coming forth. The tide is rising everywhere. God is pouring out His Spirit in the hearts of all flesh and they are crying before God. The day is at hand. God is fulfilling His promises.

Oh, regeneration is lovely—the change from nature to grace, from the power of satan to God. You who are natural are made supernatural by the divine touch of Him who came to raise you from the dead. The Holy Spirit comes to abide. He comes to reveal the fullness of God. The Holy Ghost is shedding abroad in our hearts the love of God, and He takes of the things of Jesus and shows them unto us.

I know this great salvation that God has given us today is so large that one feels his whole body is enraptured. Dare you leap into the power of faith this afternoon? Dare you take your inheritance in God? Dare you believe God? Dare you stand upon the record of His Word? If you will believe you will see the glory of God. "...All things are possible to him that believeth" (Mark 9:23). Dare you come near today and say that God will sanctify your body and make it holy? He wants you to have a pure body, a holy body, a separated body, a body presented on the altar of God that you may be no longer conformed to this world, but transformed and renewed after His image.

PERFECTED IN CHRIST

...If we love one another, God dwelleth in us, and his love is perfected in us (First John 4:12).

Everyone will endure trials in life that will challenge his or her faith. You will be sifted as wheat. You will be tried as though some strange thing happened to you. You will be put in most difficult places where all hell seems round about you, but God will sustain and empower you, and bring you into an unlimited place of faith. God will not allow you to be "...tempted above that ye are able; but will with the temptation also make a way to escape, that ye may be able to bear it" (1 Cor. 10:13). God will surely tell you when you have been tried sufficiently to bring you out as pure gold.

Every trial is to prepare you for a greater position for God. Your tried faith will make you know that you will have the faith of God to go through the next trial. Who is going to live dormant, weak, trifling, slow, indolent, prayerless, Bible-less lives when you know you must go through these things? And if you are to be made perfect in weakness, you must be tried by fire in order to know that no man is able to win a victory, only by the power of God in him.

The Holy Spirit will lead us day by day. You will know that these light afflictions, which are but for a moment, are working out for us an eternal weight of glory. Oh, beloved, what are we going to do with this day? We must have a high tide this afternoon. Some of you have been longing for the Holy Ghost. God can baptize you just where you are. There may be some here who have not yet tasted of the grace of God. Close beside you is the water of life. Have a drink, brother, sister, for God says, "...And let him that is athirst come. And whosoever will, let him take the water of life freely" (Rev. 22:17).

Living Without Condemnation

There is therefore now no condemnation to them which are in Christ Jesus, who walk not after the flesh, but after the Spirit. For the law of the Spirit of life in Christ Jesus hath made me free from the law of sin and death (Romans 8:1-2).

There is therefore now no condemnation. This means so much to me. I know I was baptized with the Holy Ghost. The Holy Ghost was not the life—Jesus is the life, but the Holy Ghost came to reveal the life. The Holy Ghost is not truth—Jesus is the truth, but the Holy Ghost is the Spirit of that truth. The Holy Ghost reveals the truth that there is no condemnation in Christ.

I am noticing that to be without condemnation, I must be in a just place with God. It is a wonderful thing to be justified by faith, but I find there is a greater place of justification than this. I find this because Abraham believed God, and God accounted it to him for righteousness. He imputed no sin to Abraham; He gave Abraham wings! When he imputed no sin, he lifted Abraham into the righteousness of God, lifted him out of himself into a place of rest and God covered him there. Abraham did not receive anything of the Lord that He is not willing to give to any of us. I now see that whatever I have reached is only on the rippling wave of the bosom of God's intense zeal of love and compassion. He is always saying—and nothing less than this—"Come on," so I am going forward. The Lord has spoken good concerning His people, and He will give us the land of promise.

THE HOPE OF GLORY

Looking unto Jesus the author and finisher of our faith; who for the joy that was set before him endured the cross, despising the shame, and is set down at the right hand of the throne of God (Hebrews 12:2).

If I can always have the hope of glory set before me, I shall not fail to find joy in every trying hour. How can we be worthy of His fullness? By keeping full of joy in the expectation of His fullness. When the Holy Ghost is very present, it is for increase. We see in the Old Testament that God is great and could fill the universe, but He can also fill the human heart, illuminating and empowering it to take in all the divine rays. Love is concentrated power; the heart is the center of strength. We are weak or powerful in proportion to the amount of love we possess.

Anything that comes to mar our peace is foreign and not of God. Jesus said, "These things I have spoken unto you, that in me ye might have peace. In the world ye shall have tribulation: but be of good cheer; I have overcome the world" (John 16:33). I count on the need always being met because the Holy Ghost abides in me. It is an attitude to a climax. Our business is to always abide in the will of God with such unction that God is able to move through us at any time. The need always makes the river flow.

The baptism of the Holy Ghost means revival. The disciples seem to have carried with them that which buoyed them. There is more in it than the salvation of the people. The Spirit always promotes faith for action. If your whole ambition is God-ward, and you feel out of place unless things are heading toward God, you are ready.

United with the Spirit of God

The sacrifices of God are a broken spirit: a broken and a contrite heart, O God, thou wilt not despise (Psalm 51:17).

Beloved, there is a deadness in us that must have the resurrection touch. Today we have the unveiled truth, for the dispensation of the Holy Ghost has come to unfold the fullness of redemption, that we might be clothed with power. A broken spirit and a contrite heart bring us into the state where God can pour His blessing upon us. We need to examine ourselves this morning to see what state we are in, whether we are just "religious" or whether we be truly "in Christ."

The human spirit, when perfectly united with the Holy Spirit, has but one place, and that is death, death, and deeper death. The human spirit will then cease to desire to have its own way, and instead of "my" will, the cry of the heart will be, "Thy will, oh Lord, be done in me." The great aim of the spirit's power within us is to so bring us in line with His perfect will that we will unhesitatingly believe the Scriptures, daring to accept them as the authentic divine principle of God. When we do, we will find our feet so firmly fixed upon the plan of redemption that it will not matter from whence come trials or other things, for our whole nature will be so enlarged, that it will be no more *I*, but, "Lord, what wilt thou have me do?"

Every believer should be a living epistle of the Word, one who is "read and known of all men" (2 Cor. 3:2). Your very presence should bring such a witness of the Spirit that everyone with whom you come in contact would know that you are a "sent" one, a light in the world, a manifestation of the Christ; and last of all, that you are a *biblical* Christian.

Listen to the Word

Seeing ye have purified your souls in obeying the truth through the Spirit unto unfeigned love of the brethren, see that ye love one another with a pure heart fervently: being born again, not of corruptible seed, but of incorruptible, by the Word of God, which liveth and abideth for ever (First Peter 1:22-23).

It takes the Master to bring the Word home to our hearts. His was a ministry that brought a new vision to humankind, for a man never spoke the way He spoke. Enter into the Scriptures and watch the Lord, follow Him, take notice of His counsel, and you will have a story of wonders. How I love to hear Him preach. How He says things. I have watched Him as He trod this earth. The Book speaks today! It is life, and it is full of glory. The Word reflects and unfolds with a new creative power. The words of Jesus are life—never think they are less. If you believe it, you will feel quickened. The Word is powerful; it is full of faith.

The Word of God is vital! Listen! "...The word preached did not profit them, not being mixed with faith in them that heard it" (Heb. 4:2). There has to be a "hearing" in order to have faith. Faith is established and made manifest as we "hear" the Word. Beloved, read the Word of God in quietude, and read it aloud, so that you can *hear* it—for "He that *heareth* my word," to them it gives life. Beloved, listen!

There are many books written on the Word, and we love clear, definite teaching on it, but go yourself to the Book and listen to what the Master says, and you will lay a sure foundation that cannot be moved.

TRIALS AS PREPARATION

For as the sufferings of Christ abound in us, so our consolation also aboundeth by Christ (Second Corinthians 1:5).

It was said of Jesus that He was in all points tempted as we are. Where did He receive strength to comfort us? It was at the end of strong crying and tears, when the angel came and ministered just in time and saved Him from death just at the end. Is He not able? Oh, God highly exalted Him. Now He can send angels to us. When? Just when we should go right down, did He not stretch out to us a helping hand? There is a sense of the power of God working in humanity, bringing us through trials, transforming our mind into the mind of Christ.

God takes us to a place of need, and before you are hardly aware of it, you are full of consolation toward the needy. How? The sufferings of Christ abound! The ministry of the Spirit abounds so often. We are members of one body in Christ. When God's breath is upon us and we are quickened by the Holy Ghost, we can pour into each other wonderful ministries of grace and helpfulness. We need a strong ministry of consolation, not deterioration, which is living below our privileges. These consolations come out of privation, endurance, and affliction.

Could you see how Paul could help and comfort and sustain because he yielded to God all the time as Jesus did? He was yielded to the Holy Ghost to work out the sentence of death—He could help others. I pray to God that He may never find us kicking against the pricks of our trials. We have to go through the testing, because we are tested in the truths we stand for. We are tested in divine healing, purity, doctrine, and in the Holy Ghost. Oh, the joy of being worthy of suffering! How shall we stand the glory that shall be after?

FIXING OUR EYES ON JESUS

Thou wilt keep him in perfect peace, whose mind is stayed on thee: because he trusteth in thee (Isaiah 26:3).

The inspiration of a living faith is not on the line of the flesh, but in God's order. God will never let us move—He is bound up in it—until this faith is perfected. In order that we may merit the quickening of our faith we must lay aside the very weight and the sin which does so easily beset us, remembering that not only earthly but also heavenly witnesses are watching to see faith established on the earth. Thus we live not unto ourselves in this race of faith. God plants faith in us so that we may endure hardships. His benevolent hand holds us. We will not have a moment's unrest or trouble if we keep our minds stayed on God. The enemy may seek to insert a dart of bitterness or hardness, but faith is the only production of what is pleasing to God. I must get my eyes fixed on Jesus, the Author and Finisher of our faith.

Salvation is the greatest and most stupendous work worked in man. The healing of the body is wonderful, but to be like-minded with Him, to think with Him—our salvation began in glory and it will be finished there. We shall be crushed by our trials if we do not fix our eyes on the right place.

Wherefore seeing we also are compassed about with so great a cloud of witnesses, let us lay aside every weight, and the sin which doth so easily beset us, and let us run with patience the race that is set before us, looking unto Jesus the author and finisher of our faith; who for the joy that was set before him endured the cross, despising the shame, and is set down at the right hand of the throne of God. For consider him that endured such contradiction of sinners against himself, lest ye be wearied and faint in your minds (Hebrews 12:1-3).

PREPARATION FOR THE GLORY

...My son, despise not thou the chastening of the Lord, nor faint when thou art rebuked of him: for whom the Lord loveth he chasteneth, and scourgeth every son whom he receiveth (Hebrews 12:5-6).

Why should sons need correcting? The sons we love need correcting because all must go so that the image of the Lord may be formed within us. He chases all away to perfect us unto Himself. As we have borne the image of the earthly, we shall also bear the image of the heavenly. The chastening is to bear the image of the heavenly, a great structure of His loveliness. As we submit, our face bears the glory. Don't think, beloved, the work is done when the gravity is removed. This is for our profit, that we might be partakers of His holiness. For our light affliction, which is but for a moment, works for us a far more exceeding and eternal weight of glory.

Isaiah was undone when he was in the glorious presence for a moment. Even the back of God caused Moses's face to reflect an expression so glorious that men could not bear to look upon him. Correction prepares us for the same holiness they experienced. It is not an earthly invention, but a divine apprehension through the Spirit. The chastening is through the Spirit that we might know the breadth of God's holiness and love for us. Oh, this wonderful inheritance—the fullness of the Spirit. Mount Zion is not far from us. The angels are close to use. We live in heavenly places where we can receive strength covered with almighty power, where you can experience the glory so much that you do not know you have a body.

A THIRSTY PEOPLE

In the last day, that great day of the feast, Jesus stood and cried, saying, If any man thirst, let him come unto me, and drink. He that believeth on me, as the scripture hath said, out of his belly shall flow rivers of living water. (But this spake he of the Spirit, which they that believe on him should receive: for the Holy Ghost was not yet given; because that Jesus was not yet glorified) (John 7:37-39).

You must know that dry conditions exist everywhere. People are longing to be filled with the Spirit. There never was such a cry. Beloved, it is because the Scriptures are being fulfilled. The former rain fell in a very blessed way, clothing the apostles with power, and the Acts of the Apostles came forth because they dared to act. In these last days, God will pour out upon all flesh the Latter Rain, and I believe all flesh will feel the effects of it. It will not be possible for anyone to miss it. They may refuse it, but it will be there for the taking, and I believe God wants us to see the Latter Rain has begun to fall.

I do not say we are anywhere near experiencing the fullness of God, but I do see a great thirst for it, and I believe that man does not thirst unless God first draws him. You cannot love righteousness and hate iniquity without a revelation of the Spirit. Likewise, you cannot desire purity in the flesh. The flesh has been regenerated, and the regenerated heart is hungry.

God is creating a hunger and a thirst in His people. This outpouring is for you. It is a personal baptism, not a church baptism. What do I mean by saying the church? When I say churches, people get their mind on buildings, when it is believers who compose the body. The Master desires a river to flow through everyone. Your salvation is like a river. Jesus came to do nothing less than embody us with the same manifestation as He had to do great works.

Doing and Teaching

The Spirit of the Lord God is upon me; because the Lord hath anointed me to preach good tidings unto the meek; he hath sent me to bind up the brokenhearted, to proclaim liberty to the captives, and the opening of the prison to them that are bound; to proclaim the acceptable year of the Lord, and the day of vengeance of our God; to comfort all that mourn; to appoint unto them that mourn in Zion, to give unto them beauty for ashes, the oil of joy for mourning, the garment of praise for the spirit of heaviness; that they might be called trees of righteousness, the planting of the Lord, that he might be glorified (Isaiah 61:1-3).

Luke opens the book of Acts by describing the Gospel of Luke as an account of "all that Jesus began both to do and teach." After Jesus was filled with the Spirit, He began to do great works and to teach with great revelation. He was ready to minister to people in the streets. He had a river flowing through Him. Believers should always be full of the Holy Ghost. They must have three things—ministration, operation, and manifestation—and those three things must always be forthcoming. We ought to be so full of the manifestation of the power of God that in the Name of Jesus we can absolutely destroy the power of satan. We are in the world, not of it. Jesus overcame the world. We are nothing, but in Christ we are more than conquerors through the blood, more than a match for satanic powers in every way.

We must be loosed from ourselves, for if you examine yourself you will be natural, but if you look at God, you will be supernatural. If you have a great God, you will have a little devil; if you have a big devil, you will have a little God. So may the Lord let us see that we must be so full of the Spirit of life that we are always overcoming satan. Jesus laid a foundation for us. It is a drink at the well; by receiving Him, you have power as the sons of God.

THE GREAT REFINER

...If any man thirst, let him come unto me, and drink (John 7:37).

Let me by the grace of God just put us into the place of where to expect and receive. Now we know as well as anything that the day of Pentecost came; we know that He was received up into glory, and that the angel spoke as He was going away and said this same Jesus would come again. We know that the disciples tarried at Jerusalem till they were endued with power from on High, and we know the Holy Ghost came.

Since we know the Holy Ghost came, it is wrong to wait for the Holy Ghost now. I know it was personally right; it was divinely right for those apostles to hear what Jesus said and to tarry for the Holy Ghost, but it is not right now to tarry for the Holy Ghost. Then why do we not all receive the Holy Ghost, you ask? Because the bodies are not ready for it, the temples are not cleansed.

When the temples are purified and the minds put in order so that carnalities and fleshly desires and everything have gone, then the Holy Ghost can take full charge. The Holy Ghost is not a manifestation of carnality. There are people who never read the Word of God who could not be led away by the powers of satan. The power of the Holy Ghost is most lovely and divine in all its construction. It is a great refiner. It is full of life but it is always divine—never natural.

THE INRUSH

And suddenly there came a sound from heaven as of a rushing mighty wind, and it filled all the house where they were sitting (Acts 2:2).

When I think about a river—a pure, holy, divine river—I say, what can stand against its inrush? Wherever it is—in a railway carriage, or in the street, or in a meeting—its power and flow will always be felt; it will always do its work. Jesus spoke about the Holy Ghost. I want you to think about how God gave it, and how His coming was manifested, about its reception, and about its outflow after it had come.

In Acts 2, we find three positions of the Holy Ghost. The first was a rushing, mighty wind. Keep that in your mind. The second were cloven tongues of fire, and then the fact of the incoming manifestations. Keep your mind for a moment on the rushing, mighty wind, and then see the cloven tongues of fire over everyone; then see the incoming and outflow through it. I am glad that the Holy Ghost manifested to us as wind, person, and fire. The fire is wonderful. Then I want you to know that the Holy Ghost is power manifested in those three ways.

Can we be filled with a river? How is it possible for a river to flow out from us? A river of water is always an emblem of the Word of God. This river flows with no effort. When the Holy Ghost takes hold of you, you will have no more cracked brains and sleepless nights through preparing your addresses—God will do it. He has no plan for you less than to make you a son of God with resurrection power.

KEEPING THE VISION

...Be filled with the Spirit (Ephesians 5:18).

Humanity is filled with failure everywhere, but when humanity is filled with God's divinity, there is no such thing as failure, and we know that the baptism of the Holy Ghost is not a failure. There are two sides to the baptism of the Holy Ghost. The first condition is that you possess the baptism; the second condition is that the baptism possesses you. God can manifest His divine power so that you can possess, if you are eligible, this blessed infilling of the baptism of the Holy Ghost. There is no limit to it. It is without measure, because God is behind it, in the midst of it, and through it. Take the epistles and read them through. I would say that God is through them, under them, and all over them. I pray it would be the same with us.

I see people from time to time very slack, cold, and indifferent, and after they get filled with the Holy Ghost they become ablaze for God. Ministers of God are to be flames of fire, nothing less than holy and mighty instruments with burning messages. We are to have hearts full of love, to live in deep consecration. Surely this is the ideal and purpose of this great plan of salvation for man, that we might be filled with all the fullness of God. This glorious baptism allows us to be a witness of Jesus, manifesting His grace and being an instrument of the saving power for humanity.

Oh, beloved, we must reach the ideal identification with the Master. It is the same baptism, the same power, with the same revelation of the King of kings. Beloved, turn to the Spirit of God and receive the baptism of the Holy Ghost.

POWER TO OVERCOME

For whatsoever is born of God overcometh the world: and this is the victory that overcometh the world, even our faith (First John 5:4).

God declared Himself mightier than every opposing power when He cast out the powers of darkness from heaven. I want you to know that the same power that cast satan out of heaven dwells in every man who is born of God. If you would but realize this, you would reign in life. When you see people laid out under an evil power, when you see the powers of evil manifesting themselves, always put the question, "Did Jesus come in the flesh?" I have never seen an evil power answer in the affirmative. When you know you have an evil spirit to deal with, you have power to cast it out. Believe it and act on it, for "…greater is he that is in you, than he that is in the world" (1 John 4:4).

God means you to be in a place of overcoming, and has put a force within you whereby you may defeat the devil. Temptations will come to all. If you are not worth tempting you are not worth powder and shot. Job said, "…when he hath tried me, I shall come forth as gold" (Job 23:10). In every temptation that comes, the Lord lets you be tempted up to the very hilt, but He will never allow you to be defeated if you walk in obedience; for right in the midst of the temptation He will always "make a way to escape" (1 Cor. 10:13).

May God help us to see it. We cannot be to the praise of His glory until we are ready for trials, and are able to triumph in them. We cannot get away from the fact that sin came in by nature, but God comes into our nature and puts it to death, that the Spirit of God may come into the temple in all His power and liberty, that right here in this present evil world satan may be dethroned by the believer.

THE POWER OF THIS LIFE

Forasmuch as ye are manifestly declared to be the epistle of Christ minis-tered by us, written not with ink, but with the Spirit of the living God; not in tables of stone, but in fleshy tables of the heart (Second Corinthians 3:3).

Satan is always endeavoring to bring the saints of God into disrepute by railing accusations against them, but the Holy Ghost never comes with condemnation. He always reveals the blood of Christ. He always brings us help. The Lord Jesus referred to Him as the Comforter. He is always on hand to help in the seasons of trial and test. The Holy Ghost is the lifting power of the Church of Christ. And Paul tells us that we "...are manifestly declared to be the epistle of Christ... written not with ink, but with the Spirit of the living God; not in tables of stone, but in fleshy tables of the heart" (2 Cor. 3:3).

The Holy Ghost begins in the heart, right in the depths of human affections. He brings the riches of the revelation of Christ into the heart, implanting a purity and holiness there, so that praises well up continually out of its depths. The Holy Ghost will make us epistles of Christ, ever telling us that Jesus our Lord is our Redeemer and that He is ever before God as a newly slain Lamb. God has never put away that revelation. And because of the perfect atonement of that slain Lamb, there is salvation, healing, and deliverance for all.

Some people think that they have only to be cleansed once, but as we walk in the light, the blood of Jesus Christ is ever cleansing. The very life of Christ has been put within us, and is moving within us—a perfect life. May the Lord help us to see the power of this life.

YIELD YOURSELF

Not that we are sufficient of ourselves to think any thing as of ourselves; but our sufficiency is of God; who also hath made us able ministers of the new testament; not of the letter, but of the spirit: for the letter killeth, but the spirit giveth life (Second Corinthians 3:5-6).

If you go back, you miss the plan. We leave the old order of things. We can never have confidence in the flesh; we cannot touch that. We are in a new order, a spiritual order. It is a new life of absolute faith in the sufficiency of our God in everything that pertains to our salvation. You could never come into this place and be a Seventh-day Adventist. The law has no place in you. You are set free from everything. At the same time, like Paul, you are "bound in the Spirit" so that you would not do anything to grieve the Lord.

It is one thing to read this, and another to have the revelation of it and to see the spiritual force of it. Any man can live in the letter and become dry and wordy, limited in knowledge of spiritual verities, and spend his time everlastingly in splitting hairs; but as soon as he touches the realm of the Spirit, all the dryness goes, all the spirit of criticism leaves. There can be no divisions in a life in the Spirit. The Spirit of God brings such pliability and such love! There is no love like the love in the Spirit. It is a pure, a holy, and a divine love that is shed in our hearts by the Spirit. It loves to serve and to honor the Lord.

I see everything a failure except that which is done in the Spirit. But as you live in the Spirit, you move, act, eat, drink and do everything to the glory of God. Our message is always this, "Be filled with the Spirit." This is God's place for you, and it is as far above the natural life as the heavens are above the earth. Yield yourselves for God to fill.

WRITTEN ON OUR HEARTS

This is the covenant that I will make with them after those days, saith the Lord, I will put my laws into their hearts, and in their minds will I write them; and their sins and iniquities will I remember no more (Hebrews 10:16-17).

Moses had a tremendous trial with the people. They were always in trouble. But as he went up onto the mount, and God unfolded to him the Ten Commandments, the glory fell. He rejoiced to bring those two tables of stone down from the mount, and his very countenance shone with the glory. He was bringing to Israel that which, if obeyed, would bring life. I think of my Lord coming from heaven. I think the sight moved all heaven. Moses brought the law of the letter and it was made glorious, but all its glory was dimmed before the excelling glory that Jesus brought to us in the Spirit of life. The glory of Sinai paled before the glory of Pentecost. Those tables of stone with their, "Thou shalt not, thou shalt not," are done away; for they never brought life to anyone, and the Lord has brought in a new covenant, putting His law in our minds and writing it in our hearts, this new law of the Spirit of life.

As the Holy Ghost comes in, He fills us with such love and liberty and we shout for joy these words: "For if that which is done away was glorious, much more that which remaineth is glorious" (2 Cor. 3:11). Henceforth there is a new cry in our hearts, "I delight to do Thy will, O God." He takes away the ministration of death, written and engraved in stones, that He might establish the second, this ministration of righteousness, this life in the Spirit.

THE SPIRITUAL COMMANDMENT

For whosoever shall keep the whole law, and yet offend in one point, he is guilty of all. ...So speak ye, and so do, as they that shall be judged by the law of liberty (James 2:10,12).

You ask, "Does a man who is filled with the Spirit cease to keep the commandments?" I simply repeat what the Spirit of God has told us, that this ministration of death, written and engraved in stones (and you know that the Ten Commandments were written on stones), is *"done away"* (2 Cor. 3:11). The man who becomes a living epistle of Christ, written with the Spirit of the Living God, has ceased to be an adulterer, a murderer, or a covetous man; the will of God is his delight. I love to do the will of God; there is no irksomeness to it. It is no trial to pray, no trouble to read the Word of God, and it is not a hard thing to go to the place of worship. Like the Psalmist, "I was glad when they said unto me, Let us go into the house of the Lord" (Ps. 122:1).

How does this new life work out? The thing works out because God works in you to will and to do of His own good pleasure (see Phil. 2:13). There is a great difference between a pump and a spring. The law is a pump; the baptism is a spring. The old pump gets out of order, the parts perish, and the well runs dry. The letter killeth. But the spring is ever bubbling up and there is a ceaseless flow direct from the Throne of God. There is life. It is written of Christ, "Thou lovest righteousness and hatest wickedness..." (Ps. 45:7). And in this new life in the Spirit, in this new covenant life, you love the things that are right and pure and holy, and shudder at all things that are wrong. Jesus was able to say, "...the prince of this world cometh, and hath nothing in me" (John 14:30). And the moment we are filled with the Spirit of God we are brought into like wonderful condition, and as we continue to be filled with the Spirit, the enemy cannot have an inch of territory in us.

VICTORIOUS LIVING

Who is he that overcometh the world, but he that believeth that Jesus is the Son of God? This is he that came by water and blood, even Jesus Christ; not by water only, but by water and blood. And it is the Spirit that beareth witness, because the Spirit is truth. For there are three that bear record in heaven, the Father, the Word, and the Holy Ghost: and these three are one (First John 5:5-7).

How wonderful is this faith that overcomes the world! But how does he overcome the world? If you believe in Him you are purified, as He is pure. You are strengthened because He is strong. You are made whole because He is whole. All of His fullness may come into you because of the revelation of Himself. Faith is the living principle of the Word of God. If we yield ourselves up to be led by the Holy Spirit, we shall be divinely led into the deep things of God, and the truths and revelations and all His mind will be made so clear unto us that we shall live by faith in Christ.

God has no thought of anything on a small scale. God's Word is without change. We are to be filled with the righteousness of God on the authority of the Word. His righteousness is from everlasting to everlasting, the same yesterday, today, and forever. If I limit the Lord, He cannot work within me, but if I open myself to God, then He will surely fill me and flow through me. If we know that He hears us, then we know we have the petitions we desire. Oh, brothers, sisters, we must go into the presence of God and get from Him the answer to our prayers.

Precious Faith

...To them that have obtained like precious faith with us through the righteousness of God and our Saviour Jesus Christ: Grace and peace be multiplied unto you through the knowledge of God, and of Jesus our Lord (Second Peter 1:1-2).

In these eventful days, we must not be content with a mere theory of faith; we must have this almighty and precious faith within us so that we may move from the ordinary into the extraordinary. We must expect Him to come forth in power through us for the deliverance of others. Peter spoke of it as "like precious faith." It is like the faith that Abraham had—the very faith of God. When Peter and John said to the lame man, "Silver and gold have I none; but such as I have give I thee: In the name of Jesus Christ of Nazareth rise up and walk" (Acts 3:6), there was a manifestation of the same faith that Abraham had. It is this same precious faith God wants us to have.

In the former days, the prophets received the Holy Spirit in a certain measure, but the Holy Spirit was given to the Lord Jesus Christ without measure. Did He not give the Holy Spirit on the Day of Pentecost in this same measureless measure? That is His thought for you and me. Since I received the mighty baptism in the Holy Spirit, God has flooded my life with His power. From time to time there have been wonderful happenings—to Him be all the glory. Faith in God will bring the operation of the Spirit and we will have the divine power flooding the human vessel and flowing out in blessing to others.

Divine Power in Operation

The sorrows of hell compassed me about: the snares of death prevented me. In my distress I called upon the Lord, and cried unto my God: he heard my voice out of his temple, and my cry came before him, even into his ears (Psalm 18:5-6).

Faith is made in hard places when we are at wit's-end corner, and there seems no way out of our adversity. Faith cries to God in the place of testing. It is in these places that God enlarges us and brings us forth into a large place, to prove Himself the God of deliverances, the One who is indeed our helper.

We read in Acts 10:38 that "God anointed Jesus of Nazareth with the Holy Ghost and with power: who went about doing good, and healing all that were oppressed of the devil; for God was with him." God wants us to have this same anointing and power through the indwelling Christ and through a living faith. It was the Lord Himself who told us before He went away, "These signs shall follow them that believe. In my name they shall cast out devils...they shall lay hands on the sick, and they shall recover" (Mark 16:17-18). God is waiting to manifest His divine power through believers.

We must so live in God that the Spirit of God can operate through us. Have you received this precious faith? If so, deal bountifully with the oppressed. God has called us to loose the bands of wickedness, undo the heavy burden, let the oppressed go free, and break the yokes that the devil has put upon them. Pray in faith. Remember, he that asks receives. Ask and it shall be given you. Live for God. Keep clean and holy. Live under the unction of the Holy Spirit. Let the mind of Christ be yours so that you live in God's desires and plans. Glorify Him in the establishment of His blessing upon the people, and in seeing God's glory manifested in the midst. Amen.

PERFECTED BY CHRIST

Ye are our epistle written in our hearts, known and read of all men: foras-much as ye are manifestly declared to be the epistle of Christ ministered by us, written not with ink, but with the Spirit of the living God; not in tables of stone, but in fleshy tables of the heart (Second Corinthians 3:2-3).

This is what the Lord does for us when we come to Him; He takes out the heart of stone and gives us a heart of flesh. The Spirit of God will write the law of Christ in both our hearts and minds. He cleanses us from all iniquity, takes away the old order and brings in the new, and He gives us His blessed Holy Spirit, who causes us to walk in a way that is pleasing to Him. The old life is brought to the cross of Calvary. Our old nature is crucified there and we are brought into the position that Paul speaks of when he says, "I am crucified with Christ: neverthe-less I live; yet not I, but Christ liveth in me: and the life which I now live in the flesh I live by the faith of the Son of God, who loved me, and gave Himself for me" (Gal. 2:20).

Beloved, God would have us see that no man is perfected except as Christ the living Word abides in him. In this new life, we must have the Word of God dwelling richly in us. This Word is living and powerful and effective. It is the sword of the Spirit that will prove an effective weapon in the hands of the Spir-it-filled warrior. By it we get complete victory over all the power of the enemy. But we need the power of the Spirit within us to enable us to wield the sword of the Spirit effectively.

As the Lord fills your heart with love and compassion, you will find the inward cry from the depths of your need is met by the depth of God's love. When God gets into the depths of our hearts He purifies every intention, and He fills us with His own joy.

THE BRIGHTNESS OF HIS GLORY

Who being the brightness of his glory, and the express image of his person, and upholding all things by the word of his power, when he had by himself purged our sins, sat down on the right hand of the Majesty on high (Hebrews 1:3).

When Moses received the tablets of stone and returned to the people, God made his face shine. There was a glory in the giving of the Law. But there is a more wonderful glory in the giving of the Spirit. More wonderful than the shine on Moses's face is the moving of the Spirit to write His commandments on our hearts. God wrote His law of love and compassion into our inner beings. O beloved, let us allow the Holy Spirit to have His way in our lives to unfold to us the grandeur of Christ's glory.

The Lord will bring us into a life of humility where we have no confidence in ourselves, but our whole trust rests upon the authority of the mighty God, who has promised to be with us at all times. He has made us able ministers of the New Testament, ministers of the Spirit that gives life. Rivers of living water will flow from us as our confidence rests in Him. As we constantly partake of the living Christ within, He will give us a message direct from heaven, a hot, burning, living message.

He will elevate our minds until we have heavenly minds. We will be able to bring the vision of heavenly things to the people until they will want more of God and more of the Spirit, till they long to be filled with Spirit that they may be fruitful in every way.

I have found that the baptism in the Holy Ghost infuses into us an intensity of zeal. He will fill us with a passion for the good and acceptable and perfect will of God. We must be continually changed from glory to glory as we behold His face, until the Spirit of God changes us into His image.

A Wonderful Place
of Rest in Faith

So then faith cometh by hearing, and hearing by the Word of God (Romans 10:17).

What is faith? It is the very nature of God. Faith is the Word of God. It is the personal inward flow of divine favor, which moves in every fiber of our being until our whole nature is so quickened that we live by faith, we move by faith, and we are going to be caught up to glory by faith, for faith is the victory (see 1 John 5:4). Faith is the glorious knowledge of a personal presence within you, changing you from strength to strength, from glory to glory, until you get to the place where you walk with God, and God thinks and speaks through you by the power of the Holy Ghost. Oh, it is grand! It is glorious!

God wants us to have far more than what we can handle and see, and so He speaks of the substance of things hoped for; the evidence of things not seen; but, with the eye of faith, we may see it in all its beauty and grandeur. It is possible for the power of God to be so manifest in your human life that you will never be as you were before; for you will be ever going forward, from victory to victory, for faith knows no defeat. The Word of God will bring you into a wonderful place of rest in faith.

God means you to have a clear conception of what faith is, how faith came, and how it remains. Faith is in the divine plan, for it brings you to the open door that you might enter in. You must have an open door, for you cannot open the door; it is God who does it, but He wants you to be ready to step in and claim His promises to all the divine manifestation of power in the name of Christ Jesus. Living faith brings glorious power and personality; it gives divine ability. Faith has power to make you what God wants you to be; only you must be ready to step into the plan and believe His Word.

FAITH FOR WORKS

Even so faith, if it hath not works, is dead, being alone (James 2:17).

Faith is an increasing position, always triumphant. It is not a place of poverty but of wealth. If you always live in fruitfulness, you will always have plenty. If your life is in the divine order, you will not only have living, active faith but you will always be building up someone else in faith. What is the good of preaching without faith? God intends that we should so live in this glorious sphere of the power of God that we will always be in a position to tell people of the act that brought the fact. You must act before you can see the fact.

What is the good of praying for the sick without faith? You must believe that God will not deny Himself, for the Word of God cannot be denied. I believe this message is given in divine order, so that you may no longer be in a place of doubt but will realize that "faith is the substance!" Beloved, even with all the faith we have, we are not even so much as touching the hem of God's plan for us. It is like going to the seashore and dipping your toe in the water, with the great vast ocean before you. God wants us to rise on the bosom of the tide and not keep paddling along the shore.

Oh, to be connected with that sublime power, that human nature may know God and the glory of the manifestation of Christ! The Word of God is eternal and cannot be broken. You cannot improve on the Word of God, for it is life, and it produces life. Listen! God has begotten you to a "lively hope." You are begotten of the Word that created worlds. If you dare to believe, it is powerful. God wants us to be powerful, a people of faith, a purified people, a people who will launch out in God and dare to trust Him in glorious faith, which always takes you beyond that which is commonplace to an abiding place in God.

For the Word of God is quick, and powerful, and sharper than any twoedged sword, piercing even to the dividing asunder of soul and spirit, and of the joints and marrow, and is a discerner of the thoughts and intents of the heart (Hebrews 4:12).

One of the greatest things in the Word of God is that it discerns the thoughts and intents of the heart. Oh, that you may allow the Word of God to have perfect victory in your body, so that it may be tingling through and through with God's divine power. Divine life does not belong to this world but to the Kingdom of Heaven, and the Kingdom of Heaven is within you. God wants to purify our minds until we can bear all things, believe all things, hope all things, and endure all things. God dwells in you, but you cannot have this divine power until you live and walk in the Holy Ghost, until the power of the new life is greater than the old life.

Jesus said to His disciples, if you will believe in your heart the mountain shall be removed. God wants us to move mountains. Anything that appears to be like a mountain can be moved—the mountains of difficulty, the mountains of perplexity, the mountains of depression or depravity, or things that have bound you for years. Sometimes things appear as though they could not be moved, but believe in your heart, stand on the Word of God, and God's Word will never be defeated. Notice again this Scripture: "…What things soever ye desire, when ye pray, believe that ye receive them, and ye shall have them" (Mark 11:24). First, believe that you get them, and then you shall have them. That is the difficulty with people. They say: "Well, if I could feel I had it, I would know I had it," but you must believe it, and then the feeling will come; you must believe it because of the Word of God. God wants to work in you a real heart faith.

BECAUSE OF RIGHTEOUSNESS

And if Christ be in you, the body is dead because of sin; but the Spirit is life because of righteousness (Romans 8:10).

The moment flesh is dealt with and judgment comes to it, we are brought to a place of helplessness. The flesh has gone—dead—but the Spirit is life within us. Then the body is helpless, but it is dominated by the power of the Spirit till it only longs to breathe and act in the Spirit. It is beautiful. One of the greatest mercies that you will ever have as long as you live will be a revelation to your heart of how to get rid of yourself. It is one of the greatest revelations that can come to the human life, and there are many after that. There are boundless resources after the flesh has gone.

The word to revel in is: "Blessed are they which do hunger and thirst after righteousness: for they shall be filled" (Matt. 5:6). You cannot hunger and thirst after righteousness if you have any tendency to the natural life. The righteousness of God is a perfect development in your life of inward heart sanctification, where no defilement can enter, and the pure in heart always see God. It is a deep death, and it is a great life. God makes it a holy sacrifice, and He accepts it as an offering, and then, when we have perfectly considered the whole thing and everything has gone, we come to the conclusion that it was a reasonable thing to do, and anything less that that is unreasonable, because God has claimed us.

There is a word in the Scriptures that we very seldom understand. It has taken me a long time to understand it. It is this: "So then death worketh in us, but life in you" (2 Cor. 4:12). Only as death was manifested in them could life come to the saints. Absolutely everything you count as your life has to go, and as it goes, it is transformed. Death works in us and produces life.

THE LIVING WORD

When he was come down from the mountain, great multitudes followed him. And, behold, there came a leper and worshipped him, saying, Lord, if thou wilt, thou canst make me clean. And Jesus put forth his hand, and touched him, saying, I will; be thou clean. And immediately his leprosy was cleansed (Matthew 8:1-3).

This Living Word is not given to us just because of the narratives or the wonderful parables that Jesus taught, but that through it we might be changed. When Jesus was on earth and beheld suffering humanity, He was moved with compassion. He met the most difficult problems; and one of the hardest conditions to meet is leprosy. The moment that leprosy is pronounced upon a person, it means they are doomed. We all know that leprosy is a type of sin. Just as there is no remedy in this world for the leper, there is no natural power that can deliver us from sin. Leprosy is the disease that has sure death in it, and sin means death to the spiritual man unless the blood of Jesus cleanses it. Here was a leper with the seal of death on him, and there was only one hope. What was it? If he could come to Jesus he would be healed! But how could a leper come to Jesus? Whenever a leper came near the people, he had to cry out "Unclean! Unclean!"—so how could a leper ever get near to Jesus? The difficulty was tremendous, but when faith lays hold, impossibilities must yield.

The leper kept close to the crowd, and as Jesus drew nearer and nearer, he began his chant, "Unclean! Unclean!" and what was the result? The crowd moved away from him, leaving the path clear for the leper to be the first to get to Jesus—and no one could turn him back. No one could stop a man whose heart was set on reaching Jesus. There is no power on earth that can stop a sinner from reaching the side of the Master, if he has faith that will not be denied.

VENTURE ON THE IMPOSSIBLE

But Jesus beheld them, and said unto them, With men this is impossible; but with God all things are possible (Matthew 19:26).

The Christian life is always moving forward, non-stop, until you reach the top. If you ever stop between Calvary and the Glory, it is you who blocked the way. There is no stop between Calvary and the Glory except by human failure, but if you allow God to have His way, He will surely transform us, for His plan is to change us from what we are to be what He intends us to be, and never to lose the ideal of His great plan for us. God wants to shake us loose and take the cobwebs away, and to remove all the husks from the wheat, that we may be pure grain for God to work upon. In order to do that, we must be willing to let go; as long as you hold on to the natural, you cannot take hold of divine life.

You will not get strong in faith until you venture on the impossible. If you ask anything six times, the first five requests are made with unbelief. You are not heard because you are speaking, but because you believe. Faith never feels and never looks. Faith is an act, and faith without an act is not faith, but doubt and disgrace. Every one of us has more faith than we are using.

God gives us this remarkable substance that is called faith. It consists of the Word of God, of the personality of God, of the nature of God, and of the acts of God, and those four things are all in faith. Faith is a deep reality caused by God's personality waking up our humanity to leap into eternal things and be lost forever in something a million times greater than ourselves. Beloved, are you living in the realm of substance that cannot be touched or living in the temporal realm?

A GROWING FAITH

But grow in grace, and in the knowledge of our Lord and Saviour Jesus Christ. To him be glory both now and for ever. Amen (Second Peter 3:18).

There is always something going on with God. We grow in our faith after we are saved. Backsliding is knowing the way of holiness and shutting the door. So if you know to do good and you do not do it, that is backsliding. What standard is holiness? There is none. A person who is newborn is as holy as the oldest saint. God took the Word and made this world out of things that were not there. He caused it all to come by the word of faith. You were born of, created by, and made anew by the same word that created the world. God, in His infinite mercy, brings His infinite light and power right into our finite being so that we have revelations of the mighty God and His wonderful power.

God has taken all ranks and conditions of people to make the eleventh chapter of Hebrews. Samson made terrible mistakes, but he is included. Then there is Barak, who wouldn't go without Deborah. He couldn't have been a strong man when a woman had to go with him, but he is mentioned. Now, why can you not believe that God will have you also included? The Acts of the Apostles finishes abruptly. It is not finished, and all believers must add to the Acts of the Apostles.

You have to be zealous. You can't let anyone stand in your way. Salvation is the beginning; sanctification is a continuation; the baptism in the Holy Ghost is the enlargement of capacity for the risen Christ. God comes along and inspires your thoughts and says, "Now go forward, My child; it will be all right. Do not give in." The life that He began cannot be taken away from you. It is His purpose that we shall be sanctified, purified, and renewed. We are a people who have been raised from the dead, and if Jesus comes, you go because you have resurrection in you.

STANDING ON FAITH

So then faith cometh by hearing, and hearing by the Word of God (Romans 10:17).

Every time I preach I am impressed with the fact that the Word of God is full of life and vitality. God's Word must come to pass in us. We receive our inheritance by faith. It's a new order. Faith is a gift, and by it we have become God's spiritual children. The moment we believed we knew we had a new nature, a new life. He had a wonderful word, a sweet influence; men saw love in those beautiful eyes and were convinced of sin in His presence.

How quickly God's Word works in our spirit, soul, and body, separating the desires of our hearts. The Word enters into the joints and the marrow. As you pray, begin in the Spirit; the Spirit leads you how to pray. After you begin, God will come in. God will lift you up and breathe encouragement into you. Come into a Person who has no end. Feed upon Him; believe Him. Look at Him. Enjoy communion with Him. Reign with Him, and live in His presence.

God gives us His sweet, sweet peace. It is the gift of God's love to us. We are standing now on the foundation, the Rock, Christ, the Word, the Living Word. The power is contained in the Word. Christ is the substance of our faith. He is the hope of our inheritance. Jesus lived in the knowledge of the power of God; the Spirit of the Lord was upon Him.

YIELD TO HIS HANDS

For I am persuaded, that neither death, nor life, nor angels, nor principalities, nor powers, nor things present, nor things to come, nor height, nor depth, nor any other creature, shall be able to separate us from the love of God, which is in Christ Jesus our Lord (Romans 8:38-39).

Oh, the joy of the thought of it! What shall separate us from the love of Christ? Nothing can separate us! God is bringing forth a new creation; the sons of God are to be manifested, and we must see our inheritance in the Holy Ghost. What is it God wants us to know? Right in our earthly temple God has brought forth a son with power, with manifestation, with grace, crowned already in the earth, crowned with glory. Where sin abounded, He has brought in His grace; where disease came in to steal our life, God raised up a standard and we are here having come through tribulation. God has been purifying us, strengthening us, and equipping us with divine audacity by His almighty power.

God is in you mightily, forming within you a new creation by the Spirit—to make you ready for the glory that shall be revealed in Him. Now that He has quickened your Spirit, allow Him to reign, for He shall reign until all flesh is subdued. He is preeminently King in your life over your affections, your will, your desires, and your plans. He rules as Lord of Hosts over you, in you, and through you to chasten you and bring you into perfection. Greater is He that is in you than all the powers of darkness. Whatever befalls you, abide in Him. He stretches out His hand to cover us with His mantle of love and brings us into the channel of His grace until our hearts have moved and yielded and turned to the Lord.

THE MOVING BREATH OF THE SPIRIT

In the beginning was the Word, and the Word was with God, and the Word was God (John 1:1).

Here is our attitude of rest. All our hope is in the Word of the Living God and in the Holy Ghost. When the Comforter comes to you, He will enrich us and give us a perfect revelation. He came to fill the body and to bring forth that which all the prophets had spoken of—taking of the things of Jesus and showing them to us. Oh the joy of being filled with divine purpose in the Holy Ghost. We are to be filled with the fullness of God just as the apostles were filled. We have the same warmth, same divine approval, same life, same heaven in our souls. The Holy Ghost brings heaven to us as He reveals Jesus, who is the King of heaven.

The Spirit of the Lord is upon us. Experience the wonder of His breath, lifting the Word up, making all things new, meeting our present needs. These are the last days. They are very wonderful and blessed with signs. The breath of the Spirit is unfolding and helping.

May God move in our hearts to act in the Holy Ghost. Do you long to be with God in His splendid palace? God can only choose those filled to the uttermost. Are you hungering and thirsting for God's fullness?

BELIEVE

...I have chosen you, and ordained you, that ye should go and bring forth fruit, and that your fruit should remain: that whatsoever ye shall ask of the Father in my name, he may give it you (John 15:16).

I believe God wants us to know that our fruit has to remain. Beloved, we should recognize that our prayers are in vain unless we really expect what we ask to be granted to us. May God give us the word of faith so we know for a fact that there is a great change in us.

Oh, it is lovely to think that God can change in a moment, and can heal in a moment. When God begins, who can hinder Him? You can be saved by the power of the faith that I am speaking about. Only believe. You cannot save yourself. The more you try in your own strength, the more you get fixed up; but oh, if you will believe God will save you, He will do it. Oh, bless the Lord, oh my soul, and all that is within me bless His holy name!

Sometimes we are tested in our faith. For twenty-five years, Abraham believed God would give him a son, and every year Abraham's wife grew weaker. Did he look at her weakness? No—he looked at the promise. God tested Abraham for twenty-five years, but he gave glory to God and did not doubt. Nothing is impossible for those who believe. All who believe are blessed. People say to me, "How long will it be before I am healed?" And I ask: "How long will it be before you believe God?"

For Preachers

I therefore, the prisoner of the Lord, beseech you that ye walk worthy of the vocation wherewith ye are called (Ephesians 4:1).

I believe there is no way to make proclamation but by the Spirit. And I believe that those who are sent are called and chosen of God to be sent. We should be able, in the face of God and in the presence of His people, to behave ourselves so comely and pleasing to the Lord that we always leave behind us a life of blessing and power without strife.

It is a great choice to become a preacher of the Gospel, to handle the Word of life. We who handle the Word of life ought to be well built on the lines of common sense, judgment, and not given to anything that is contrary to the Word of God. We should have a deep reverence toward God and His Word that under all circumstances we would not forfeit our principles on the lines of faith that God revealed unto us by the truth. God wants us to know that there is strength by the power of the Spirit. We must know that to be baptized in the Holy Ghost is to leave your own life, as it were, out of all questioning; leave yourself out of all pleasing and come into like-mindedness with Jesus.

We want to be sent. It is a great thing to be called of God to preach the unsearchable riches of Christ. When we come into this blessed calling, we know that we are teaching principles and ideals for eternal life. We should be spiritual all the time. God has given His Spirit to us, and we are His spiritual children. Beloved, walk worthy of your calling in Christ.

DON'T GET ESTABLISHED

Let no man despise thy youth; but be thou an example of the believ-ers, in word, in conversation, in charity, in spirit, in faith, in purity (First Timothy 4:12).

Some believers get an idea that a preacher ought not say anything till they are established. I like to hear the bleating of the lambs. I like to hear the life of the young believer. I like to hear something coming right down from heaven into the soul as they rise the first time with tears coming down their eyes, telling of the love of Jesus.

The Holy Ghost fell upon a young man outside a church. He went into the church, and they were all so sedate. And this young man with his fullness of life and zeal for the Master got into expostulating and praising the Lord, and mak-ing manifest the joy of the Lord, and he disturbed the old saints. The father of the young man was one of the deacons of the church, and the other deacons got round him and said, "You must talk to your boy, and give him to understand that he has to wait till he is established before he manifests those things." So his father had a long talk with the boy, and he told him what the deacons said. "You know," he said, "I must respect the deacons. You have to wait until you are established."

As they neared their home, their horse made a full stop. He tried to make it go forward and back but the horse would not move for anything. "What is up with this horse?" asked the father. "Father," replied the boy, "this horse has got established."

I pray God the Holy Ghost that we will not get established in that way. God, loose us up from these old, critical, long-faced, poisoned kind of countenances. May the Lord save Pentecost from going to dry rot. We must have the reality of the supernatural quickening till we are sane and active, and not in any way dor-mant, but filled with life so God is working in us mightily by His Spirit.

Be Transformed

And be not conformed to this world: but be ye transformed by the renewing of your mind, that ye may prove what is that good, and acceptable, and perfect, will of God (Romans 12:2).

We must always be transforming, not conforming; always renewing the mind, always renovated by the mighty thoughts of God, always being brought into line with what God has said to us by His Spirit, "…This is the way, walk ye in it" (Isa. 30:21). Walk in the Spirit, and you will not fulfill the lusts of the flesh.

Lord, how shall we do it? Can a man be meek and lowly and filled with joy? Do they work together? Out of the abundance of the heart the mouth speaks. The depths of God come in, in lowliness and meekness, and make the heart love. There is no heart that can love like the heart that God has touched.

Oh, that love that embraces the sinner! There is no love like it. I always feel I can spend any time with the sinner. Oh, brother, there is a love that is God's love! There is a love that only comes by the principles of the Word of God. He loved us and gave Himself up for us. Oh, beloved, God is a real essence of joy to us in a time when it seems barren, when it seems nothing can help us but the light from heaven. We must have ideals that come from the throne of God. We must live in that place and let Him be enthroned.

It is only the broken, contrite heart that has received the mark of God. In that secluded place, He speaks to you alone; when you are down and out, and when no hand is stretched out to help you, He stretches out His hand with mercy and brings you into a place of compassion.

FORBEARING ONE ANOTHER IN LOVE

I therefore, the prisoner of the Lord, beseech you that ye walk worthy of the vocation wherewith ye are called, with all lowliness and meekness, with longsuffering, forbearing one another in love (Ephesians 4:1-2).

Isn't it glorious? You cannot find these words anywhere else. You cannot get these pictures in any place you go to. These revelations are not from nature's garden; they are from God's garden. The Spirit explains these things to us, for He alone can explain this ideal of beatitudes. They are marvelous, they are beautiful, they are full of grandeur, and they are God's. Hallelujah!

In the Church of God, where a soul is on fire, kindled with the love of God, there is a deeper love between me and that brother than there is between my earthly brother and me. Oh, this love that I am speaking of is divine love; it is not human love. It is higher than human love; it is more devoted to God. It will not betray. It is true in everything. You can depend upon it. His love will not change in character; His love demonstrates His character.

As you rise into association with Him in the Spirit, as you walk with Him in the light as He is in the light, then your fellowship becomes unique. I pray God that He will help us to understand that we shall be able to be clothed as we have never been, with another majestic touch, with another ideal of heaven. No one can love like God. And when He takes us into this divine love, we shall exactly understand this Word, this verse, for it is full of entreaty, passion, and compassion. It has every touch of Jesus right in it.

UNITY IN THE SPIRIT

Endeavouring to keep the unity of the Spirit in the bond of peace (Ephesians 4:3).

It should never be known that any preacher caused any distraction, or detraction, or split, or disunion in a meeting. The preacher has lost his unction and his glory if he ever stoops to anything that would weaken the assembly in any way.

The greatest weakness of any preacher is to draw men to himself. It is a fascinating point, but you must be away from fascination. If you don't crucify your "old man" in every way, you are not going into divine lines with God. When they wanted to make Jesus king, He withdrew Himself to pray. Why? It was a human desire of the people. What did He want? His Kingdom was a spiritual Kingdom. He was to reign over demon powers. He was to have power over the passions of human life. He was to reign so supremely over everything which was earthly that all the people might know He was divine.

He is our pattern, beloved. When they want to make anything of us, He will give you grace to refuse it. The way to get out is to find there is nothing in the earth that is worthy of Him; that there is no one in the world who is able to understand but He; that everything will crumble to the dust and become worthless. Only that which is divine will last.

Every time you draw anyone to yourself it has a touch of earth. It does not speak of the highest realm of thought. There is something about it that cannot bear the light of the Word of God. Keep men's eyes off you, but get their eyes on the Lord. Live in the world without a touch or taint of any natural thing moving you. Live high in the order and authority of God and see that everything is bearing you on to greater heights and depths and greater knowledge of the love of God.

The Fullness of Pentecostal Power

...I will pray with the spirit, and I will pray with the understanding also: I will sing with the spirit, and I will sing with the understanding also (First Corinthians 14:15).

God is bringing us right into the fullness of the Pentecostal power that was given in the first days of the Church. God wants us to know that after we have been brought into this divine life with Christ, we are able to speak in the Spirit, and we are able to sing in the Spirit; we are able to speak with understanding, and we are able to sing with understanding.

Beloved, I want you, above all things, to remember that the Church is one body. She has many members, and we are all members of that one body. At any cost, we must not break up the body but rather keep the body in perfect unity. Never try to get the applause of the people by any natural thing. Yours is a spiritual work. Yours has to be a spiritual breath. Your word has to be the Word of God. Your counsel to the Church has to be so that it cannot be gainsaid. You have to have such solid, holy reverence on every line so that every time you handle anybody, you handle him or her for God, and you handle the Church as the Church of God. By that means, you keep the Church bound together.

As the Church is bound together in one Spirit, we grow into that temple in the Lord, and we all have one voice, one desire, and one plan. And when we want souls saved, we are all of one mind. I am speaking now about spiritual power. If you get them into the mind with Christ, all their desires will be the same desires of Christ the Head.

PASSING THE TORCH

My little children, of whom I travail in birth again until Christ be formed in you (Galatians 4:19).

Unless we pass on what we receive, we shall lose it. If we didn't lose it, it would become stagnant. Virtue is always manifested through blessings that you have passed on. Nothing will be of any importance to you except that which you pass on to others. God wants us in the order of the Spirit, and He breaks upon us the alabaster box of ointments of His precious anointing that He has for every child of His. He wants us to be filled with perfumes of holy incense that we may be poured out for others and that others may receive the graces of the Spirit so that all the Church may be edified.

We must have this inward burning desire for more of God. We must not be at any stationary point. We must always have the highest power telescopes looking and hasting toward that which God has called us to that He may perfect that forever.

Oh, what a blessed inheritance of the Spirit God has for us in these days, that we should be no longer barren, nor unfruitful, but rather filled with all fullness, unlimited, increasing with all increasings, with a measureless measure of the might of the Spirit in the inner man, so that we are always like a great river pressing on and healing everything that it touches. Oh, let it be so today! We must always be hungry and ready for every touch of God.

ONE HOPE, ONE CALLING

There is one body, and one Spirit, even as ye are called in one hope of your calling (Ephesians 4:4).

Many people get called and have missed it because they are dull of hearing. There is something in the call, beloved. Many are called, but few are chosen. I have a big heart to believe that all shall be chosen. You ask, "Can it be so?" Yes, beloved, it can—not a few chosen, but many chosen.

And how shall the choice be? The choice is always your choice first. You will find that gifts are your choice first. You will find that salvation is your choice. God has made it all, but you have to choose. And so God wants you to make an inward call, to have a great intercessory condition of beseeching the Holy One to prepare you for that wonderful, mystical body.

If you want to grow in grace and in the knowledge of the grace of God, get hungry enough to be fed, be thirsty enough to cry, be broken enough you cannot have anything in the world unless He comes Himself. Oh, the baptism in the Holy Ghost! The baptism of fire! The baptism of power! The baptism of oneness! The baptism of association! The baptism of communion! The baptism of the Spirit of life that takes the man, shakes him through, builds him up, and makes him know he is a new creature in the Spirit. Beloved, receive the Holy Ghost afresh today.

THE REVELATION OF THE SPIRIT

One Lord, one faith, one baptism (Ephesians 4:5).

Just in the proportion that you have the Spirit unfolding to you, you have the Holy Ghost bringing into you a revelation of the Word. Nothing else can do it, for the Spirit gave the Word through Jesus. Jesus spoke by the Spirit that was in Him, He being the Word. The Spirit brought out all the Word of this life. Then we must have the Spirit.

If you take up John's gospel, you will find that when Jesus came, it wasn't to speak about Himself but to bring forth all He said. Just as we have the measure of the Spirit, there will be no measure of unbelief. We shall have faith. The Church will rise to the highest position when there is no schism in the Body of the lines of unbelief. When we all, with one heart and one faith, believe the Word as it was spoken, then signs, wonders, and diverse miracles will be manifested everywhere. Hallelujah!

If this spiritual life be in us, we will find we have no fear. We would have no nervous debility; it would vanish. Every time you have fear, it is imperfect love. Every time you have nervous weaknesses, you will find it is a departing from an inner circle of truth faith in God.

There is no fear in love; but perfect love casteth out fear: because fear hath torment. He that feareth is not made perfect in love (1 John 4:18).

I see that the pure heart can come into such closeness with God that the graces are so enriched, and the measure of Christ becomes so increased, that you know you are going on to possess all things. Nothing comes up in mind as beautiful as a soul just developing in their first love. I believe that God would have us to know this first love, the great love that Jesus gives us to love others.

IMMERSED IN THE HOLY GHOST

Now the God of hope fill you with all joy and peace in believing, that ye may abound in hope, through the power of the Holy Ghost (Romans 15:13).

The Christian ought to realize that at any moment, whether in the presence of others or alone, he is with God. He can have a vision in the tramcar, or in the railway train, alone, or in a crowd.

Nehemiah stood before the king because of trouble in Jerusalem, and it had nearly broken his heart. He was sorrowful, and it affected His countenance; but he was so near to God that he could say, "I have communed with the God of heaven." And if we believers are to go forth and fulfill God's purpose with us, the Holy Spirit must be constantly filling us and moving upon us until our whole being is on fire with the presence and power of God. That is the order of the baptism of the Holy Ghost.

The Holy Ghost has come into us to give us divine revelations for the moment. The man that is a "parktaker of the divine nature" has come into a relationship where God imparts His divine mind for the comprehension of His love and of the fellowship of His son. We are only powerful as we know the source; we are only strong as we behold the beatitudes and all the wonderful things and graces of the Spirit.

Some people get a wrong notion of the baptism. The baptism is nothing less than the third person of the blessed Trinity coming down from the glory, the executive Spirit of the triune God indwelling your body, revealing the truth to you, and causing you to sometimes say, "Ah!" till your bowels yearn with compassion, as Jesus yearned, to travail as He travailed, to mourn as He mourned, to groan as He groaned. Oh, that God might bring from our hearts the cry for such a deluge of the Spirit that we could not get away till we were ready for Him to fulfill His purpose in us and for us.

THE GLORY REVEALED

And the glory of the LORD shall be revealed, and all flesh shall see it together: for the mouth of the LORD hath spoken it (Isaiah 40:5).

The quickening of the Spirit results in an inspired life. I want you to notice also that when a man is born of God, or when, as it were, God is born into the man, and he becomes a quickened soul to carry out the convictions of the life of the Spirit of God in him, there comes a vision of what his life is to be.

The question is whether you dare go through with it, whether you are going to hold on to the very thing the Holy Ghost brought to you and never lose sight of it, but press on in a life of devotion to God and of fellowship and unity with Him. That is what Paul did, that is what Jesus did, and that is what we all have to do. We must not allow tongues to entertain us, nor be entertained with speaking in tongues. When you have accomplished one thing in the purpose of God for you, He means you to go forward and accomplish another. As soon as you accomplish one thing, it is, so to speak, no more to you, and God will enlarge you and fit you for the next thing He wants you to do.

If you are careful to watch for God, God is always caring for you. Jesus said, "If you honour Me here, I will honour you yonder." Whatever it may be that you are working out for God here, He is working out a far greater and divine glory for you. You have no need to be constantly talking of what you are going to appear like in the glory. The chief thing you are to watch is that you realize within your-self a deeper manifestation of the power of God today than yesterday, that you have something more clear today of the mind of the Spirit than you had the day before, that nothing comes between you and God to cloud your mind. You are to see a vision of the glory of God more today than yesterday, and to be living in such a state of bliss that it is heavenly to live.

LAYING ON THE ALTAR

I beseech you therefore, brethren, by the mercies of God, that ye present your bodies a living sacrifice, holy, acceptable unto God, which is your reasonable service (Romans 12:1).

Paul lived in an ecstasy of glory because he got into a place where the Holy Ghost could enlarge him more and more. I find that, if I continually keep my mind upon God, He unfolds things to me, and if I obediently walk before God and keep my heart pure and clean and holy and right, He will always be lifting me higher than I have expected to be.

How does it come? In Romans 12:1, Paul spoke about a certain place being reached—he speaks about an altar on which he had laid himself. When he had experienced the mercies of the Lord, he could do no other than make a presentation of his body on the altar, and it was always to be on the altar and never to be taken off. Paul so lived in the Spirit so that God brought His mind into Paul's mind, so that the apostle could write and speak, as an oracle of the Holy Ghost, things which had never been in print before, things portraying the mind of God. We read them today and drink them as in a river, and we come out of the epistles, as it were, clothed with mighty power—the power of God Himself.

It comes when we are in a place low enough and where God can pour in, pour in, pour in. Paul could say that not one thing that God had spoken of him had failed. In Acts 26 and Romans 15, you will find that he accomplished the whole of what Jesus said he would accomplish when he was filled by the mighty power of God. God wants to do the same for you and for me, according to the gifts He has bestowed upon us. To what profit will to be if we hold back anything from Him who gives us a thousand times more than ever He asks from us? In Hebrews 2 He says He is going to bring many sons to glory. It means that He is going to clothe them with glory. Let that be your vision. If you have lost the vision, He is tender to those who cry to Him; from the broken heart He never turns away, and they that seek Him with a whole heart will find Him.

THE LORD'S BANQUET

Whereby are given unto us exceeding great and precious promises: that by these ye might be partakers of the divine nature, having escaped the corruption that is in the world through lust (Second Peter 1:4).

A fter Jesus was dead, He rose to carry out His own will. And now we may have all that has been left to us by Him, all the inheritances, all the blessings, all the power, all the life, and all the victory. All the promises are ours because He is risen.

Because He is risen as a faithful High Priest, he is here to help us this morning to understand what it means by these divine principles that we have been reading. I pray God that we may have a clear knowledge today of what God means for us in these days, for He has called us to great banquets, and we must always have a good appetite at the Lord's banquets. It is a serious thing to come to a banquet of the Lord and have an anemic stomach, something that cannot take anything. We must have great appetites and be hungry souls when we come to the Lord's table. And then we can have what is laid up for us. We can be strengthened by the might of the power of God in the inner man. May the Lord take us into His treasures now.

There are no limitations. He is the executive of the Kingdom of heaven. He has power in our body as we open ourselves to Him. He displays the fullness of God to us. He reveals the full measure of His presence. So, beloved, God wants us to understand that whatever it costs, whatever it means, we must have a personal incoming of this life of God, this Holy Ghost, this divine Person.

Touched by Divine Power

...My grace is sufficient for thee: for my strength is made perfect in weakness. Most gladly therefore will I rather glory in my infirmities, that the power of Christ may rest upon me (Second Corinthians 12:9).

I want you to think about what it really means to receive the Holy Ghost. We are born again of the incorruptible Word. It liveth and abideth forever. And we are born again of that incorruptible power. It is God's plan for us. This divine power is beyond what the human mind has ever been able to fully receive. We must be made divine in order to understand all things that are divine.

We must understand that this matter must return into grace. We must understand this body must be changed into a temple of the Spirit. And we must understand that even the mind must be the mind of Christ. And we must understand that the very inner moving and crying must be of the divine plan, for God has come to change us into the same image, into the same process of power.

Just as He was in this world, so are we to be. John clearly saw it. As He is, so are we. I find that God has always, in order to encourage His people, been speaking to them in the future tense. Remember, Jesus lived in the present tense, but He always spoke in a future tense. And beloved, there is a future tense. We must come now to a place of present tense. Whatever God desired for man we must claim it now, and we shall always have greater manifestations of power if we are living now instead of living future. We must live in a now power, a now blessing, a now God, a now heaven, a now glory, and in a now virtue.

He wants us to go higher and higher. Oh, for a heavenly sight this morning, a divine touch of God, of Jesus. His touch is divine!

It Comes in Floods

According as his divine power hath given unto us all things that pertain unto life and godliness, through the knowledge of him that hath called us to glory and virtue (Second Peter 1:3).

Oh, this divine presence, this virtue! It is eminently real, and we have no sense of its presence, and that is what I believe we ought to be in. Stephen was a man full of faith and of the Holy Ghost. And you take Barnabas and read of him. Barnabas was a good man filled with the Holy Ghost and faith. It seems to me that God has a plan through holiness; you cannot get into it but through holiness. It seems there is a pure place, a pure heart that sees God. There is a divine place of purity, where the unclean never put their feet.

God has a way. It is called the way of holiness, and He can bring us into that place. He has a divine longing to bring us into that place where we hear the voice of God, we see the form of God, we understand the way of God, and we walk in communion with God. These are the places where divine virtue flows. We must have life in this glorious order of the Spirit—united, illuminated, transformed all the time by this glorious regenerating power of the Spirit, of life, of God.

May God open the door for us this morning to see that it is all for us. Oh, brothers and sisters, do not tell me that we have the fullness. Oh, the fullness of the Spirit, an immeasurable measure! Oh, don't tell me there are any limitations of it. It comes in floods we cannot contain. I drink and drink and drink again and yet we are still thirsty. Oh saints of God, the more of this joy we get, the more we require, the more we desire. It is God in you that longs for all the fullness of God to come into you. Praise His name! The divine order is in the wind, and all the manifestation of the glory is in the wind.

THE GLORY WITHIN, THE GLORY WITHOUT

Therefore my heart is glad, and my glory rejoiceth: my flesh also shall rest in hope (Psalm 16:9).

The inward man receives the Holy Ghost and instantly has great joy and blessedness. He cannot express it. It is beyond His expression. The Holy Ghost takes of the things of Jesus and utters them by this expressive wind and sends forth as a river the utterances of the Spirit.

When I come into the presence of God, He does take the things of the Spirit and reveals them to me. Our hearts are comforted and built up. And there is no way to warm a heart more than by the heart that first touched the flame. There must be the heavenly fire burning and moving us within. We are born of the Spirit and nothing but the Spirit of God can feed that spiritual life. We must live in it, feed in it, walk in it, talk in it, and sleep in it. Hallelujah! We must always be in the Holy Ghost.

You will find that virtue has to be transmitted, and you will find that glory has to be expressed. And so God, by filling us with the Holy Ghost, has brought into us that which He has in the glory, so that out of us may come forth that which He has in the glory. The world needs our manifestations and revivals; all conditions are settled in heaven and then worked out on the earth.

RECEIVE THE VIRTUE OF GOD

One thing have I desired of the LORD, that will I seek after; that I may dwell in the house of the LORD all the days of my life, to behold the beauty of the LORD, and to enquire in his temple (Psalm 27:4).

The spiritual life is so mighty in all its branches to bring to death the natural man so that the righteousness of the Spirit of the life of God can so permeate the whole body till the virtues of Christ are as much in His fingers as in His hand. It is the divine life, the divine virtue of our Lord Jesus Christ.

And then while we walk about, we have no desire for the world, because our desires are greater than the world. You cannot fascinate a man of God with gold, or houses, or lands. We seek a country, a city, which hands have not made, that is eternal in the heavens. And if this mortal body shall be put off, the heavenly body shall be put on. And we are waiting and longing with an expression, with an inward joy, with a great leap of life.

Beloved, there is a longing in the soul, a travail in the Spirit, a yielding of the will, and a blending of the life that only gives utterances as He wishes. And this morning, I believe God the Holy Ghost is bringing us to a longing for these utterances in the Spirit. You cannot get away from Him. He is the center of all things. He moves the earth, transforms beings, can live in every mind, and can plan every thought. Oh, He is there all the time. Sometimes it feels as if we have just as much as we can digest, yet there are such divine nuggets of precious truth held before our hearts, so full that it makes you understand that there are yet heights, and depths, and lengths, and breadths of the knowledge of God that God has laid up for us.

There is a principle in Scripture that may free humanity from the natural order of every institution and bring him unto a place of holiness, righteousness, and peace with God. We must touch it. We must receive all the fullness of God into our lives.

THE FIRSTFRUITS OF THE KINGDOM

For as in Adam all die, even so in Christ shall all be made alive. But every man in his own order: Christ the firstfruits; afterward they that are Christ's at his coming (First Corinthians 15:22-23).

In First Corinthians 15, we read of the glorious fact of Christ the firstfuits. A farmer goes over his land eagerly scanning the first ears of corn that show themselves above the soil because he knows—as the first beginnings, so may the harvest be. And just in the measure as Jesus Christ is risen from the dead, so are we (see 1 John 4:17).

Paul and Peter were very little together, but both were inspired to bring this wonderful truth of transformation before the Church. If Christ rose not, our faith is in vain. We are yet in our sins. But Christ has risen and become the firstfruits, and we have now the glorious hope that we shall be so changed. We who were not a people are now the people of God. Born out of due time, out of the mire, to be among princes. Beloved, God wants us to see the preciousness of it. It will drive away the dullness of life; it is here set above all other things. Jesus gave all for this treasure. He purchased the field because of the pearl of great price—the substratum of humanity. Jesus purchased it, and we are the pearl of great price for all time. Our inheritance is in heaven.

There is something very wonderful about being undefiled in the presence of my King, never to change, only to be more beautiful. Unless we know something about grace and the omnipotence of His love, we should never be able to grasp it. His love is as fathomless as the sea. His grace is flowing for you and me.

The Great Inheritance Within

To an inheritance incorruptible, and undefiled, and that fadeth not away, reserved in heaven for you, who are kept by the power of God through faith unto salvation ready to be revealed in the last time (First Peter 1:4-5).

The poor in spirit, the mourners, the meek, the hungry and thirsty, the merciful, the pure—all these are ready to be revealed at the appearing of Jesus Christ. You could not remain there but for the purifying, the perfecting, the establishing, and the working out of His perfect will in your life.

The trial of your faith is more precious than gold that perishes. (Men are losing their heads for gold.) And we must give all, yield all, as our Great Refiner puts us again and again in the melting pot. What for? So that we lose the chaff and the pure gold of His presence is so clearly seen and His glorious image reflected. We must be steadfast and immovable until all His purposes are worked out. Praising God like this in a church meeting is a different thing to the time when you are faced with a hard career; there must be no perishing though we are tried by fire.

The Spirit's grace establishes your heart to refine and enlarge you, not to destroy you. Oh, beloved, to make you know the enemy as a defeated foe, to see Jesus not only conquering but also displaying the spoils of conquest. The pure in heart shall see God. Did you know your inheritance within you is more powerful than all that is without? He will only remove hindrances from within you. Who is looking into your heart? Who is the refiner? My Lord. Oh, I know the love of God is working out in my heart a great purpose of reality.

The Mighty Shout

And when they had prayed, the place was shaken where they were assembled together; and they were all filled with the Holy Ghost, and they spake the Word of God with boldness (Acts 4:31).

Today we praise God for the fact that our glorious Jesus is the risen Christ. Those of us who have tasted the power of the indwelling Spirit know something of the manner in which the hearts of those two disciples burned as they walked to Emmaus with their risen Lord as their companion. "And when they had prayed, the place was shaken…." There are many churches where they never pray the kind of prayer that you read of here. A church that does not know how to pray will never be shaken. If you live in a place like that, you may as well write, "Ichabod—the glory of the Lord has departed" over the threshold. It is only when men have learned the secret of prayer, of power, and of praise that God comes forth. Some people say, "Well, I praise God inwardly," but if there's an abundance of praise in your heart, your mouth cannot help speaking it.

Our Christ is risen. He is a living Christ who dwells within us. We must not have this truth merely as a theory. Christ must be risen in us by the power of the Spirit. The power that raised Him from the dead must animate us, and as this glorious resurrection power surges through your being, you will be freed from all your weaknesses and you will become strong in the Lord and in the power of His might. There is a resurrection power that God wants you to have today. Why not? Receive your portion here and now.

SHOUTING IN THE RIVER

And when they heard that, they lifted up their voice to God with one accord, and said, Lord, thou art God, which hast made heaven, and earth, and the sea, and all that in them is (Acts 4:24).

God, help us understand this. It is time people knew how to shout in faith. I come across some who would be giants in the power of God, but they have no shout of faith. I find everywhere people who go down even when they are praying, simply because they are just breathing sentences without uttering speech, and you cannot get victory that way. Contemplate the eternal power of our God to whom it is nothing to quicken and raise the dead. You must learn to take the victory and shout in the face of the devil, "It is done!"

People do not expect to see signs and wonders today, as the disciples saw them of old. Has God changed? Or has our faith waned so that we are not expecting the greater works that Jesus promised? We must not harp on any minor key. Our message must rise to concert pitch, and there must be nothing left out of it that is in the Book.

There is no man who can doubt if he learns to shout. When we know how to shout properly, things will be different, and tremendous things will happen. When the apostles "lifted up their voice to God with one accord," it surely must have been a loud prayer. We must know that God means us to have life. If there is anything in the world that has life in it, it is this Pentecostal revival we are in. I believe in the Holy Ghost. And if you are filled with the Spirit, you will be superabounding in life—living waters will flow from you.

THE SPIRIT DWELLS WITHIN

But if the Spirit of him that raised up Jesus from the dead dwell in you, he that raised up Christ from the dead shall also quicken your mortal bodies by his Spirit that dwelleth in you (Romans 8:11).

Our Christ has risen. His salvation was not a thing done in a corner. Truly, He was a man of glory who went to Calvary for us, in order that He might free us from all that would mar and hinder, that He might transform us by His grace, and bring us out from under the power of satan into the glorious power of God. One touch of our risen Christ will raise the dead. Hallelujah!

Oh, this wonderful Jesus of ours! He comes and indwells us. He comes to abide. It is He who baptizes us with the Holy Ghost and makes everything different. We are to be a kind of firstfruits unto God and are to be like Christ—walking in His footsteps, living in His power—as He is the firstfruit.

Dare you take your inheritance from God? Dare you believe God? Dare you stand on the record of His word? What is the record? If you believe, you will see the glory of God. The trial that tries your faith will take you on to the place where you will know that the faith of God will be forthcoming in the next test. No man is able to win any victory save through the power of the risen Christ within him. You will never be able to say, "I did this or that." You will desire to give God the glory for everything. If you are sure of your ground, if you are counting on the presence of the living Christ within, you can laugh when you see things getting worse. God would have you settled and grounded in Christ, and you become steadfast and unmovable in Him. He will never be satisfied until He has us with Himself, sharing His glory and sharing His throne.

THE GREAT CLIMAX

...Have ye received the Holy Ghost since ye believed? (Acts 19:2)

When I think about Pentecost, I am astonished from day to day because of its mightiness, of its wonderfulness, and how the glory overshadows it. And we have only just touched it. Truly, it is so, but we must thank God that we have touched it. We must not give in because we have only touched it. Whatever God has done in the past, His name is still the same. When hearts are burdened and they come face to face with the need of the day, they look into God's Word and it brings in a propeller of power or an anointing that makes you know He has truly visited.

It was a wonderful day when Jesus left the glory. I can imagine all the angels and God the Father and all heaven so wonderfully stirred that day when the angels were sent to tell that wonderful story: "Peace on earth and good will to men." It was a glorious day when they beheld the Babe for the first time and God was looking on. It would take a very big book to record all that happened from that day until He was thirty years old. It was working up to a great climax.

I know that Pentecost in my life is working up to a great climax as well—it is not all done in a day. There are many waters and all kinds of times until we get to the real summit of everything. The Power of God is here to prevail, for God is with us.

Touches of His Wonderful Power

Mary kept all these things, and pondered them in her heart (Luke 2:19).

The mother of Jesus hid a lot of things in her heart. The time came when it was made manifest at Jordan that Jesus was the Son of God. Oh, how beautifully it was made known! It had to be made known first to one that was full of the vision of God. The vision comes to those who are full. Did it ever strike you we cannot be too full for a vision, we cannot have too much of God? When God has you in His plan, what a change in how things operate. You wonder and you see things in a new light. And how God is being glorified as you yield day to day, and the Spirit seems to lay hold of you and bring you on. Yes, it is pressing on, and then He gives us touches of His wonderful power, manifestations of the glory of these things, and indications of great things to follow—these days that we are living in now speak of better days. How wonderful!

Where should we have been today if we had stopped short, if we had not fulfilled the vision that God gave us? I am thinking about that time when Christ sent the Spirit to Paul, and he did not know much about it. His heart was stirred, his eyes were dim, and he was going to put the whole thing to an end in a short time, but Jesus was looking on. We can scarcely understand the whole process, only as God seems to show us, when He gets us into His plan and works with us little by little.

We are all amazed that we are amongst the "tongues people"—it is out of order according to the natural realm. Some of us would have never been in this Pentecostal movement had we not been drawn, but God has a wonderful way of drawing us. Paul never intended to be among the disciples, Paul never intended to have anything to do with this Man called Jesus, but God was working. God has been working with us and has brought us to this place. It is marvelous.

THE KNOWLEDGE OF GOD

O the depth of the riches both of the wisdom and knowledge of God!
(Romans 11:33)

It is necessary for me to get the knowledge of God if I want to do anything for God. I must get the vision of God, for I cannot work on my own. It must be a divine revelation of the Son of God. It must be that. I can see as clearly as anything that Paul had to be stopped in his mad pursuit. After he was stopped and had the vision from heaven, he instantly realized he had been working the wrong way. As soon as the power of the Holy Ghost fell upon him, he began in the way in which God wanted him to go.

And what is belief? To believe is to have the knowledge of Him in whom you believe. It is not to believe in the Word Jesus, but to believe in the nature, to believe in the vision, for all power is given unto Him, and greater is He that is within you in the revelation of faith than he that is in the world.

The power of the Holy Ghost has to come to be enthroned in the human life, so it does not matter what state we are in. You have to have holiness, the righteousness and Spirit of the Master, so that in every walk of life everything that is not like our Lord Jesus will have to depart. That is what is needed today. Seek the place where He is in power.

The fear of the Lord is the beginning of wisdom: and the knowledge of the holy is understanding (Proverbs 9:10).

ABIDING IN HIS PRESENCE

I am the vine, ye are the branches: He that abideth in me, and I in him, the same bringeth forth much fruit: for without me ye can do nothing (John 15:5).

Oh, to abide in Him and discover the joy of being at that place where I can always count upon being in the presence of power, where I know God's presence is leading me to a place where victory is assured. Let us get hold of this thought—if we keep in a certain place with God, wonderful things may happen.

As Jesus was baptized, we saw power and majesty falling on Him. He was no longer the same man. He received a mighty anointing power of God, and in this place He realizes that the only thing for Him to do is to submit to God, and as He submits He is more and more covered with power and led by the Spirit.

The Holy Spirit takes Him away into the wilderness, with its darkness and great privations. For forty days, He was without food, but because of the presence and the power within and on Him, He was certain of victory. He faced the wild beasts of the wilderness with this power. He faced satan with this power. Jesus returned in the power of the Spirit. After all the trials, temptations, and everything, Jesus came out more full of God, more clothed in the Spirit, more ready for the fight. The endowment with power had such an effect upon Him that other people saw it and flocked to hear Him, and great blessings came to the land.

Beloved, receive the Holy Ghost. As the Holy Ghost comes upon an individual, He is capable of changing him and fertilizing his spiritual life and filling him with such power and grace. Oh, what a blessed thing this is to be so filled with God.

Yielded and Full of the Spirit

I was in the Spirit on the Lord's day... (Revelation 1:10).

John the Divine preached all over the country, and the enemies of Christ gnashed upon him with their teeth, and they tried to the best of their power to destroy him. Tradition says that they even put him in a pot of boiling oil, but, like a cat, he seemed to have nine lives. I tell you there is something in the power of the Holy Spirit. When God wants to keep a man, nothing can destroy him.

My life is in the hands of God. What can separate us from the love of God? Can heights or depths? Is there anything that can separate us? No, praise God! Nothing can separate us. No, his enemies said they could not kill him, so they cast him away on the rocky and desolate island of Patmos. They thought that would be an end of him; and there, on that lonely isle, he was "in the Spirit."

Have you ever been there? The very place that was not fit for humanity was the place where he was most filled with God, and where he was most ready for the revelation of Jesus. Oh, beloved, I tell you there is something in the baptism in the Holy Ghost worthy of our whole attention, worthy of our whole consideration in every way. Yes, the barren wilderness, the rocky and desolate isle, the dry land, and the unfriendliest place may be filled with God.

The revelation given to him was a series of holy truths that have yet to be fulfilled and will be fulfilled to the letter. You will see you are in a thousand times better position than John. In that barren place he was filled with the Spirit. You can have no excuse, for the lines have fallen to you in pleasant places. You say, "How can I have it?" Let heaven come in; let the Holy Ghost take possession of you, and if you allow the Holy Ghost to have full control you will find you are living in the Spirit.

Breathing Life into Dry Bones

And he said unto me, Son of man, can these bones live? And I answered, O Lord GOD, thou knowest (Ezekiel 37:3).

Only one thing can accomplish the purposes of God, and that is being *in the Spirit*. I don't care how dry the land is; I don't care how thirsty the land is. Only the Holy Ghost can breathe life into barrenness. When you are in the Spirit, and the dry bones are round about you, and you think everything is exactly opposite to your desires, and you can see no deliverance by human power, then—knowing your condition is known to God and that He wants men and women who are willing to submit and yield to the Holy Spirit until their bodies are saturated and soaked with God—you will realize that God your Father has you in such a condition that at any moment He can reveal His will to you.

God speaks so loud and clear that Ezekiel could hear every word. There was no move in the valley until the Word of the Lord was uttered. God spoke and His message went forth through His servant the prophet. The world has to be brought to a knowledge of the truth, but that will only be brought about through human instrumentality. Ezekiel rose up, and clothed with divine power he began to speak and prophesy. There was a rattling among the bones as Ezekiel's voice filled with the Spirit of the Living God. God gave him the victory.

Beloved, this is the place that we reach. This prophecy is for us. Truly God wants to begin this in us. There are many dry places. The Lord's hand is not shortened that it cannot save. It is in man's extremity that God finds His opportunity. "All things are possible to him that believeth" (Mark 9:23). But if we are to do the will of God at the right time and place, we must get into the Spirit and give God a fair chance.

Entering into Rest

There remaineth therefore a rest to the people of God. For he that is entered into his rest, he also hath ceased from his own works, as God did from his. Let us labour therefore to enter into that rest, lest any man fall after the same example of unbelief (Hebrews 4:9-11).

God wants me to speak about the rest where you cease from your own works, and where the Holy Ghost begins to work in you and where you know that you are not your own but are absolutely possessed by God.

I believe that God can bring us into places of rest this day where we will cease from our own works, our own planning, our own human individuality that so interferes with God's power within us. God wants to fill the body with Himself, for God shall take use into His plan, His pavilion, His wisdom, and the government shall be upon His shoulders.

The baptism of the Holy Ghost is necessary, for then the Holy Ghost will so reveal the Word in the body that it will be like a sword: it will cut between the soul and the Spirit till the soul can no longer desire indulging in the things contrary to the mind and will of God. I want to show you the need for the Holy Ghost, by which you know there is such a thing as perfect rest, a perfect Sabbath coming to your life. I want you to see Jesus—He was filled with the Holy Ghost and lay asleep peacefully when the storm began to blow so terribly and filled the ship with water. He was filled with the Holy Ghost and lived in perfect rest.

Don't you want rest? How long are you going to be before you enter into that rest? Enter into rest, get filled with the Holy Ghost, and unbelief will depart.

The Spirit Within You

In the last day, that great day of the feast, Jesus stood and cried, saying, If any man thirst, let him come unto me, and drink. He that believeth on me, as the scripture hath said, out of his belly shall flow rivers of living water. (But this spake he of the Spirit, which they that believe on him should receive: for the Holy Ghost was not yet given; because that Jesus was not yet glorified.) (John 7:37-39).

It is a wonderful thing to get in touch with the Living God; it is a glorious thing. The Holy Spirit came as a breath, as the moving of a mighty wind. When you are filled with the breath of the Spirit, the breath of God, the holy fire, and the Word, Christ is within you.

He never separates power from holiness; the pure in heart shall see God. But I believe that if He has come to reveal Himself, you cannot lack, because he that believes that Jesus is the Christ overcomes the world. He is the purifier; He is the abiding presence, the one great source of righteousness.

He does not want any of us to be thirsty, famished, naked, full of discord, full of evil, full of carnality, full of sensuality. And so He sends out in His own blessed way the old prophetic cry: "Ho, every one that thirsteth, come ye to the waters, and he that hath no money; come ye, buy, and eat…" (Isa. 55:1).

The Master can give you that which will satisfy. He has in Himself just what you need at this hour. He knows your greatest need. You need the blessed Holy Ghost, not merely to satisfy your thirst, but to satisfy the needs of thirsty ones everywhere; for as the blessed Holy Spirit flows through you like rivers of living water, these floods will break what needs to be broken.

CLOTHED WITH DIVINE FULLNESS

And I will pray the Father, and he shall give you another Comforter, that he may abide with you for ever; even the Spirit of truth; whom the world cannot receive, because it seeth him not, neither knoweth him: but ye know him; for he dwelleth with you, and shall be in you (John 14:16-17).

Abraham believed God, and we are all blessed through faithful Abraham. As we believe God, many will be blessed through our faith. Abraham was an extraordinary man of faith. He believed God in the face of everything. God wants to bring us to the place of believing, where, despite all contradictions around, we are strong in faith, giving God glory. As we *fully believe God,* He will be glorified, and we will prove a blessing to the whole world as was our father Abraham.

In John 14, we see the promise that ignorant and unlearned fisherman were to be clothed with the Spirit, anointed with power from on high, and endued with the Spirit of wisdom and knowledge. As He imparts divine wisdom, you will not act foolishly. The Spirit of God will give you a sound mind, and He will impart to you the divine nature. How could these weak and helpless fishermen, poor and needy, ignorant and unlearned, do the works of Christ and greater works than He had done? They were incapable. None of us is able. But our emptiness has to be clothed with divine fullness, and our helplessness has to be filled with the power of His helpfulness. Paul knew this when he gloried in all that brought him down in weakness, for a mighty deluge of divine power came flowing into his weakness.

When the Lord reveals to you that you must be filled with the Holy Ghost, seek Him until He gives you a revelation. The Holy Ghost takes of the words of Christ and makes them life to us.

TOWARD THE MARK

Brethren, I count not myself to have apprehended: but this one thing I do, forgetting those things which are behind, and reaching forth unto those things which are before, I press toward the mark for the prize of the high calling of God in Christ Jesus (Philippians 3:13-14).

The Lord would have us preach by life and by deed, always abounding in service—living epistles, bringing forth to men the knowledge of God. If we went all the way with God, what would happen? What should we see if we would only seek to bring honor to the name of our God? We must move on to a fuller power of the Spirit, so that we are never satisfied that we have apprehended all, but rather are filled with the assurance that God will take us on to the goal we desire to reach, as we press on for the prize ahead.

You say, "I am in a needy place." It is in needy places that God delights to work. For three days, the people who were with Christ were without food, and Jesus asked Philip, "Whence shall we buy bread, that these may eat?" (John 6:5). That was a hard place for Philip, but not for Jesus, for He knew perfectly what He would do. The hard place is where He delights to show forth His miraculous power. And how fully was the need provided for—bread enough and to spare!

There is power in the name of Jesus. Let us apprehend it—the power of His resurrection, the power of His compassion, the power of His love. Love will break the hardest thing—there is nothing love cannot break.

Delighting to Do the Will of God

For we are the circumcision, which worship God in the spirit, and rejoice in Christ Jesus, and have no confidence in the flesh (Philippians 3:3).

Beloved, it is God's thought to make us all very rich in grace and in the knowledge of God through our Lord Jesus Christ. There is a circumcision of the heart by faith, a wonderful circumcision made without hands, where God brings into the heart such perfection that all the law is fulfilled and we delight to do the will of God.

Some people are very much perplexed in regard to keeping the Sabbath Day. Why should I go back under law when God has worked the whole law into my heart, and I have great joy to keep the Sabbath? Every day is a Sabbath with me; every day is a day unto the Lord. It is grand to be in a place where we have "no confidence in the flesh." When God holds the reins of our lives, we no longer have anything to boast about.

Oh, it is beautiful to gaze upon the perfected Jesus! Jesus so outstrips everything else. Beloved, I see there is no hope for us except through broken conditions. Pentecost came to a broken heart. It was there on the Cross—Christ died with a broken heart. Oh, glory to God, "It is finished" for you. And now because it is finished, we can take the same place Jesus took and rise out of death into majestic glory with the resurrection touch of Heaven, so that all will know that God has done something for us. Every day there must be a revival touch in our hearts. We are to be made new all the time.

Beloved, do not go back to works; abide in the finished work of Christ. Rest in His great love for you.

THE EXCELLENCE OF CHRIST

For ye had compassion of me in my bonds, and took joyfully the spoiling of your goods, knowing in yourselves that ye have in heaven a better and an enduring substance (Hebrews 10:34).

I am positive that no man can ever come into like-mindedness on these lines except by the illumination of the Spirit. I see in the baptism of the Holy Ghost unlimited grace and endurance in that revelation by the Spirit. The excellence of Christ can never be understood except by illumination. The Holy Ghost is the great Illuminator who makes me understand all the depths of Christ.

Paul never saw Christ but by the Spirit's revelation. Before his conversion Paul would do anything to put Christians to death, and that passion within him raged like a mighty lion. But as he was on the way to Damascus, he heard the voice of Jesus saying, "Saul, Saul, why persecutest thou Me?" (Acts 9:4.) It was the tenderness of God that broke his heart.

Beloved, it is always God's tenderness that brings us to brokenness. If somebody tried to thwart us, we could stand our ground, but when we go to One who forgives us all, we know not what to do except to surrender all to Him. Oh, to win Christ, beloved! There are many things in the human heart that need softening a thousand times a day. There are things in us that will never be broken and brought to ashes unless God shows us the excellence of the knowledge of Christ.

Yield to the Power of God

And be found in him, not having mine own righteousness, which is of the law, but that which is through the faith of Christ, the righteousness which is of God by faith (Philippians 3:9).

We must not depend upon our own works but upon the faithfulness of God, being able under all circumstances to be hidden in Him, covered by the Almighty One in the presence of God. Oh, I must be found in Him! There is seclusion, a place of rest and faith in Jesus, and nothing else is like unto it.

He came to the disciples on the water when they were terrified and He said to them, "It is I, be not afraid" (John 6:20). Yes, He is always there in the storm; He is there in the peace; He is there in the trouble; He is there in the adversity. When shall we know He is there? When we are found in Him, not having our own work, our own plan, but resting in the omnipotent plan of God, resting in the finished work of Christ.

Beloved, today is a resurrection day. Jesus said, "Greater things shall ye do." Then we must know the power of His resurrection. To know this rest of faith, to know the supplanting of His power in you, to make you see that every one of us without exception can reach these beatitudes in the Spirit. The Lord wants us to come to the place where we cease living our own lives, where by the power of God we rise out of our natural life into a life where God rules and reigns. Beloved, do you long to win Him? Do you long to know Him? Do you long to be found in Him? That longing shall be satisfied. This is a day of being clothed by God. All who want to know the power of God should yield to the mighty power of God and obey the Spirit.

BLESSED THROUGH SIMPLE FAITH

...Blessed is the womb that bare thee, and the paps which thou hast sucked. But he said, Yea rather, blessed are they that hear the Word of God, and keep it (Luke 11:27-28).

No doubt some have thought what a blessed thing it would be if you had been the Virgin Mary. Listen! You can attain a higher position than Mary's through simple faith in what the Scriptures say.

If we receive the Word of God as it was given to us, there will be power in our bodies to claim the gifts of God, and it will amaze the world when they see the power of God manifested through these gifts. I am convinced that there is nothing in the world that is going to convince men and women of the power of the Gospel like the manifestation of the Spirit. God has baptized us in the Holy Ghost for a purpose—that He may show His mighty power in human flesh, as He did in Jesus. And He is bringing us to a place where He may manifest these gifts.

Wherever there is a child of God who dares receive the Word of God and cherishes it, God is manifest in the flesh, for the Word of God is life and Spirit and brings us into a place where we know that we have power with God and with men, in proportion to our loyalty of faith in the Word of God. Now, beloved, I feel somehow that we have missed the greatest principle that underlies the baptism of the Holy Spirit. The greatest principle is that God the Holy Ghost came into my body to make manifest the mighty works of God and that I may profit as well. It so fills us that we feel we can command demons to come out of possessed people. It is not our own power. It is the power of the Holy Ghost that makes manifest the glorious presence of Christ.

THE POWERFUL NAME OF JESUS

God also hath highly exalted him, and given him a name which is above every name: that at the name of Jesus every knee should bow... (Philippians 2:9-10).

All things are possible through the name of Jesus. There is power to overcome everything in the world through the name of Jesus. I want you to see the power, the virtue, and the glory of that name.

Six people went into the house of a sick man to pray for him. He was an Episcopalian vicar, and he lay in his bed utterly helpless, without even strength to help himself. He had read a little tract about healing and had heard about people praying for the sick and sent for these friends, who, he thought, could pray the prayer of faith. They anointed him according to James 5:14, but, because he had no immediate manifestation of healing, he wept bitterly.

The six people walked out of the room, somewhat crestfallen to see the man lying there in an unchanged condition. When they were outside, one of the six said, "There is one thing we might have done. I wish you would all go back with me and try it." They went back and all got together in a group. This brother said, "Let us whisper the name of Jesus." At first when they whispered this worthy name, nothing seemed to happen. But as they continued to whisper, "Jesus! Jesus! Jesus!" the power began to fall. As they saw that God was beginning to work, their faith and joy increased and they whispered the name louder and louder. As they did so the man arose from his bed and dressed himself.

The secret was just this, those six people had gotten their eyes off the sick man, and they were just taken up with the Lord Jesus Himself, and their faith grasped the power that there is in His name. Oh, if people would only appreciate the power that there is in this name, there is no telling what would happen. I know that through the power of His name we have access to God. The very face of Jesus fills the whole place with glory. All over the world there are people magnifying that name, and oh, what a joy it is for me to utter it.

SAVED, FILLED, TRANSFORMED

That at the name of Jesus every knee should bow, of things in heaven, and things in earth, and things under the earth (Philippians 2:10).

It is a blessed thing to learn that God's Word can never fail. Never hearken to human plans. God can work mightily when you persist in believing Him in spite of discouragements from the human standpoint. Peter and John were helpless, illiterate, and had no college education. They had some training with fish, and they had been with Jesus. A wonderful revelation of the power of the name of Jesus came to them. The handed out the bread and fish after Jesus had multiplied them. They had sat at the table with Him, and John had often gazed into His face. Peter had to be rebuked often, but Jesus manifested His love to Peter through it all. Yes, He loved Peter, the wayward one. There is power in Jesus and in His wondrous name to transform anyone, to heal anyone.

The name of Jesus is so marvelous. Peter and John had no conception of all that was in that name; neither had the lame man who lay daily at the gate; but they had faith to say, "In the name of Jesus Christ of Nazareth, rise up and walk" (Acts 3:6). And as Peter took him by the right hand, and lifted him up, immediately his feet and anklebones received strength, and he went into the temple with them, walking and leaping and praising God.

Poor Peter and poor John! They had no money! But they had faith and the power of the Holy Ghost. You can have God even though you have nothing else. Even though you have lost your character you can have God. I have seen the worst men saved by the power of God—saved by the name of Jesus and filled with the Holy Ghost! God wants you to see more of this sort of thing done.

MEMORIAL STONES

That this may be a sign among you, that when your children ask their fathers in time to come, saying, What mean ye by these stones? Then ye shall answer them, That the waters of Jordan were cut off before the ark of the covenant of the Lord; when it passed over Jordan, the waters of Jordan were cut off: and these stones shall be for a memorial unto the children of Israel for ever (Joshua 4:6-7).

Do you keep in memory how God has been gracious in the past? God has done wonderful things for all of us. If we keep these things in memory we shall become strong in faith. We should be able to defy satan in everything. Remember all the ways the Lord has led you through trials and valleys. When Joshua passed over Jordan on dry land, he told the people to pick up twelve stones and pitch them in Gilgal. These were to remind the children of Israel that they came over the Jordan River on dry land.

There is something in the Pentecostal work that is different from anything else in the world. Somehow in Pentecost you know that God is a reality. Wherever the Holy Ghost has right of way, the gifts of the Spirit will be in manifestation; and where these gifts are never in manifestation, I question whether He is present. Pentecostal people are spoiled for anything other than Pentecostal meetings. We want none of the entertainments that the churches are offering. When God comes in, He entertains us Himself. Entertained by the King of kings and Lord of lords! Oh, it is wonderful.

Do you remember the wonderful ways God has met with you? Think of the first time you were baptized in the Holy Ghost. Oh, consider the blessed event when He opened rivers of living water within you. All His words are spirit and life to you. If you will only have faith in Him, you will find that every word that God gives is life. You cannot be in close touch with Him, and you cannot receive His Word in simple faith, without feeling the effect of it in your body as well as in your spirit and soul. Remind yourself of the great words and works of God, and you will not doubt.

Who Do You Say I Am?

When Jesus came into the coasts of Caesarea Philippi, he asked his disciples, saying, Whom do men say that I the Son of man am? And they said, Some say that thou art John the Baptist: some, Elias; and others, Jeremias, or one of the prophets. He saith unto them, But whom say ye that I am? And Simon Peter answered and said, Thou art the Christ, the Son of the living God (Matthew 16:13-16).

Jesus asked His disciples what men were saying about Him. Peter answered, "Thou art the Christ, the Son of the living God." It is so simple. Whom do you say He is? Who is He? How can you know who He is?

This is an inward revelation. God wants to reveal His Son within us and make us conscious of an inward presence. Then you can cry, "I know He's mine. He is mine!" Seek God until you get from Him a mighty revelation of the Son, until that inward revelation moves you on to the place where you are always steadfast, unmovable, and always abounding in the work of the Lord. There is a wonderful power in this revelation.

...Upon this rock I will build my church; and the gates of hell shall not prevail against it. And I will give unto thee the keys of the kingdom of heaven: and whatsoever thou shalt bind on earth shall be bound in heaven: and whatsoever thou shalt loose on earth shall be loosed in heaven (Matthew 16:18-19).

Was Peter the rock? No. A few minutes later he was so full of the devil that Christ had to say to him, "Get thee behind me, Satan: thou art an offence unto me..." (Matt. 16:23). This rock was Christ. And to every one who knows that He is the Christ, he gives the key of faith, the power to bind, and the power to loose. Establish your hearts with this fact. God wants you to have the inward revelation of this truth and of all the power contained in it. God is pleased when we stand upon this Rock and believe that He is unchangeable. If you will dare to believe God, you can defy all the powers of evil.

The Place of Reigning

There is therefore now no condemnation to them which are in Christ Jesus, who walk not after the flesh, but after the Spirit. For the law of the Spirit of life in Christ Jesus hath made me free from the law of sin and death (Romans 8:1-2).

We need to be very near God so that every day brings us nearer to the goal, which has so many things in it. The terrestrial body will be so beautiful in every way to take in all the glories and all the expression of heaven. I want to provoke you to this holy, inward interest so that you may have a share. I look forward to the Word of God where it says that He will bring many sons into glory (see Heb. 2:10). God has so many things for us in this day that we must be ready. That is the reason why I try to provoke you to holiness, an intense desire, and an inward cry after God.

If you are going on with God, you cannot be fed with natural bread. The people of God need to have the fresh bread that comes down from heaven. It is very special bread because it just meets the need of every heart. The disciples knew it. They were listening to His voice. Jesus was saying marvelous words, yet they knew that there was such freshness about it that they said, "Evermore give us this bread" (John 6:34). Now this is the bread that came down from heaven, even the Son of God, who gave His life for the world.

Remember that He has so wonderfully overcome the power of satan and all the powers of disease and all the powers of sin till there is a perfect place in Christ Jesus where we may be free from sin, sickness, disease, and death. It is one of the greatest positions that God has for us.

FEEDING ON GOD'S WORD

So then faith cometh by hearing, and hearing by the Word of God
(Romans 10:17).

All lack of faith is due to not feeding on God's Word. You need it every day. How can you enter into a life of faith? Feed on the living Christ of whom this Word is full. As you get taken up with the glorious fact and the wondrous presence of the living Christ, the faith of God will spring up within you.

You see, it is as clear, as definite, and as personal as it could be. As we enter into these divine, personal plans today, we will find that sin is dethroned, disease can't hold its seat, death has lost its sting, and victory is in Christ Jesus. How? It comes by reigning in life through Christ Jesus. To reign in life means that you are conquering every human weakness you have. To reign means to say that you are on the rock and everything else is under your feet. Jesus has made a place of victory for all of us, that we may reign as king over our bodies in every way and over all thoughts of evil. He will always heal you if you dare believe Him. Men are searching everywhere today for things with which they can heal themselves, and they ignore the fact that the balm of Gilead is within easy reach.

The new creation is God's masterpiece, His poem. Praise is God's sunlight in the heart. It destroys sin germs and ripens the fruits of the Spirit. It is the oil of gladness that lubricates life's activities. There can be no holy life without it. It keeps the heart pure and the eye clear. Praise is essential to the knowledge of God and His will. The strength of a life is the strength of its song. When the pressure is heavy that is the time to sing. Pressure is permitted to strengthen the attitude and spirit of praise. It takes a man to sing in the dark when the storm and battle are raging, and it is such singing that makes the man.

CLOTHED WITH GOD

And the disciples were filled with joy, and with the Holy Ghost (Acts 13:52).

Our hearts are moved. God is moving us to believe that He is on the throne, waiting for us to make application. Stretch out your hands to God to believe that the almightiness of His grace is available to us in a most marvelous way. Whatever yesterday was, today is to be greater.

Are you ready? What for? To come to a place where you will not give way, a place where you will dare believe that God is the same today as He was yesterday and that He will surely satisfy you because He longs to fill you. Those who believe shall be satisfied.

Are you ready? What for? To so apply your heart to the will of God, to so yield yourself to the purposes of God that He will work a plan through your life that has never been before.

Are you ready? What for? To come into such like-mindedness with Christ today that you will have no more human desire but will be cut short from all human bondages and be set free. Come to God in all the depths of His fullness, His revelation, and His power so that you may be clothed with God today.

And, behold, I send the promise of my Father upon you: but tarry ye in the city of Jerusalem, until ye be endued with power from on high (Luke 24:49).

The Ministry of Transformation

Therefore if any man be in Christ, he is a new creature: old things are passed away; behold, all things are become new. And all things are of God, who hath reconciled us to himself by Jesus Christ, and hath given to us the ministry of reconciliation; to wit, that God was in Christ, reconciling the world unto himself, not imputing their trespasses unto them; and hath committed unto us the word of reconciliation. Now then we are ambassadors for Christ, as though God did beseech you by us: we pray you in Christ's stead, be ye reconciled to God (Second Corinthians 5:17-20).

Paul wrote many things that are hard to understand. Unless you are spiritually enlightened, you will not be able to comprehend the attitude of the place of ascension he had reached. Always keep in mind that to be conformed to this world is loss, but to be transformed from this world is gain.

Transformation comes about through the working of His mighty power in the mind. The body and the soul can be so preserved in this wonderful life of God that nothing can hinder us from living as those who are dead to sin and alive unto God. In the life of Christ's resurrection, we find that sin has been destroyed, disease has been absolutely put aside, and death has been abolished!

The Spirit of the Lord is giving us revelation that will teach us a supernatural plan that enables us to absolutely live as a new creation, if we dare believe. You will go by leaps and bounds into all the treasury of the Most High, as you believe. Nothing will interfere with you but yourself. And I believe God can even change your mind.

THE BODY MUST BE CHANGED

For we that are in this tabernacle do groan, being burdened: not for that we would be unclothed, but clothed upon, that mortality might be swallowed up of life (Second Corinthians 5:4).

No flesh can come into the presence of God. If you do die, a process occurs to get rid of all that is in the body, the very body that you are in must be disposed of. It must come to ashes.

In that moment, the very nature of Christ, the life of God in you, will be clothed with a body that can stand all eternity. The very nature that came into you when you were born again is of a spiritual quality. It can understand supernatural things. And only those who are born of God can understand spiritual things. Nonbelievers cannot understand spiritual things. But the moment we are quickened, born again, made anew, this nature takes on its supernatural power and it begins travailing and groaning to be delivered from the body.

We want to be so clothed with God while we are in our bodies, clothed with life from heaven, so that no natural thing would be in evident in us. We would then be absolutely made alive in Christ, living only for the glory and the exhibition of the Lord of life. This is the clothing we want, that we might not be naked.

You know exactly what nakedness is. Nakedness is a sense of consciousness that there is something that has not been dealt with, that has not been judged; hence, the blood has not had its perfect application. Nakedness means that you are inwardly conscious that there is some hidden thing, something that has not been absolutely brought to the blood, something that could not possibly stand in God's presence, something that is not ready for the absolute glory. The Word of life is preached through the Gospel, and it has a wonderful power in it. It brings immortality into that which is natural in a person.

LIFE IN THE SPIRIT

And this is life eternal, that they might know thee the only true God, and Jesus Christ, whom thou hast sent (John 17:3).

The Scriptures are very clear: we must allow ourselves to come in touch with this great life in us. Do not forget, the Holy Ghost did not come as a cleanser. The Holy Ghost is not a cleanser. The Holy Ghost is a revealer of imperfection, which takes the blood of Jesus to cleanse. After the blood has cleansed the imperfections in us, you need the Word of God, for the Word of God is the only power that creates anew.

Life comes through the Word. The Word is the Son. He that has received the Son has received life; he that has not received the Son does not have life (see 1 John 5:12). Millions of people living today don't have eternal life. Only one life is eternal life, and that is the life of the Son of God. One is the life of eternal death, the other of eternal life. One is the life of destruction, the other of eternal deliverance. One is a life of bondage, the other of freedom. One is a life of sorrow, the other of joy. I want you to see that you are to live so full of the life divine that you are not moved by any wind of doctrine or anything that comes along. People make the biggest mistake in the world and miss the greatest things of God today by turning to the letter instead of the Spirit.

The letter kills, but the Spirit always gives life! Do not be carnally minded. Be spiritually minded, for then you will know the truth, and the truth will make you free. See to it that you know and affirm that it is Christ who gives life. Division in your thinking gives sorrow. It brings remorse, trials, and difficulties. Let Christ dwell in your hearts richly, by faith.

THE SEALING OF THE SPIRIT

Ye were sealed with that holy Spirit of promise, which is the earnest of our inheritance until the redemption of the purchased possession, unto the praise of his glory (Ephesians 1:13-14).

The Lord wants to bring us to the place of real foundational truth. Build upon the foundation of truth. Don't be twisted aside by anything. Let this be your chief position: you are living to catch more of the Spirit—only the Spirit! I clearly know that the baptism in the Holy Ghost is not the only thing that makes me eligible for the coming of the Lord. People have gone mad, thinking it is. They have gone mad because they have gotten baptized with the Spirit and think no one is right with God but those who are baptized with the Spirit. It is the biggest foolishness in the world.

Why is it foolishness? Because the Truth bears it out. The thief on the cross went right up to meet Jesus in Paradise, and he was not baptized with the Spirit! But just because a thief missed some good things, should you miss them? No! It was the great grace of the Lord to have mercy upon him who didn't have them. There is not a gift, not a grace, not a position that God will not give you to loosen you from your bondages. He wants you to be free in the Spirit. He wants to fill you with the Holy Ghost and the Word until He brings you to the sealing of the Spirit. You say, "What is the sealing of the Spirit?" The sealing of the Spirit is when God has put His mark upon you and you are tagged.

It is a wonderful thing to have the tag of almightiness. It seals you so the devil cannot touch you. It proves the Lord has preserved you for Himself. There is a covenant between you and God, and the sealing of the Spirit keeps you in that covenant, where evil powers have no more dominion.

Drunk in the Spirit

For whether we be beside ourselves, it is to God: or whether we be sober, it is for your cause (Second Corinthians 5:13).

There is a place to reach in the Holy Ghost that is mystifying to the world and to many people who are not going with God. It is remarkable: we can be so filled with the Spirit, so clothed with Him, so purified within, so made ready for the Rapture, that we are drunk in the Spirit all the time!

Oh, to be so filled with the Spirit of life that you are absolutely drunk and completely beside yourself! Now, when I come in contact with people who would criticize my drunkenness, I am sober. I can be sober one minute and drunk the next. But I tell you to be drunk is wonderful! Ephesians 5:18 admonishes us, "Be not drunk with wine, wherein is excess; but be filled with the Spirit." A drunken man stops at a lamppost, and he has a lot to say to it. He talks the most foolish things possible. The people say, "He's gone."

Beloved, pray, "O, Lord that I may be so drunk that it makes no difference what people think!" I am not concerned about what people think. I continue to speak to the Lord in hymns and spiritual songs, making my boast in the Lord. The Lord of hosts is round about me, and I am so free in the Holy Ghost.

Let no man think that he cannot fall because he stands. No, don't think that. Remember this: you need not fall. Grace abounds where sin abounds, and where weakness is, grace comes in. Your very inactivity becomes divine activity.

RECONCILED TO CHRIST
THROUGH RIGHTEOUSNESS

And if Christ be in you, the body is dead because of sin; but the Spirit is life because of righteousness (Romans 8:10).

There is no such thing as having liberty in your body if there is sin there. Only when righteousness is there does righteousness abound. When Christ is in your heart, enthroning your life, and sin is dethroned, righteousness abounds, and the Holy Ghost has great liberty. My, what triumphs of heights, of lengths, of depths, of breadths there are in the holy place! And where is the holy place? Right inside us! Right inside the children of God, the heirs of God, the joint heirs with Christ!

> *And all things are of God, who hath reconciled us to himself by Jesus Christ, and hath given to us the ministry of reconciliation; to wit, that God was in Christ, reconciling the world unto himself, not imputing their trespasses unto them; and hath committed unto us the word of reconciliation* (2 Corinthians 5:18-19).

What is reconciliation? To be absolutely joined to Christ and blended with Him in atonement. Reconciliation is a glorious thing! We remember the blessed Son of God, taking our place in reconciliation, becoming the absolute position of all uncleanness, of every sin. God laid upon Him the iniquity of all, that every iniquity might go, every bondage might be made free.

I know that this divine life—which is free from bondage, free from the power of satan, and free from evil thoughts—is for us. God is reconciling us in such a way to Himself that He abounds to us. In Him, we have freedom, purity, power, separateness, and we are ready for the great trumpet!

THE HOLY FIRE

But put ye on the Lord Jesus Christ, and make not provision for the flesh, to fulfil the lusts thereof (Romans 13:14).

The seed of the Lord Jesus Christ is mightily in you, which is a seed of purity, a seed of truth and knowledge, a seed of life, and a seed of transformation. This is the great hope of the future day.

This is the day of purifying. This is the day of holiness. This is the day of separation. This is the day of waking. Oh God, let us wake today! Let the inner spirit wake into consciousness and hear that God is calling us. And it is coming. It is upon us. Paul said he travailed in birth. Jesus did the same. John had the same. So brothers and sisters, may God bless you and make you see that this is a day of travailing for the Church of God that she might be formed so that she is ready for putting on the glorious clothing of heaven forever and forever.

I want you to be so acquainted with the Word of Life that you will have no doubt that you are coming to a precious faith, or that you are coming to the life divine, or that you have knowledge of a Greater Being than you who is working out this mighty power of redemption in your mortal bodies.

I see the Holy Spirit as a breath, or as the moving of a mighty wind. When you are filled with the breath of the Spirit, the breath of God, the holy fire, and the Word, Christ is within you. It is a wonderful thing to get in touch with the Living God; it is a glorious thing. Beloved, He will sustain you. Look unto Him and be lightened. Look unto Him now.

Joy in This Life

And these things write we unto you, that your joy may be full (First John 1:4).

The Word of Life makes your joy full. We must remember that what is absent in the world is joy. The world has never had joy. The world never will have joy. Joy is not in the five senses of the world. Feelings are there, happiness is there, but joy can only be produced where there is no alloy. Now, there is no alloy in heaven. Alloy means that there is a mixture. In the world there is happiness, but it is a mixture. Very often it comes up very close to sorrow. Very often in the midst of the ballroom there comes a place of happiness, and right underneath that there is a very heavy heart and a strange mixture. So in those five senses that the world has, they have happiness. But we have *joy* without alloy, without mixture.

Joy is inwardly expressive. It rises higher and higher till, if it had its perfect order, we would drown everything with a shout of praise coming from His holy presence. We want all the people to receive the Holy Ghost, because the Holy Ghost has a very blessed expression to the soul and heart. The Holy Ghost has an expression of the Lord in His glory, in His purity, in His power, and in all His beatitudes. All these are coming forcefully through as the Holy Ghost is able to witness to you of Him. And every time the Son is made manifest in your hearts by the Holy Ghost, you get a real stream of glory on earth. Joy in the Holy Ghost does not come by eating and drinking; it comes from something higher and better, something more substantial. Our joy is from the Holy Ghost. Only the Holy Ghost can bring joy to us.

TRIUMPHANT UNTIL HE COMES

Jesus answered, Verily, verily, I say unto thee, Except a man be born of water and of the Spirit, he cannot enter into the kingdom of God. That which is born of the flesh is flesh; and that which is born of the Spirit is spirit (John 3:5-6).

This new birth is the life of God. It is a spiritual life, as real and as true as God. God is a formation, and we are formed after His formation, for He made us in His very image. But He is a spiritual God and He has quickened us and made us inwardly like Him.

The first Adam was formed, and we were born in his likeness. When we were born, we were formed in the image of the earth; when we are reborn, we bear the image of heaven. When you are born of God, God's nature comes in. Scripture says we are conceived by the Word. That which is from above has entered into that which is below, and you have now become a quickened spirit. You were dead, without aspiration, without desire. As soon as you are born again, aspiration, desire, and prayer ascend from within you toward heavenly things. You are a new creation who cannot live on the earth. Your spiritual life lifts you higher and higher until you are soaring over all natural things.

The Sons of God are coming forth with power. May God the Holy Ghost sanctify us and purify us with a perfect purification till we stand white in the presence of God. Let us do some repenting. Let us tell God we want to be holy. If you are sure you have this eternal life in you, I want you to consider that it is not worth looking back. Keep your eyes upon the plan and look toward the Master. Believe that God is greater than your heart. Believe that God is greater than your thoughts. Believe that God is greater than the devil. Believe He will preserve you. Believe in His almightiness. And on the authority of God's faith in you, you will triumph till He comes.

SPIRITUALLY AWAKE

Wherefore he saith, Awake thou that sleepest, and arise from the dead, and Christ shall give thee light (Ephesians 5:14).

Being awakened does not mean particularly that you have been actually asleep. Sleeping doesn't mean actually asleep. It means dense to activity of spiritual relationship. Sleeping does not mean that you are fast asleep. Sleeping means to say that you have lost apprehension and you are dull of hearing and your eyes are heavy because they are not full of light. So God is making us understand that we have to be alive and awake. They that enter into this spiritual awakening have no more bondage.

God desires us to be holy, pure, and perfect right through. Our spiritual inheritance is an incorruptible inheritance, it is undefiled, and it does not fade away. Many people have fallen asleep. Why? They did not listen to the Lord's correction. Some have been sickly, and God has dealt with them. The Holy Ghost desires that we judge ourselves so that we are not condemned! What is it to judge yourself? If the Lord speaks, if He says, "Let it go," no matter if it is as dear as your right eye, you let it go. If it is as costly as your right foot, you let it go. It is far better to let it go than to perish. Be willing, beloved, for the Lord Himself to deal with you.

Oh beloved, may you have a great spiritual appetite for the Word; savor it with joy and grace, for Jesus is the Bread of Life. The process of the Word of God must kindle in us a separation from all that is not holy. It must bring to death everything except the life of the Word of Christ in our hearts. God will sift believers, and it is important to be separated from the chaff, from fear and all sin. God has to deal with His people, and if God deals with the house of God, then the world will soon be dealt with. All the world needs and longs to be right, and so we have to be salt and light to guide them, to lead them, to operate before them so that they see our good works and glorify our Lord.

A FORETASTE OF DIVINE LIFE

Blessed are the poor in spirit: for theirs is the kingdom of heaven (Matthew 5:3).

I believe that everyone who receives the baptism in the Spirit has a real foretaste of millennial blessing, but the Lord Jesus is setting forth present-day blessings that we can enjoy here and now. As we let the truth grab hold of us, we will press on for the mark ahead and enter more fully into our birthright. If the baptism means anything to you, it should bring you to the death of the ordinary, where you are no longer putting faith in your own understanding; but, conscious of your own poverty, you are ever yielded to the Spirit.

It seems to me that every time I open my Bible I get a new revelation of God's plan. God's Spirit takes man to a place of helplessness and then reveals God as his all in all. This is one of the richest places into which Jesus brings us. The poor have a right to everything in heaven—"Theirs is." Dare you believe it? Yes, I dare. When God's Spirit comes in as a ruling, controlling power of a life, He gives us God's revelation of our inward poverty, and shows us that God has come with one purpose, to bring heaven's best to earth, and that with Jesus He will indeed "...freely give us all things" (Rom. 8:32).

An old man and an old woman had lived together for seventy years. Someone said to them, "You must have seen many clouds during those days." They replied, "Where do the showers come from? You never get showers without clouds." It is only the Holy Ghost who can bring us to the place of realizing our poverty; but, every time He does it, He opens the windows of heaven and the showers of blessing fall.

Filled with Righteousness

Blessed are they which do hunger and thirst after righteousness: for they shall be filled (Matthew 5:6).

Note that phrase, *"shall* be filled." If you ever see a "shall" in the Bible, make it yours. Meet the conditions and God will fulfill His Word to you. The Spirit of God is crying, "Ho, everyone that thirsteth, come ye to the waters, and he that hath no money; come ye, buy and eat; yea, come, buy wine and milk without money and without price" (Isa. 55:1). The Spirit of God will take of the things of Christ and show them to you in order that you may have a longing for Christ in His fullness, and when there is that longing, God will not fail to fill you.

See that crowd of worshipers who came up to the feast. They were going away utterly unsatisfied, but on the last day, the great day of the feast, Jesus stood up and cried, "If any man thirst, let him come unto me, and drink. He that believeth on me, as the scripture hath said, out of his belly shall flow rivers of living water" (John 7:37-38). Jesus knew that they were going away without the living water, and so He directed them to the true source of supply. Are you thirsty today? The living Christ still invites you to Himself, and I want to testify that He still satisfies the thirsty soul and still fills the hungry with good things.

Oh, if you won't resist the Holy Ghost, the power of God will melt you down. The Holy Ghost will so take charge of you that you will be filled to the uttermost with the overflowing of His grace.

A DIVINE THIRST

And immediately he arose, took up the bed, and went forth before them all; insomuch that they were all amazed, and glorified God, saying, We never saw it on this fashion (Mark 2:12).

If anything stirs me in my life it is such words as these, "We never saw it on this fashion." Something ought to happen all the time so that people will say, "We never saw it like that." If there is anything that God is dissatisfied with, it is stationary conditions. So many people stop on the threshold when God, in His great plan, is inviting them into His treasury. Oh, this treasury of the Most High, the unsearchable riches of Christ, this divine position which God wants to move us into so that we are altogether a new creation. You know that the flesh profits nothing, for "...the carnal mind is enmity against God: for it is not subject to the law of God, neither indeed can be" (Rom. 8:7). As we cease to live in the old life and know the resurrection power of the Lord, we come into a place of rest, faith, joy, peace, blessing, and everlasting life. Glory to God!

May the Lord give us a new vision of Himself, fresh touches of divine life, and may His presence shake off all that remains of the old life and bring us fully into His newness of life. May He reveal to us the greatness of His will concerning us, for there is no one who loves us like Him. Yes, beloved, there is no love like His, no compassion like His. He is filled with compassion, and He never fails to take those who will fully obey Him into the Promised Land. You know, beloved, in God's Word there is always more to follow, always more than we know, and oh, if we could only be babies this afternoon, with a childlike mind to take in all the mind of God, what wonderful things would happen. I wonder if you take the entire Bible for yourself. It is grand. Never mind who takes only a part—you take it all. When we get such a thirst upon us that nothing can satisfy us but God, we shall have a royal time.

JESUS HAS MET THE NEED

For ye are bought with a price: therefore glorify God in your body, and in your spirit, which are God's (First Corinthians 6:20).

Thank God some of the molds have been broken. It is a blessed thing when the old mold gets broken, for God has a new mold. Oh, how He can make something perfect out of the imperfect by His own loving touch. I tell you, my sister, my brother, that since the day that Christ's blood was shed, since the Day of Atonement, He has paid the price to meet all the world's need and its cry of sorrow. Truly Jesus has met the need of the broken hearts and sorrowful spirits and also the withered limbs and broken bodies. God's dear Son paid the debt for all, for He took our infirmities and bore our sicknesses. In all points He was tempted as we are, so that He might be able to succor those who are tempted.

Oh, beloved, I have seen wonderful things like this worked by the power of God. We must never think about our God on small lines. He spoke the Word one day and created the world from things that did not exist. That is the kind of God we have, and He is just the same today. There is no change in Him. Oh, He is lovely and precious above all thought and comparison. There is none like Him.

I am certain today that nothing will profit you but that which you take by faith. God wants you to come into a close place with God where you will believe and claim the promises, for they are yes and amen to all who believe. Let us thank God for this full Gospel which is not hidden under a bushel today. Let us thank Him that He is bringing out the Gospel as in the days of His flesh. God is all the time working right in the very midst of us, but I want to know, what are you going to do with the Gospel today? There is greater blessing for you than you have ever received in your life. Do you believe it and will you receive it?

TAKE UP YOUR CROSS

And he said to them all, If any man will come after me, let him deny himself, and take up his cross daily, and follow me (Luke 9:23).

Revival is coming. God's heart is in the place of intense passion. Let us bend or break, for God is determined to bless us. Oh, the joy of service and the joy of suffering to be utterly cast upon Jesus. God is coming forth with power. The latter rain is appearing.

We must not climb down from the cross we bear, but we must go on from faith to faith and from glory to glory, with an increasing diligence to ensure we are found blameless in Him without spot or blemish (see 2 Pet. 3:14). Worship is higher than fellowship. Oh, the calmness of meeting with Jesus. All fears are gone. His tender mercy and indescribable peace are ours. I have all if I have Jesus. God's plan is that we yield our wills to Him. He is waiting for the precious fruit of the earth.

The early rain has been to get us ready for what is to come. The Holy Ghost wakes up every passion, permits every trial. His object is to make our vessels pure. We must yield to the call of martyrdom—to death of spirit, soul, and body—so that we might live! We must have absolute abandonment in order to receive divine equipment. Wake up—the air is full of revival, but we look for a mighty outpouring, shaking all that can be shaken. Take all, but give me a vision and revelation of the purposes of God and a wonderful burning love.

The fiery breath of revival is coming. There is a ripple on the lake, a murmur in the air. The price is tremendous; we must die to receive more. When the latter rain appears, God will move mightily, and millions will be ingathered, and the heart of God will be satisfied.

THE DAY OF VISITATION

And the very God of peace sanctify you wholly; and I pray God your whole spirit and soul and body be preserved blameless unto the coming of our Lord Jesus Christ (First Thessalonians 5:23).

May the Lord of Hosts so surround us with revelation and blessing till our bodies get to the place they can scarcely contain the joys of the Lord. Why not live in so rich a place of divine order that we should forever know we are only the Lord's? What a blessed state of grace to be brought into, where we know that the body, the soul, and the spirit are preserved blameless till the coming of the Lord! Jude takes us one step higher and says, "…to present you faultless before the presence of his glory" (Jude 1:24). What a blessed state of grace!

When our hearts are moved to believe God, God is greatly desirous for us to have more of His presence. Our human nature may be brought to a place where it is so superabundantly attended to by God that in the body we will know nothing but the Lord of Hosts. To this end, I bring you to the banquet that cannot be exhausted, a supply beyond all human thought and abundance beyond all human extravagances. No matter how you come into great faith and believing in God, God tells us He has so much more for us. So I trust you will be moved to believe for more.

Are you ready? What for? That you might be so in God's plan that you may know that the good hand of God is upon you, that He has chosen you that you might be a first fruits unto God. Are you ready? What for? That the Lord shall have His choice, that His will and purpose shall be yours, that the "Amen" of His character may sweep through your very nature, and that you may know as you have never known before that this is the day of the visitation between you and Him. Beloved, receive it today!

THE GLORIES OF HIS TREASURY

He made known unto me the mystery... Which in other ages was not made known unto the sons of men, as it is now revealed unto his holy apostles and prophets by the Spirit; that the Gentiles should be fellowheirs, and of the same body, and partakers of his promise in Christ by the gospel (Ephesians 3:3,5-6).

The God of all grace is bending over us. He sees us, he knows us, and He is acquainted with us. He is bending over us that His infinite, glorious, exhaustless pleasure may move us today. What can please Him more than to see His sons and daughters in their right mind, listening to His voice, their eyes and ears awake, coming into the treasury of the Most High?

Oh! That we might be so clothed by the ministry of His grace and understand the mystery of His wonderful initiative, that we may comprehend today more than ever before why the Gentiles have been brought into the glories of His treasury to feed on the finest of the wheat, to drink at the riches of His pleasure, to be filled with the God of love that has no measure. Without doubt the greatest mystery of all time from the commencement of creation to now is Christ made manifest in human flesh.

Oh, that the breath of heaven would move us today to get ready for Him. The fullness of the expression of Jesus through the Holy Ghost is giving us a glimpse into what has been provided for by the Father. Hallelujah!

THE GIFT OF SALVATION

And, behold, a woman of Canaan came out of the same coasts, and cried unto him, saying, Have mercy on me, O Lord, thou son of David; my daughter is grievously vexed with a devil. But he answered her not a word. And his disciples came and besought him, saying, Send her away; for she crieth after us. But he answered and said, I am not sent but unto the lost sheep of the house of Israel. Then came she and worshipped him, saying, Lord, help me. But he answered and said, It is not meet to take the children's bread, and to cast it to dogs. And she said, Truth, Lord: yet the dogs eat of the crumbs which fall from their masters' table. Then Jesus answered and said unto her, O woman, great is thy faith: be it unto thee even as thou wilt. And her daughter was made whole from that very hour (Matthew 15:22-28).

Abraham, Isaac, Jacob, and the twelve patriarchs had great faith in the promise of God, but they missed their opportunity. They might have gone on to have been the greatest miracle workers, the most profound teachers of the truth. They might have been everywhere, all over the world, bringing such glorious revivals, because they were entrusted to it. But they failed God. There was no hope for us Gentiles at all. A very few of the apostles felt sure that the inward power of the Holy Ghost should not be unleashed in vain, so God moved upon them to turn to the Gentiles. Then God gave Paul a special revelation about the Gentiles.

Paul spoke about it, knowing that he belonged to that royal aristocracy of Abraham's seed, but the Gentiles had no legal right to it. Jesus said to the woman, "Shall I take the bread of the children and give it to the dogs?" Did Jesus mean that the Gentiles were dogs? No, He did not mean that, but He meant that the whole race of Gentiles knew that they were far below the standard and order of those people who belonged to the royal stock of Israel. The Samaritans all felt it. "But isn't it possible for dogs to have some crumbs?" was the woman's question.

God has something better than crumbs. God has turned to the Gentiles and He has grafted us into Israel's inheritance. We are now of the same body, of the same heirs to the Kingdom. He has put no difference between them and us, and He has joined us up in that blessed order of coming into the promise through the blood of Christ. Hallelujah!

BREATHING THE HOLY SPIRIT IN

For this cause I bow my knees unto the Father of our Lord Jesus Christ, of whom the whole family in heaven and earth is named (Ephesians 3:14-15).

God's Son is in you, with all the power of development, till you shall be so enriched by this divine grace, till you live in the world knowing that God is transforming you from grace to grace, from victory to victory. The Spirit in you has no other ultimate goal than to bring you from glory to glory. Paul was so enlarged in the Spirit in this third chapter of Ephesians that his language failed him. And when he failed to go on, he bowed his knees to the Father. Oh, this is supreme! When language failed, when prophecy had no more room, it seems that he came to a place that he got down on his knees. Then we hear by the power of the Spirit language beyond all Paul could ever say.

God has something for us here in the language of the Holy Ghost. He wants us to enlarge our hearts and to take a breath of heaven. Let your whole soul waft out unto God—dare to breathe heaven in, dare to be awakened to all God's mind. Listen to the Holy Ghost. Paul is praying in the Spirit (see Eph. 3:16-21):

That he would grant you, according to the riches of his glory, to be strengthened with might by his Spirit in the inner man; that Christ may dwell in your hearts by faith; that ye, being rooted and grounded in love, may be able to comprehend with all saints what is the breadth, and length, and depth, and height; and to know the love of Christ, which passeth knowledge, that ye might be filled with all the fulness of God. Now unto him that is able to do exceeding abundantly above all that we ask or think, according to the power that worketh in us, unto him be glory in the church by Christ Jesus throughout all ages, world without end. Amen.

DRAW NEAR TO GOD

Draw nigh to God, and he will draw nigh to you. … Humble yourselves in the sight of the Lord, and he shall lift you up (James 4:8,10).

How may I get nearer God? How may I be helpless and dependent on God? I see a tide rising. God is making us very poor, but we are rich in it because our hands are stretched out toward God in this holy day of His visitation to our hearts. Believe that He is in you. Believe that He is almightiness. Believe that He is all fullness. Then let yourself go till He is on the throne. Let everything submit itself to the throne and the King. Yield yourself unto Him in such a sublime position that He is in perfect order over everything. Let God have His perfect way through you. If you will let go, God will take hold and keep you up.

Oh, to seek only the will of God, to be only in the purpose of God, to seek only that God shall be glorified! What a word we get over and over in our hearts, "Not I, but Christ." I believe God wants to send you forth filled with the Spirit. Oh beloved, are you ready? What for? To say, "Father, have Your way. Do not let my human will spoil Your divine plan. Father, so take charge of me today that I will be wholly, entirely on the altar for Your service." And I am sure He will meet us in this.

Let us draw near with a true heart in full assurance of faith, having our hearts sprinkled from an evil conscience, and our bodies washed with pure water (Hebrews 10:22).

PURSUE RIGHTEOUSNESS

Thou hast loved righteousness, and hated iniquity; therefore God, even thy God, hath anointed thee with the oil of gladness above thy fellows (Hebrews 1:9).

It is the purpose of God that we, as we are indwelt by the Spirit of His Son, should likewise love righteousness and hate iniquity. There is a place for us in Christ Jesus where we are no longer under condemnation but where the heavens are always open to us. God is opening up to us a realm of divine life where there are boundless possibilities, where there is limitless power, where there are untold resources, where we have victory over all the power of the devil. I believe that, as we are filled with the desire to press on into this life of true holiness, desiring only the glory of God, there is nothing that can hinder our true advancement.

It is through faith that we realize that we have a blessed and glorious union with our risen Lord. When He was on earth, Jesus told us, "...The Father that dwelleth in me, he doeth the works...I am in the Father, and the Father in me..." (John 14:10-11). And He prayed to His Father, not only for His disciples, but for those who should believe on Him through their words, "That they all may be one; as thou, Father, art in me, and I in thee, that they also may be one in us: that the world may believe that thou hast sent me" (John 17:21). Oh, what an inheritance is ours when the very nature, the very righteousness, the very power of the Father and the Son are made real in us. This is God's purpose, and may we be ever conscious of the fact that greater is He that is in us than he that is in the world. The purpose of all Scripture is to move us on to this wonderful and blessed elevation of faith where our constant experience is the manifestation of God's life and power through us.

GOD'S FAITHFULNESS

Grace and peace be multiplied unto you through the knowledge of God, and of Jesus our Lord (Second Peter 1:2).

We can have the multiplication of this grace and peace only as we live in the realm of faith. Abraham attained to the place where he became a friend of God, on no other line than that of believing God. He believed God and God counted that to him for righteousness. Righteousness was imputed to him on no other ground than that he believed God. Can this be true of anybody else? Yes, every person in the whole wide world who is saved by faith is blessed with faithful Abraham.

Abraham believed God and God gave him a promise that all the families of the earth should be blessed through his line. When we believe God, there is no knowing where the blessing of our faith will end. Some are tied up because, when they are prayed for, the thing that they are expecting does not come off the same night. They say they believe, but you can see that they are really in turmoil of unbelief. Abraham believed God. You can hear him saying to Sarah, "Sarah, there is no life in you and there is nothing in me, but God has promised us a son and I believe God." And that kind of faith is a joy to our Father in heaven.

Oh, beloved, your faith is a great joy to God. Believe Him at His word and receive the full blessings of His faithfulness to you. Our holy God is faithful to His children.

PEACE IN THE LION'S DEN

Whoso looketh into the perfect law of liberty, and continueth therein, he being not a forgetful hearer, but a doer of the work, this man shall be blessed in his deed (James 1:25).

What was the difference between Daniel and the king that night when Daniel was put into the den of lions? Daniel knew, but the king was experimenting. The king came around the next morning and cried, "...O Daniel, servant of the living God, is thy God, whom thou servest continually, able to deliver thee from the lions?" (Dan. 6:20). Daniel answered, "My God hath sent his angel, and hath shut the lions' mouths..." (Dan. 6:22). The thing was done. It was done when Daniel prayed with his windows open toward heaven. All our victories are won before we go into the fight. Prayer links us on to our lovely God, our abounding God, our multiplying God. Oh, I love Him! He is so wonderful!

Grace and peace are multiplied through the knowledge of God, but our faith comes through the righteousness of God. Note that righteousness comes first and knowledge afterward. It cannot be otherwise. If you expect any revelation of God apart from holiness, you will have only a mixture. Holiness opens the door to all the treasures of God. He must first bring us to the place where we, like our Lord, love righteousness and hate iniquity, before He opens up to us these good treasures. When we regard iniquity in our hearts the Lord will not hear us, and it is only as we are made righteous and pure and holy through the precious blood of God's Son that we can enter into this life of holiness and righteousness in the Son. It is the righteousness of our Lord Himself made real in us as our faith is stayed in Him.

EMBRACING HIS EXCELLENCE

Yea doubtless, and I count all things but loss for the excellency of the knowledge of Christ Jesus my Lord: for whom I have suffered the loss of all things, and do count them but dung, that I may win Christ (Philippians 3:8).

There is something in the new birth of our divine character that makes us long all the time that we may be like Him. It is not so much an impression but something in our life, words, and acts that make people know we have been with the Master and that we have learned of Him.

Paul was not seeking the knowledge of salvation. He wanted to experience the fullness of salvation. Salvation brought a spring into Paul's soul, and he received all the life of God, which had within itself divine resources. Paul longed for more of God. Oh, that I might win Him. All of us must reach the state of the crucifixion. Paul had heard about the crucifixion—how Jesus uttered not a word before Pilate; how they smote Him with a rod and gave Him vinegar to drink; and how in the midst of the crucifixion, He had love for His enemies: "Father, forgive them, for they know not what they do" (Luke 23:34).

Have we become like Him in persecution? Do we return harsh words with soft answers, and do we respond to criticism with love? Is this the true picture within our hearts this morning? God has apprehended us so we may be perfect sons and daughters who walk in holiness. "Be ye therefore perfect..." (Matt. 5:48). It is important to become like Him. His excellent character is before us, and His divine purpose is working through us. These days are days of quickening, reviving, stirring, and moving us. Oh, yes, the Master is before us in many revelations. As we receive from Him, the Lord opens the door so that we can have a new vision and enter into the divine character of the Lord. We find that the Word of God lives when we stand on the rock. Being found in Him is so remarkable; it is so right for every emergency. Can we reach the place where we can be in the Master's will, where we can absolutely see God's plan for us? His righteousness and revelation come by faith.

WALKING IN GREATER WORKS

Verily, verily, I say unto you, He that believeth on me, the works that I do shall he do also; and greater works than these shall he do; because I go unto my Father (John 14:12).

The Lord can enlarge us if we are ready. He has a wonderful way of enlarging things. Paul said, "If only I can get to the place of Christ's righteousness, then God could meet all of my needs." Nothing is too much if we can only reach the state where Christ is living and active in us. He brings us to the place where we count all as loss that we may gain Him. Our new nature helps us manifest His divine plan for the people in our day.

It is glorious to read of the prophets Isaiah, Ezekiel, Enoch, and Lot, but this is our day. God's plan for me is the outpouring of the Holy Ghost. Within this great plan is an elevation of our minds so that we may be associated with this great principle of faith.

When Dorcas died they sent for Peter, and he came. They brought out the things she had made and showed them to Peter. This woman had lived in benevolence and gave her life for the people. What moved Peter to sit with her corpse? It was the longings and cry of the people around her; her ministry to them had been the ministry of Christ.

Beloved, we must have great faith for the works of today. We need to imitate Peter and recognize the potential miracles in our midst. Jesus's compassion is greater than death. He can do great and mighty things if we would just believe. May we be found in Him, manifesting His divine nature, walking in the power of God.

VICTORY OVER TRIALS

Blessed be the God and Father of our Lord Jesus Christ, which according to his abundant mercy hath begotten us again unto a lively hope by the resurrection of Jesus Christ from the dead, to an inheritance incorruptible, and undefiled, and that fadeth not away, reserved in heaven for you, who are kept by the power of God through faith unto salvation ready to be revealed in the last time (First Peter 1:3-5).

God wants to speak to us to strengthen our position in faith and grace. Beloved, I want you to understand that you will get more than you ask for. God always gives you more. No man gets answers to his prayers—he never does, for God answers his prayers abundantly above what he asks or thinks. Yield and consecrate your heart to Him, and He will answer your prayers with great abundance and grace.

Throughout history, whenever there has been a divine rising of revelation, with God coming forth with new dispensational orders of the Spirit, you will find that persecution also increases. You take the cases of Daniel and the three Hebrew children and of Jeremiah. With any person in the old dispensation, as much as in the new, when the Spirit of the Lord has been moving mightily, there has arisen trouble and difficulty. Humanity, flesh, and natural things are all against divine things.

Divine order is very often in minority, but always in majority. Wickedness may increase and abound, but when the Lord raises His flag over the saints it is victory, though it is in minority, and always triumphs. Even in the days of John Knox, the people who served God had to be in very close quarters, because the Roman church set out to destroy them, nailed them to judgment seats, and destroyed them in all sorts of ways. They were in minority, but they swept through in victory, and the Roman power was crushed and defeated. Revelation brings persecution, but the Holy Spirit enables us to be victorious.

A REVELATION OF ELECTION

Peter, an apostle of Jesus Christ, to the...elect according to the foreknowledge of God the Father, through sanctification of the Spirit, unto obedience and sprinkling of the blood of Jesus Christ: Grace unto you, and peace, be multiplied (First Peter 1:1-2).

The Holy Ghost wants us to understand our privileges. We are the elect, according to the foreknowledge of God through sanctification of the Spirit. Now this sanctification of the Spirit is not along the lines of sin cleansing. It is a higher order than the redemption work. The blood of Jesus is rich and cleanses us from other powers and transforms us by the mighty power of God. When sin is gone, when we are clean, and when we know we have the Word of God right in us and the power of the Spirit is bringing everything to place where we triumph, then comes revelation by the power of the Spirit, which lifts you onto higher ground.

I don't want you to stumble at the word *elect*—it is a most blessed word. You might say we are all elect. God has designed that all men should be saved. This is the election, but whether you accept and come into your election, whether you prove yourself worthy of your election, whether you allow the Spirit to fortify you, I don't know, but this is your election, your sanctification, and you are seated at the right hand of God.

This word *election* is a very precious word to me. God has designed *elected*, *foreordained*, and *predestinated* before the world was to bring us into triumph and victory in Christ. Some people play round about it and make it a goal. They say, "Oh, well, you see, *we* are elected, *we* are all right." God elects everybody to be saved, but whether they come into it, that is another thing. Beloved, have you come into your election?

Confirmed Election

Peter, an apostle of Jesus Christ, to the...elect according to the foreknowledge of God the Father, through sanctification of the Spirit, unto obedience and sprinkling of the blood of Jesus Christ: Grace unto you, and peace, be multiplied (First Peter 1:1-2).

Beloved, I want you to see this election I am speaking about, to catch a glimpse of heaven, with your heart always on the wing, where you grasp everything spiritual so that everything divine makes you hungry. Sanctification of the Spirit comes through obedience and the sprinkling of the blood of Jesus Christ. There is no sanctification if it is not sanctification unto obedience.

Beloved, if there are any *buts* in your attitude toward the Word of truth, there is something unyielded to the Spirit. I do pray to God the Holy Ghost that we may be willing to yield ourselves to the sanctification of the Spirit, that we may be in the mind of God in the election, and that we may have the mind of God in the possession of it. Perhaps to encourage people, it would be helpful to show you what election is, because there is no difficulty in proving whether you are elected or not.

If you have a holy calling, a strange inward longing for more of God, you could say it was the sanctification of the Spirit that is drawing you. Who could do that but He who has elected you for it? It is a blessed thought that we have a God of love, compassion, and grace, who wills not the death of one sinner. He made it possible for all men to be saved, and caused Jesus, His well beloved Son, to die for the sins of the people. It is true He took our sins; it is true He paid the price for the whole world; it is true He gave Himself a ransom for many; it is true, beloved.

Through sanctification of the Spirit, according to the election, you will get to a place where you are not disturbed. There is a peace in the sanctification of the Spirit, because it is a place of revelation, taking you into heavenly places. When you are face to face with God, you get a peace that passes all understanding. It really is a wonderful state of inexpressible wonderment.

Our Heavenly Destination

To an inheritance incorruptible, and undefiled, and that fadeth not away, reserved in heaven for you (First Peter 1:4).

Glory to God! I tell you this is great. May the Lord help us to thirst after this glorious life of Jesus. Oh, brother, it is more than new wine; the Holy Ghost is more than new wine. The Holy Ghost is the manifestation of the glories of the new creation. Our inheritance is incorruptible. *Incorruptible* is one of those delightful words that God wants all saints to grasp—everything corruptible fades away, everything seen cannot remain.

Oh, beloved. God desires that every soul reach out to ideal perfection. God has ten thousand more thoughts for you than you have for yourself. Our inheritance does not fade away. What a heaven of bliss, a joy of delight, a foretaste of heaven on earth.

It is so lovely to think of that great and wonderful city we read about in Revelation. "And I John saw the holy city, new Jerusalem, coming down from God out of heaven, prepared as a bride adorned for her husband" (Rev. 21:2). Think about the glorious marriage! I see the holy city as a bride adorned for her husband, undefiled, pure, glorious, all white, and all pure. Who are the members of this city? They were once in the world, once corruptible, once defiled, now made holy and spiritual by the blood, now lifted from corruptible to incorruptible, and now undefiled in God's presence. This is our destination, beloved. It is glorious!

SALVATION AND PURIFICATION

Who are kept by the power of God through faith unto salvation ready to be revealed in the last time (First Peter 1:5).

Salvation is very much misunderstood. It comes to you in a moment of time; believing unto salvation is only the beginning. Salvation is so tremendous, mighty, and wonderful, as the early apostles said, "Being saved every day." You begin with God and go right on to being saved day by day; forgetting the things that are behind and pressing forward through the power of the blood you go onto salvation.

Salvation is like sanctification of the Spirit. It is not a goal. It is only a goal as you limit yourself. There is no limitation as we see the great preservation of the Master. We should never stand still for a moment, but we must mightily move on in God. Ah, what a blessing He is to us in trials and temptations. It is then that we receive the purification of the Spirit. "That the trial of your faith, being much more precious than of gold that perisheth, though it be tried with fire, might be found unto praise and honour and glory at the appearing of Jesus Christ" (1 Pet. 1:7).

I went into a place one day and a gentleman said to me, "Would you like to see purification of gold this morning? I replied, "Yes." He got some gold and put it in a crucible and put a blast of heat on it. First, it became blood red, and then it changed and changed. Then he took an instrument and passed it over the gold, which drew something foreign off. He did this several times until every part was taken away, and then at last he showed it to me, "Look," and there we both saw our faces in the gold. It was wonderful.

Beloved, the trials of your faith are much more precious than the gold that perishes. As you are tested in fire, the Master is cleaning away all that cannot bring out the image, cleaning away all the dross from your life, till He sees His face right in your life. It is lovely to know that in the times of chastening and hard tests, God is meeting and blessing you.

THIRSTING AFTER GOD

In the last day, that great day of the feast, Jesus stood and cried, saying, If any man thirst, let him come unto me, and drink. He that believeth on me, as the scripture hath said, out of his belly shall flow rivers of living water (John 7:37-38).

These verses are filled with vital power and wonderful revelation. There is an inflow of life that is sufficient to meet the world's need. These revelations are stepping stones and gateways to life in God, and we are reaching out to such splendors from which we never turn back. Thousands came to the feast from all parts of the world, but Jesus saw that thousands came who never had their needs supplied, so He cried out with a broken spirit and a in a lamentable voice, "If any man thirst let him come unto me and drink."

As he spoke, real springs came to many hearts. Here was a supply for every need. Only the thirsty ones can be needy. If the Son of God were preaching, not everyone would come—only the thirsty ones!

I traveled on a train in America and we stopped at a mineral spring. I filled all the containers I had that would hold water, but the time came when this supply was exhausted and I was thirsty again. How many around us are thirsty with broken, empty, unsatisfied lives, wanting something that will touch the mainspring of life? Have you ever been thirsty enough to drink? "If any man thirst, let him come unto Me and drink." Between this invitation and the outpouring in Acts 2 there is a great gulf.

Jesus left Heaven and all the glory. When He submitted to John's baptism, the "Spirit descended from heaven like a dove and rested on him" (see John 1:32). The whole countryside was filled with the glory and John cried, "Behold! The Lamb of God." The wonderful presence of God manifested in human form and revival came! Wonderful things appeared! Fields white to harvest were seen! In the cities people thronged to him. Not only was the thirsty land satisfied, but those around Him were satisfied with the Spirit of God.

A REVELATION OF SAVING GRACE

For by grace are ye saved through faith; and that not of yourselves: it is the gift of God (Ephesians 2:8).

Jesus came with a perfect purpose that many might hear His message and come into His divine life. Saving grace is a revelation from heaven. Christ sets up His heavenly standard in our mind, so that we can live, act, and think in a new world. To be saved is to have the revelation of the glory of Christ. It is our inheritance to have the evidence of the Holy Ghost coming upon us. God is visiting the earth with His resplendent glory. He comes to revive us, to heal us, and to deliver us from the power of the pit. The ransom is the Lord, and He comes to save the oppressed, whose eyes, ears, and heart shall see, hear, and feel with a new beauty.

Our King has come to fill us with the Holy Ghost, to rule our bodies, and to transform our lives. We have become new creations. The Holy Spirit will bring forth divine character in us if we yield to His work. God has saved, chosen, and equipped believers so that those bound by satan may go free. Jesus taught His disciples that, as they believed, greater things would be accomplished because He was going. And He gave His disciples this promise: "And I will give unto thee the keys of the kingdom of heaven: and whatsoever thou shalt bind on earth shall be bound in heaven: and whatsoever thou shalt loose on earth shall be loosed in heaven" (Matt. 16:19).

Have you received the Holy Ghost since you believed? After God has saved you by His power, He wants you to be illuminators of the King as new creations. The King is already on the throne, and the Holy Ghost has come to reveal the fullness of the power of His ministry. To be filled with the Holy Ghost is to be filled with prophetic illumination. The baptism in the Holy Ghost brings divine utterance. We are here to glorify God. We must be ready for the opportunities before us. God wants to give us divine life from heaven to share with the world.

POWER TO OVERCOME

He that dwelleth in the secret place of the most High shall abide under the shadow of the Almighty (Psalm 91:1).

The crown of life is for the overcomer. God never wants you to retreat before the enemy, but to learn the song of victory and overcome! Praise the Lord! There are two kinds of shouts—a shout that is made and a shout that makes you. There are men of God, but there are also men who are God's men. There is a place where you take hold of God, but there is a better place where God takes hold of you. "He that dwelleth in the secret place of the most High shall abide under the shadow of the Almighty." Do *you* know the presence of the Almighty? It is wonderful. His presence is a surety, and there is no wavering, no unbelief, and no unrest there. It is perfect.

My greatest desire is to see men become strong in the Lord by dwelling in the secret place, which is known to all who fear Him. Now, there are two kinds of fear. One fear involves being afraid of God. I hope you are not there. Unbelievers are there. But the believer should desire rather to die than to grieve God by fearing Him in this way. Fellowship with God, His peace, and His power—this is God's will for us, so don't fear that it isn't. No price is too great to pay to have it. It is our inheritance. Christ purchased it for us. Through Him we have the covering of the presence of the Almighty. What a covering the unfolding of His will is. The secret place of the Lord is with those who fear Him in the second way—with respect and honor. Moses knew something about it. He feared God and said to Him, "If thy presence go not with me, carry us not up hence" (Exod. 33:15).

Oh, to dwell in the secret place, in His presence! What will this presence do? It will dare us to believe all God says. We have a great salvation filled with inspiration. It has no limitations. It makes known the immeasurable wonders of God.

An Antidote to Evil

I will say of the Lord, He is my refuge and my fortress: my God; in him will I trust (Psalm 91:2).

He who abides in the Lord knows he can trust in the Lord to protect him from harm. There is no *kick* in the secret place—no evil temper, no irritability. All is swept away while one is dwelling in the presence of the Almighty, under the covering of God.

God sent forth Jesus in the mightiness of His power. The law of the Spirit of life was destroying all that must be destroyed. Dead indeed unto sin, but alive unto God. It is the gift of God from heaven. We belong to the new creation, and we are in a wonderful place in life. It is a life free from the law of sin and death. Can we keep ourselves there? *God* can keep us there. He never forgets to keep me. He *never* forgets to keep me. God has much in store for you; you are far from being out of His thoughts.

There was a time when the children of Israel hung their harps on the willows in defeat. Sometimes the believer does the same. The song of joy leaves his heart. It doesn't have to happen. You see, "There is no fear in love; but perfect love casteth out fear..." (1 John 4:18). God has embodied Himself in the Word. The Word spells destruction to all evil, because God is in the Word, and He is greater than all evil. Therefore, he that dwelleth in love is master of evil situations. He that dwelleth in God, in His presence and in His Word, is master of evil situations. We have no fear. We are over every sickness! Ours is a perfect redemption!

ESTABLISHED IN FAITH

He shall cover thee with his feathers, and under his wings shalt thou trust: his truth shall be thy shield and buckler. Thou shalt not be afraid for the terror by night; nor for the arrow that flieth by day; nor for the pestilence that walketh in darkness; nor for the destruction that wasteth at noonday. A thousand shall fall at thy side, and ten thousand at thy right hand; but it shall not come nigh thee. Only with thine eyes shalt thou behold and see the reward of the wicked. Because thou hast made the Lord, which is my refuge, even the most High, thy habitation; there shall no evil befall thee, neither shall any plague come nigh thy dwelling (Psalm 91:4-10).

"How can I get established in the faith?" you ask. Abide under the shadow of the Almighty. Don't change your position, but always have the presence of God, the glory of God. Pay any price to abide under that covering, for the secret of victory is to abide where the victor abides.

Jesus is the Author and Finisher of your faith. Through faith in Him, you came to the Father, "For with the heart man believeth unto righteousness; and with the mouth confession is made unto salvation" (Rom. 10:10). Your life is hid with Christ in God. You have no limitation when the holy breath blows an inward cry after Him. Oh, do you know His name? If you do, God will set you on high (see Ps. 91:14). And you can ask what you will—communion with Jesus, divine fellowship—and it shall be given to you! It comes through knowledge of Jesus's name, not just by whispering it now and then. Call upon the Lord, and He will answer you (see Ps. 91:15). Feed upon His word. To those who do, God has said, "With long life will I satisfy him, and shew him my salvation" (Ps. 91:16).

POSSIBILITY BELONGS TO GOD

Because it is written, Be ye holy; for I am holy (First Peter 1:16).

You never have to struggle to be holy. Holiness will keep you without a struggle. If you "try" to be holy you cannot, but if you will "be holy" you can. If you simply trust, you are kept by the power of God. You can never have abundant life in the flesh. It is in the spirit, and the Spirit can keep you in liberty and in freedom. There is a law of sin and death, and there is a law of the life of the Spirit that shall make you free from the law of sin and death. Wherever faith is manifested, fear cannot abide there. You can have anything from God if you are hungry enough. God's fullness cannot be reached when you are running over. Then you are emptied out and you get a larger vessel for more. It is the expansiveness that comes from God.

You cannot teach people anything better than what you know. Don't be satisfied with anything less than the duplication of the Son of God. There are three positions—good, better, and best. Never be satisfied with the best without some improvement. I hope there is something moving you that will not let you stop. The Holy Ghost can so stir within you that you begin to stir everything else. Limitation belongs to you, possibility to God.

CONFIDENCE IN OUR ADOPTION

For ye have not received the spirit of bondage again to fear; but ye have received the Spirit of adoption, whereby we cry, Abba, Father (Romans 8:15).

The Spirit brings us to a place where we see that we are sons of God. And because of this glorious position, we are not only sons but also heirs, and not only heirs, but joint-heirs. And because of that, I want you to see that all the promises of God are yea and amen to us through Jesus in the Holy Ghost. If the Spirit of God that raised Jesus from the dead is in you, that power of the Spirit is going to quicken your mortal body. And it brings me into a place of life, where I believe that as an adopted child I may lay hold of His promises.

It is no small thing to be brought into fellowship with the Father through Jesus Christ. The Spirit that is in you not only puts to death all other power, but He is showing us our privilege and bringing us into a faith that we can claim all we need. The moment a man comes into the knowledge of Christ, he is made an heir of heaven. By the Spirit, he is being changed into the image of the Son of God, and it is in that image that we can definitely look into the face of the Father and see that the things we ask for are done.

I see two wonderful things for us. First, I see the power of the Spirit in sonship raising us up. I also see us pressing onward to transformation through faith in the Lord Jesus Christ.

WALKING IN GREATER WORKS

For I reckon that the sufferings of this present time are not worthy to be compared with the glory which shall be revealed in us. For the earnest expectation of the creature waiteth for the manifestation of the sons of God (Romans 8:18-19).

The glory has already been revealed in us. We are being changed from glory to glory. I want you to know you are a son; you are a daughter. I want you to know that the Spirit that raised Jesus from the dead is dwelling in your mortal body. "We shall be like him; for we shall see him as he is" (1 John 3:2). It does not mean that we shall have faces like Jesus, but we will have the same Spirit within us. When they look at us and see the glory, they will say, "Yes, it is the same Spirit," for they will see the luster of the glory of Jesus Christ. Beloved, we are being changed.

Every one of us who is born of God, and who has the Holy Spirit in him, is longing for the manifestation of sonship. You say, when shall these things come forth? Paul explains:

For we know that the whole creation groaneth and travaileth in pain together until now. And not only they, but ourselves also, which have the firstfruits of the Spirit, even we ourselves groan within ourselves, waiting for the adoption, to wit, the redemption of our body (Romans 8:22-23).

The Holy Spirit is working in us and bringing us to a condition where we know He is doing a work in us. You live in resurrection power. Embrace this power and do greater works than Jesus did when He walked the earth.

CONFORMED TO HIS IMAGE

For we know that the whole creation groaneth and travaileth in pain together until now. And not only they, but ourselves also, which have the firstfruits of the Spirit, even we ourselves groan within ourselves, waiting for the adoption, to wit, the redemption of our body (Romans 8:22-23).

The baptism of the Spirit links heaven to earth, and God wants us to be so filled with the Spirit, and to walk in the Spirit, that while we live here on earth our heads will be right up in heaven. Brothers and sisters, the Spirit can give you patience to wait. The baptism in the Holy Ghost is the essential power in the body that will bring rest from all your weariness and will give you a hopeful expectation that each day may be the day we go up with Him. We must not be foolish people folding our hands and giving up everything. I find there is no time like the present to be up and active.

"The Spirit helpeth our infirmities" (Rom. 8:26). We need the Spirit to help our infirmities so that our bodies are not taxed out of measure. The Holy Spirit Himself will pray through you and bring to remembrance the things you ought to pray for, according to the mind of the Spirit. The highest purpose God has for us is that we shall be transformed into the image of His Son. We have seen a measure of God's purpose in filling us with His Spirit, so that He might bring about in us the image of His Son. Examine yourself and see where you stand. Have you surrendered all so that He can conform every part of you into the image of His Son?

PURPOSED FOR RIGHTEOUSNESS

But when it pleased God, who separated me from my mother's womb, and called me by his grace, to reveal his Son in me, that I might preach him among the heathen; immediately I conferred not with flesh and blood (Galatians 1:15-16).

It is a sad thing today to see how people are astonished at the workings of God. Millions of years ago He purposed in His heart to do mighty things in us. Are you going to refuse them, or will you yield to them? I thank God He predestinated me to be saved. You see, it is a mystery, but God purposed it before the foundation of the world. And if you yield, He will put in you a living faith, and you cannot get away from the power of it. Oh, brothers and sisters, let us come a little nearer. How amazing it is that we can be so transformed that the thoughts of Christ will be first in our minds. What a blessing you are to God when you are thinking about Jesus Christ and everyone around you is thinking of other things. Brothers and sisters, let us get a little nearer still.

It is the purpose of God that you should rise into the place of sonship. Don't miss the purpose God has in His heart for you. If you could only realize that God wants to make you first fruits so you are separated unto Him. God has lifted some of you up over and over again. It is amazing how God in His mercy has restored and restored. It does not matter who is against us. If there be millions against you, God has purposed it and will bring you right through to glory. Human wisdom has to stand still. It is with the heart that man believes unto righteousness. Beloved, do you believe with your whole heart?

DISPLAYING THE MAJESTY OF GOD

Ye are of God, little children, and have overcome them: because greater is he that is in you, than he that is in the world (First John 4:4).

Any person who has come to this word, which is a divine proposition, is mightier than all the powers of darkness, is mightier than the power of disease, and is mightier than his own self. Beloved, you must come to the place of knowledge. It is not sufficient for you to quote the Word of God. You never come to a place of righteousness, of truth, until you are in possession of these things that I am giving you by the Word. Beloved, God wants us to be something more than ordinary people. Remember this, whoever you are—if you are ordinary you have not touched the ideal principles of God. The only thing God has for a man is to be extraordinary. God has no room for an ordinary man. There are millions of ordinary people in the world. But when God lays hold of a man, He makes him extraordinary in personality, power, unction, thought, and activity.

Beloved, we are now sons of God. It is His divine will. God does not offer us anything He does not mean for us to possess. God has such purposes to perform in us that He has a great desire to utter these words in our hearts that we may rise. You will never reach ideal purposes on any line without the Word becoming a living epistle to you. Then you become a living epistle by the power of the Holy Spirit. You manifest the Spirit of God to the world. You are a body filled with the fullness of God, and He is displaying His majesty through you.

THE TREASURES OF GOD

Behold, what manner of love the Father hath bestowed upon us, that we should be called the sons of God... (First John 3:1).

We are sitting at a banquet of love, where Jesus is looking over us and making Himself known to us. This is surely the manifestation of His love that we read about in God's Word. As high as the heavens are above the earth, so is His love and His mercy for us.

Beloved, God surely means to strengthen us by drawing us near to Him, so that our weaknesses are turned into strength. Our unbelief shall be made into living faith, so that the dew of His presence and the power of His love are so active upon us that we are all changed by this powerful Word. I want to see you lifted to a place that you dare believe that God is waiting to bless you abundantly, beyond all that you can ask or think.

This day you shall come before God with such living faith to dare believe that all things are possible concerning you. You will not experience barrenness, for surely God will surely grant unto you a very rich blessing that you shall forget all your poverty and come into a bountiful supply. God means it. You shall be brought into His treasures, and He shall cover you with His bountifulness, and you shall know that the God of the Most High reigns.

Living as Children of God

In this the children of God are manifest, and the children of the devil: who-soever doeth not righteousness is not of God, neither he that loveth not his brother (First John 3:10).

This is one of the pinnacles of truth. A pinnacle of truth leads you to a place of sovereignty, of purity, a place where you cannot be moved by a situation. You have a fixed position. You take the position clearly on the authority of the Word of Jesus. God means to let it ring through our hearts distinctly, clearly, marvelously, so that we are free from sin, children of God, heirs of the Kingdom of His righteousness.

God looks past your weaknesses, your human depravities, all your issues that you know are absolutely out of order, and He washes you, cleanses you, and beautifies you. He looks at you and says, "You are lovely! I see no spot of sin upon you. There is no spot. You are now My sons."

The world does not know us in our sonship. We have to be strangers to the world's knowledge. Let us examine ourselves to see if this sonship is ours, if we are in the order of perfect sonship. And after that, may you strengthen yourself in God and believe for anything to come to pass. But you must examine yourself to see if you are in the Father. The greatest blessing that can come to you will be that the Word of life will go forth and create an inwardly deep desire for God. If you are right with Him, the Spirit of God will make you long more for God, more for the holiness of God, more for the righteousness of God. Let us be pure as He is pure.

KEPT IN PERFECT PEACE

Thou wilt keep him in perfect peace, whose mind is stayed on thee: because he trusteth in thee (Isaiah 26:3).

Don't stumble at the Word. If Jesus says anything, if the Word conveys anything to your mind, don't stumble at the Word. Believe that God is greater than you are, greater than your heart, greater than your thoughts, and can establish you in righteousness even when your thoughts and knowledge are absolutely against it.

Often I find that people misunderstand God's Word because they bring their mind to the Word, and because the Word does not exactly fit their mind they do not get liberty. They want the Word to come to their mind. It will never do it. You have to be submissive to God. The Word of God is true. If you understand truth and righteousness, you can always gain strength, overcome obstacles, live above the world, not in it, and make everything subject to you.

This is what God wants us to learn: whatsoever we do, do it to the glory of God. If you listen to the Word of God this morning, it shall make you strong. You will find out that whatever work you have to do will be made easier if you keep your mind stayed on the Lord. Blessed is the man who has his mind stayed upon the Lord. We must see to it that in the world we are not moved.

One day God revealed to me that if I had any trouble in my body, in my heart, I had missed it. He showed me that if I had trouble in my heart, I had taken on something that did not belong to me, that I was out of the will of God. So I investigated it and found it was true, on this line: "They that keep their minds stayed on God shall be kept in perfect peace."

SONS OF GOD

Behold...that we should be called the sons of God (First John 3:1).

A son of God must excel in every way. God says to you more than you dare say about yourself, "Behold, ye are sons of God." So do not be afraid. Take the stand, come into line, and say, "I will be a son." God spoke and the heavens gave place to His voice, and He cried, "This is my beloved Son: hear him" (Mark 9:7). And afterward Jesus always said, "I am the Son of God."

God also comes to us and says, "Behold, you are the sons of God!" Oh, that we could have a regiment rising, claiming their rights, standing erect with a holy vision, and full of inward power, saying, "I am, by the grace of God, a son of God!"

You may have felt, in many ways, that you were never worthy, but God makes you worthy. And who shall say you are not worthy?

Beloved, now are we the sons of God, and it doth not yet appear what we shall be: but we know that, when he shall appear, we shall be like him; for we shall see him as he is (1 John 3:2).

I am not talking about the Second Coming of Christ. I am dealing with the life of the believer. I am talking about sonships in the earth—what we are to be like, what will take place, and how we shall overcome the world. Beloved, believe you are a son of God. Walk in the fullness of the Spirit of God.

THE LIFE OF THE SPIRIT

It is the spirit that quickeneth; the flesh profiteth nothing: the words that I speak unto you, they are spirit, and they are life (John 6:63).

Jesus says, "My Word is the Spirit of life," so we need the Spirit to bring life into the believer. Why? How? There is a deep secret in the midst of this: "Every man that hath this hope in him purifieth himself..." (1 John 3:3). Beloved, our faith in God purifies us. The Spirit brings life into us through the Word and we are transformed and purified by the renewing of our minds. Saints, we do not need to know how to merely quote Scripture, but how the Spirit should breathe on Scripture so that the Spirit imparts life as the Word is given.

God wants to make you sound. He wants to make you restful. God wants to give you peace, and He wants to cause you to live in the world with peace. The very first message the angel gave was, "On earth peace, good will toward men" (Luke 2:14). If you are not at peace, there is something wrong. If you are not at rest, something has taken place. You must know that God means you to be at peace as if you were in heaven. We are to be as much at peace as if we were in the glory.

Beloved, come into this royal place of peace as sons and daughters of God. Do not allow your own reasoning to defeat the power that God has for you. You cannot forgive yourself, but He can. You cannot find your own peace and sound mind, but He can give them to you. God has promised to give you life through His Spirit. Receive it.

MASTER OVER EVIL THOUGHTS

Casting down imaginations, and every high thing that exalteth itself against the knowledge of God, and bringing into captivity every thought to the obedience of Christ (Second Corinthians 10:5).

Evil thoughts are from satan. Satan does not know your thoughts. He does not know your desires. God hides these things from him. God can search our hearts, but satan cannot. Nobody can know you like God. The devil has no chance of really knowing you.

So, what does satan do? He came to Jesus and suggested evil things, but he could not arouse a single response in Him. When does he arouse a response in you? When he suggests a thought in you that you embrace. And he gets you the moment he does this. But if you are so delivered by the blood and made holy, the devil cannot arouse you.

Nevertheless, if you are troubled because he suggests an evil thought, you are in a good place. But if you are not troubled, you are in a bad place. Suppose he is continually after you like that. Is there a way? Of course there is. How can you deal with it? Say to him, "Did Jesus come in the flesh?" And the evil one will say, "No." There is not a demon power out of hell or in hell that has ever been willing to say Jesus came in the flesh. And when he says no, you can say, "Get behind me, satan! I rebuke you in the name of Jesus."

Oh, it is wonderful to be able to test the spirits to see if they are of God. We are brought into liberty, power, blessing, and strength, till we live in the earth like the Lord did.

Sin Dethroned

And every man that hath this hope in him purifieth himself, even as he is pure. Whosoever committeth sin transgresseth also the law: for sin is the transgression of the law. And ye know that he was manifested to take away our sins; and in him is no sin. Whosoever abideth in him sinneth not: whosoever sinneth hath not seen him, neither known him (First John 3:3-6).

There is no sin in us. We are pure as He is pure. Sin has been destroyed in us. Do not be afraid to claim your place. Do not be afraid to see the Word of God. It is true. "Ye are dead indeed unto sin, but alive unto God" (see Rom. 6:11). As sin had reigned unto death, so now Christ comes and reigns in life over you. You reign in life over sin, disease, and the devil. You reign over principalities and powers. He is manifested in our flesh to destroy the emotions of our bodies, to bring carnality to an end, and to bring of human depravity to an end.

Christ is in the body; sin is dethroned. Sin shall not reign over you. Believe that God is bringing you to this place. This is a dethronement of human helplessness. It is an enthronement of Christ's righteousness in us. He comes in and begins to rule over our bodies by another plan. God's purity makes you hate sin. You must have a righteous indignation against the powers of evil and the devil. And all the time you are being purified, and you get to the place where you cannot sin. This is a glorious position of victory. This is a place of rest for your feet. This is a great place for enduement of power, for holiness is power and sins is weakness and defeat. Beloved, believe that God is purifying you.

PRAYER AND FASTING

Lift up your heads, O ye gates; and be ye lift up, ye everlasting doors; and the King of glory shall come in (Psalm 24:7).

God has given you a rising tide of expectancy or adaptability within your soul that will bring you into the very place God has made for you. It is as easy as possible if you can touch it by faith this morning. I am the last man to say anything about fasting, or about praying, or about anything that has been a source of blessing to others. But I have learned by personal experience that I can get more out of one moment's faith than I can get out of a month's yelling. I can get more by believing God a moment than I can get by screaming for a month.

I am also positive that blessing comes out of fasting when fasting is done the right way. So many people make up their mind to fast and finish off with a thick head, troubled bones, and sleepy conditions. I am as satisfied as possible that that is no way to fast.

When you pray and fast, the Spirit is leading you to pray. The Spirit lays hold of you till you forget even the hour or the day, and you are so caught up by the power of the Spirit that you want nothing, not even meat or drink. Then the Lord of hosts, I trust, will so encamp round about us with songs of deliverance, and give us inward revelations, till the whole of our being shall absolutely be on the rising tide. May God the Holy Ghost wake us up to see we must rise with the tide.

CLAIMING OUR RIGHTS

Beloved, now are we the sons of God, and it doth not yet appear what we shall be: but we know that, when he shall appear, we shall be like him; for we shall see him as he is. And every man that hath this hope in him purifieth himself, even as he is pure (First John 3:2-3).

W ho dares to believe God? Who dares to claim his rights? What are these rights? "Now we are the sons of God." This is absolutely a position of rest and of faith. It brings us perfect trust, perfect habitation, no disturbance, and peace like a river. Look at the face of God. Hallelujah! The very Word itself that comes to judge comes to help.

Look! The law came as judgment, but when the Spirit comes and breathes through the law, He comes to lift us higher and higher. Oh, hallelujah! We must go a little further. God comes to us and says, "I will make it all right if you dare believe it." All the great revelations of God come to clothe our nakedness. Nakedness is everything that is coinciding with worldly evil. If you can be attracted by anything earthly, you have missed the greatest association that God has for you. If any natural, human thing can attract you from God, you are not a son in this respect.

Hallelujah! So you see, beloved, the importance of coming into line with God's Word. The reality of sonship is as clear as anything. Look at the tremendous, gigantic power of almightiness behind sonship. This is what you come into. Will you shiver on the edge of it like children do at a bath? Or will you take a plunge into omnipotence and find the waters are not as cold as people told you? Dare you let the warmth of the power of God make you see your inheritance in the Spirit? Glory! Glory! Glory to God!

A HOLY GHOST MOVEMENT

I press toward the mark for the prize of the high calling of God in Christ Jesus (Philippians 3:14).

You want the association with God, and God says, "I will come and walk with you. I will sup with you and you with Me, and I will live in you." A joyful hallelujah! We are attaining to a spiritual maturity, a fullness of Christ, a place where God becomes the perfect Father, and the Holy Ghost has a rightful place as never before.

The Holy Spirit breathes on you so that you can recognize and say, "You are my Father; You are my Father." The Spirit cries, "Abba Father, My Father." Oh, it is wonderful! And God the Holy Ghost will grant us that richness of His pleasure, that unfolding of His will, that consciousness of the beaming of His countenance on us. There is no condemnation, for the law of the Spirit of life is making us free from the law of sin and death. Glory!

We are to face God with facts. He has shown us different aspects of the Spirit. He has shown us the pavilion of splendor. He has unfolded to us the power of the relationship of sonship. And the perfection of sonship is being so manifested that there is absolutely a rising tide of the sons of God.

Beloved, God the Holy Ghost has a perfect plan for us to become a movement. There is a difference between a movement and a monument. A monument is something that is fixed at a corner and neither speaks nor moves, but there is a tremendous lot of humbug and nonsense to get it there. It is silent and does nothing. A movement is where God has come into the very being of a person, where he becomes active for God. He is God's property, God's mouthpiece, God's eyes, and God's hands. Beloved, are you a part of a monument or a movement?

DESIRING MORE

But as it is written, Eye hath not seen, nor ear heard, neither have entered into the heart of man, the things which God hath prepared for them that love him (First Corinthians 2:9).

Y̶ou have to embrace what God has prepared for you and make it yours. He has laid it up for you already. You don't want a stepladder to get it. God will hand it to you when you become joined with Him. When you walk with Him, He will either drop all that He has on you or take you where you are to remain forever. Enoch could not understand all the weights of glory, so God took Enoch into it as soon as He could.

Beloved, it is impossible to estimate the loving-kindness of God or the measureless mind of God in our finite condition. When we come into like-mindedness with the Word, we begin to see what God has for us in the Word instead of just seeing the Word. This is a very exhaustless subject, but I pray God He will make us an exhaustless people. I want something to happen on the line of this verse:

> *Me with a quenchless thirst inspire,*
> *A longing, infinite desire*
> *Fill my craving heart.*
> *Less than Thyself You do not give,*
> *Thy might within me now to live.*
> *Come, all Thou hast.*

God, just come and make me so that there is not a possibility for me to ever be satisfied but to have a quenchless thirst for the Living God! And then I shall not be overtaken. Then I shall be ready. Then I shall have eyes that beam and are filled with the extremity of delight, as I look at the Master.

No Difference Between Us

…What is man, that thou art mindful of him? or the son of man that thou visitest him? Thou madest him a little lower than the angels; thou crownedst him with glory and honour, and didst set him over the works of thy hands: thou hast put all things in subjection under his feet. For in that he put all in subjection under him, he left nothing that is not put under him. But now we see not yet all things put under him. But we see Jesus, who was made a little lower than the angels for the suffering of death, crowned with glory and honour; that he by the grace of God should taste death for every man (Hebrews 2:6-9).

Oh, this second chapter of Hebrews is one of the mighty, glorified positions for the children of God! God would have me herald, like a great trumpet call, to speak to every heart. Brother, God's design is to bring you as a son, clothed with the power of the gifts and graces, the ministries and operations, and to bring you into glory. We will be clothed with heaven's majesty, for He shall bring many sons into glory, into the perfected likeness of His Son. Oh, this is like heaven to me! My very body is filled with heaven.

Oh, what an exhaustless position we are in! Oh, brothers, sisters, what immensity of pleasure God has for us! What unbounded conditions of sober-mindedness God is bringing us to that we may be able to apprehend that for which God has apprehended us in the Spirit. Oh, that we may look not on the things that are, but with eyes of chaste virgin purity, as we gaze solely upon the invisible Son! And so having our whole bodies illuminated by the power of the Holy Spirit, we grow in grace—from grace to grace, from faith to faith, and in the personality and likeness of His son, till there is no difference between us and Him.

WHOLLY SURRENDERED

And we have known and believed the love that God hath to us. God is love; and he that dwelleth in love dwelleth in God, and God in him. Herein is our love made perfect, that we may have boldness in the day of judgment: because as he is, so are we in this world. There is no fear in love; but perfect love casteth out fear: because fear hath torment. He that feareth is not made perfect in love. We love him, because he first loved us (First John 4:16-19).

Let me give you this word if you can receive it: "As He is, so are we in this world." What a word! Who dares believe it? Only God can take us on to such heights and depths and lengths and breadths in the Spirit. Brother, sister, are you prepared to go all the way? Are you willing for heights and depths and lengths and breadths? Are you willing for your heart to have only one attraction? Are you willing to have only one Lover? Are you willing for Him to become the very perfect Bridegroom?

For I understand the more bride-like we are, the more we love to hear the Bridegroom's voice, and the less bride-like we are, the less we long for His Word. If you cannot rest without it, if it becomes your meat day and night; if you eat and drink of it, His life will be in you; when He appears you will go. Help us, Jesus!

How many are prepared to be unclothed before the King, prepared to yield to His call, His will, and to His desires? Everybody knows just how far he or she has missed the plan. The Word has gone forth, the Spirit has been quickening you. How many are going to say, "At all costs I will go through!" Are you determined? Is your soul on the wing? Make a full consecration to God today. It is between you and God this morning. It is nothing to do with your next door neighbor. You are now going to get in the presence of God. Make a full breast of everything in the presence of God!

Endowed with the Spirit of God

The Spirit of the Lord is upon me, because he hath anointed me to preach the gospel to the poor; he hath sent me to heal the brokenhearted, to preach deliverance to the captives, and recovering of sight to the blind, to set at liberty them that are bruised (Luke 4:18).

Jesus took up the book in the temple and read these words and impressed the fact because of the manifestation of the work He was doing. I believe God is bringing us to a place where we know the Spirit of the Lord is upon us. If we have not got to that place, God wants to bring us to the fact of what Jesus said in John 14, "I will pray the Father, and he shall give you another Comforter, that he may abide with you for ever" (John 14:16). Because the Spirit of the Lord came upon Him who is our head, we must see to it that we receive the same anointing and that the same Spirit is upon us.

The devil will cause us to lose the victory if we allow ourselves to be defeated by him. But it is a fact that the Spirit of the Lord is upon us, and as for me I have no message apart from the message He will give, and I believe the signs He speaks of will follow. I believe that Jesus was sent forth from God to be the propitiation for the sins of the whole world, and we see the manifestation of the Spirit resting upon Him so that His ministry was with power. May God awaken us to the fact that this is the only place where there is any ministry of power.

THE COMFORTER HAS COME

In whom ye also trusted, after that ye heard the word of truth, the gospel of your salvation: in whom also after that ye believed, ye were sealed with that holy Spirit of promise, which is the earnest of our inheritance until the redemption of the purchased possession, unto the praise of his glory (Ephesians 1:13-14).

Beloved, the promised Comforter has come. He is come, and He has come to abide forever. Are you going to be defeated by the devil? No, for the Comforter has come that we may receive and give forth the signs that must follow, so that we may not by any means be deceived by the wiles of the devil. There is no limit as to what we may become if we dwell and live in the Spirit. In the Spirit of prayer, we are taken from earth right away into heaven. In the Spirit, the Word of God seems to unfold in a wonderful way, and it is only in the Spirit that the love of God is shed abroad in us.

We feel as we speak in the Spirit that the fire that burned in the hearts of the two men on their way to Emmaus, when Jesus walked with them, is burning in our heart (see Luke 24:13-32). It is sure to come to pass when we walk with Him—our hearts will burn; it is the same power of the Spirit. They could not understand it then, but a few hours later they saw Him break the bread, and their eyes were opened.

Beloved, our hearts ought to always burn. There is a place where we can live in the unction and the clothing of the Spirit, where our words will be clothed with power. "Be not drunk with wine…but be filled with the Spirit" (Eph. 5:18). It is a wonderful privilege to be filled with the Spirit. It brings us great revelation, and I see that it was necessary for John to be in the Spirit on the Isle of Patmos for the revelation to be made clear to him. Brothers, sisters, be filled with the Spirit so that the Word of God may be made clear to you.

ANOINTED BY THE SPIRIT

The Spirit of the Lord God is upon me; because the Lord hath anointed me to preach good tidings unto the meek; he hath sent me to bind up the brokenhearted, to proclaim liberty to the captives, and the opening of the prison to them that are bound; to proclaim the acceptable year of the Lord, and the day of vengeance of our God; to comfort all that mourn; to appoint unto them that mourn in Zion, to give unto them beauty for ashes, the oil of joy for mourning, the garment of praise for the spirit of heaviness; that they might be called trees of righteousness, the planting of the Lord, that he might be glorified (Isaiah 61:1-3).

There is a measure of power that we have not yet claimed, and we shall not be able to claim this manifestation of the Spirit unless we live in the Spirit. He says, "I will give you power to bind and I will give you power to loose." When are you able to bind and able to loose? It is only in the Spirit. You cannot bind things in the human or with the natural mind. This power was never demonstrated apart from Jesus. I feel that there is a great lack of it in most of us. God help us! "The Spirit of the Lord is upon me." Beloved, there was a great purpose in this Spirit being on Him, and there is a special purpose in your being baptized in the Spirit. We must not forget that we are members of His body, and by this wonderful baptismal power, we are partakers of His divine nature.

What does it mean to this generation for us to be kept in the Spirit? All human reasoning and all human knowledge cannot be compared to the power of the life that is lived in the Spirit. We have power to loose and power to bind in the Spirit. There is a place where the Holy Ghost can put us where we cannot be anywhere else but in the Spirit. But if we breathe His thoughts into our thoughts, and live in the unction of the Holy Spirit as He lived, then there will be evidences that we are in Him; and His works we will do. But it is only in the Spirit.

IMPOSSIBLE WITHOUT GOD

The hand of the Lord was upon me, and carried me out in the spirit of the Lord... (Ezekiel 37:1).

The only need of Ezekiel was to be in the Spirit, and while he was in the Spirit the Lord asked him to prophesy to the dry bones, "...Oh ye dry bones, hear the word of the Lord" (Ezek. 37:4). And as he prophesied according to the Lord's command, he saw an "exceeding great army" rising up about him. The prophet obeyed God's command, and all we have to do is exactly this—obey God. What is impossible with man is possible with God.

I pray God that your spirit, soul, and body may be preserved holy, and that you may be always on fire and always ready with the unction on you. If this is not so, we are out of divine order, and we ought to cry to Him until the glory comes back upon us.

"The Spirit of the Lord is upon me." There must have been a reason why it was upon Jesus. First of all, it says here, "...because he hath anointed me to preach the gospel to the poor; he hath sent me to heal the brokenhearted...." What a Gospel! "...To preach deliverance to the captives...." What a wonderful Spirit was upon Him! "...And recovering of sight to the blind, to set at liberty them that are bruised, to preach the acceptable year of the Lord" (see Luke 4:18-19).

You missionaries who are going to India and Africa and China and other places have a wonderful Gospel to take to these people who know nothing about God—a Gospel of salvation and healing and deliverance. When you go forth to these dark lands where the Holy Ghost has sent you to preach the unsearchable riches of Christ, to loose the bands of satan, and to set the captives free, be sure you can say, "The Spirit of the Lord is upon me," and remember that Christ is made unto us not only salvation but wisdom and redemption. Filled with God leaves no room for doubting or fearing. We have no idea of what being filled with God fully means. It means emptied of self. Do you know what it means to be filled with God? It means you have no fear, for when you are filled with God, you are filled with love, and perfect love casts out fear.

MADE FLAMES OF FIRE

In the same quarters were possessions of the chief man of the island, whose name was Publius; who received us, and lodged us three days courteously. And it came to pass, that the father of Publius lay sick of a fever and of a bloody flux: to whom Paul entered in, and prayed, and laid his hands on him, and healed him (Acts 28:7-8).

I want to know more about this manifestation of the power of the Holy Spirit. At the end of the book of Acts, Paul was shipwrecked on an island called Melita. Here we find the chief of the island had the bloody flux, and when Paul ministered to him he was healed, and they honored Paul with many gifts for his ministry.

When we think the church is so poor and needy, we forget that the spirit of intercession can unlock every safe in the world. What did God do for the children of Israel? He took them to vineyards and lands flowing with milk and honey, and all they did was walk in and take possession. If we will only live in the Spirit and the unction of the Spirit, there will be no lack. There is only lack where faith is not substance, but the Word says faith is the substance, and whatsoever is not of faith is sin. Things will surely come to pass if you will believe this.

It is true: we must be filled with the Spirit. Father, teach us what that means! It was only because He had knowledge of it that He could stand and say before those men, to the demon, "Come out of him." Who is the man that is willing to lay down all that he may have God's all? Begin to seek and don't stop seeking until you know the Spirit of the Lord is upon you. "I thank Thee, Father, Thou hast hid these things from the wise and prudent, and revealed them unto babes." If you are in the babe class, the Spirit must have revealed your lack to you. We need to seek with all our hearts. We need to be made flames of fire.

ALONE WITH GOD

And Jacob was left alone; and there wrestled a man with him until the breaking of the day (Genesis 32:24).

As we look back over our spiritual career, we shall always see there has been a good deal of our own day and that the end of our day was the beginning of God's day. "Can two walk together, except they be agreed?" (Amos 3:3). "...Flesh and blood cannot inherit the Kingdom of God; neither doth corruption inherit incorruption (1 Cor. 15:50), and we cannot enter into the deep things of God until we are free from our own ideas and ways.

Jacob! The name means *supplanter*, and when Jacob came to the end of his way God had a way. How slow we are to see that there is a better way. Beloved, the glory is never so wonderful as when God has His plan and we helplessly throw down our sword and give up our authority to Him. Jacob was a great worker, and he would go through any hardship if he could have his way. In many ways he had his way, in ignorance of how gloriously God preserved him from calamity. There is a good and there is a better, but God has a best—a higher standard for us than we have yet attained. It is a better thing if it is God's plan and not ours. Jacob and his mother had a plan to secure the birthright and the blessing, and his father agreed to his going to Padan-aram, but God planned the ladder and the angels.

...The land whereon thou liest, to thee will I give it...I am with thee, and will keep thee in all places whither thou goest, and will bring thee again into this land; for I will not leave thee, until I have done that which I have spoken to thee of (Genesis 28:13,15).

What a good thing for the lad—in the midst of the changes, God obtained the right place. The planning for the birthright had not been a nice thing, but there at Bethel Jacob found God was with him.

God First

There is a way that seemeth right unto a man, but the end thereof are the ways of death (Proverbs 16:25).

Jacob had been out in the bitter frost at night watching the flocks. He was a thrifty man, a worker, a planner, a supplanter. We see the whole thing around us in the world today—supplanters. There may be a measure of blessing, but God is not first in their lives. We are not judging them, but there is a better way, better than our best—God's way. God first!

After encountering the ladder at Bethel, Jacob spent twenty-one years wandering and fighting and struggling. Listen to his conversation with his wives. "Your father hath deceived me, and changed my wages ten times; but God suffered him not to hurt me" (Gen. 31:7). To his father-in-law: "Except the God of my father...had been with me, surely thou hadst sent me away now empty. God hath seen mine affliction and the labour of my hands..." (Gen. 31:42).

But there is a way that God establishes us, and I want us to keep that way before us. God desires to be first so that He can make our paths straight.

In all thy ways acknowledge him, and he shall direct thy paths (Proverbs 3:6).

In our own natural planning and way we may have much blessing, of a kind; but oh, beloved, the trials, the hardships, and the barrenness we encounter. Jacob encountered God at Bethel, but he had not made God first in all things and he endured many hardships. Oh, the things we miss that God could not give us! There is a freshness, a glow, a planning in God where you can know that God is with you all the time. Can we know that God is with us all the time? Yes! Yes! Yes! I tell you there is a place to reach where all that God has for us can flow through us to a needy world all the time.

ALONE WITH GOD

And Jacob was left alone; and there wrestled a man with him until the breaking of the day (Genesis 32:24).

Oh, to be left alone! Alone with God! In Genesis 32 we read that several things had gone on to meet Esau. Jacob's wives had gone on, his children had gone on—all had gone on. His sheep and oxen had gone on, his camels and asses had gone on—all had gone on. He was alone.

You will often find you are alone. Whether you like it or not, your wife will go on, your children will go on, your cattle will go on. Jacob was left alone. His wife could not make atonement for him, his children could not make atonement for him, and his money was useless to help him. What made Jacob come to that place of loneliness, weakness, and knowledge of himself? The memory of the grace with which God had met him twenty-one years before, when he saw the ladder and the angels and heard the voice of God.

And, behold, I am with thee, and will keep thee in all places whither thou goest, and will bring thee again into this land; for I will not leave thee, until I have done that which I have spoken to thee of (Genesis 28:15).

He remembered God's mercy and grace. Jacob was returning to meet Esau. His brother had become very rich, he was a chief, he had been blessed abundantly in the things of this world, and he had authority and power to bind all Jacob had and to take vengeance upon him. Jacob knew this. He knew also that there was only one way of deliverance. What was it? The mind of God. Jacob knew that no one could deliver him but God. God had met him twenty-one years before when he went out empty. He had come back with wives and children and goods, but he was lean in soul and impoverished in spirit. Jacob said to himself, "If I do not get a blessing from God I can never meet Esau," and he made up his mind he would not go on until he knew that he had favor with God. Jacob was left alone, and unless we get alone with God, we shall surely perish.

Victory is Ours

...Hold fast the confidence and the rejoicing of the hope firm unto the end (Hebrews 3:6).

Jacob was left alone. He knelt alone. The picture is so real to me. Alone! Alone! Alone! He began to think. He thought about the ladder and the angels. I imagine as he began to pray, his tongue would cleave to the roof of his mouth. Jacob had to get rid of a lot of things. It had all been Jacob! Jacob! Jacob! He got alone with God and he knew it. If you get alone with God, what a place of revelation!

We stay too long with our relations, our camels, and our sheep. Jacob was probably left alone in the afternoon. Hour after hour passed. He began to feel the presence of God. But God was getting disappointed with Jacob. If ever God is disappointed with you when you tarry in His presence, it will be because you are not white hot. If you do not get hotter, and hotter, and hotter, you disappoint God. If God is with you and you know it, be in earnest. Pray! Pray! Pray! Lay hold! If you do not, you disappoint God. Jacob was that way. God said, "You are not real enough; you are not hot enough; you are too ordinary; you are no good to Me unless you are filled with zeal—white hot!" He told Jacob, "Let me go, for the day breaketh" (Gen. 32:26).

Jacob was wrestling with equal strength. Nothing is obtained that way. You must always master that which you are wrestling with. If darkness covers you, if it is fresh revelation you need, or your mind to be relieved, always get the victory. God says you are not in earnest enough. "Oh," you say, "the Word does not say that." But it was God's mind. In wrestling, the strength is in the neck, chest, and thigh; the thigh is the strength of all. So God touched his thigh. With our strength gone, defeat is sure. What did Jacob do? He hung on. God means to have a people touched by His power, so hold fast; He will never let go. And if we do let go, we shall fall short. You must never let go; whatever you are seeking—fresh revelation, light on the path, some particular need—never let go. Victory is ours if we are in earnest enough.

HOLDING HIM

Thy name shall be called no more Jacob, but Israel... (Genesis 32:28).

Now a new order is beginning, sons of God. How wonderful the change of Jacob to Israel! Israel! The name change meant victory all the time, God building all the time, God enough all the time. Israel had power over Esau, power over the world, power over the cattle. The cattle were nothing to him now. All is in subjection as he came out of the great night of trial. The sun rose upon him. Oh, that God may take you on, the sun rising, God supplanting all! What happened after that? Read how God blessed and honored Jacob.

Esau met him. There was no fighting now—what a blessed state of grace! They kissed each other. "When a man's ways please the Lord, he maketh even his enemies to be at peace with him" (Prov. 16:7). "What about all these cattle. Jacob?" "Oh, it's a present." "Oh, I have plenty; I don't want your cattle. What a joy it is to see your face again!" What a wonderful change! Who worked it? God.

Can you hold God? Oh, you say, it is irreverent to say so. Oh, yes you can! Sincerity can hold Him, dependence can hold Him, and weakness can hold Him. When you are weak, then are you strong (see 2 Cor. 12:10). I'll tell you what cannot hold Him. Self-righteousness cannot hold Him, pride cannot hold Him, assumption cannot hold Him, and high-mindedness cannot hold Him.

You can hold Him in the closet, in the prayer meeting, everywhere. "...If any man hear my voice, and open the door, I will come in to him, and will sup with him, and he with me" (Rev. 3:20). Can you hold Him? There may be a thought, sometimes, that He has left you. Oh, no! You can hold Him with great sincerity.

THE GREAT TRANSFORMATION

Thy name shall be called no more Jacob, but Israel... (Genesis 32:28).

God did not leave Jacob the same. Jacob became Israel. What changed his name? The wrestling? What changed his name? The holding on, the clinging, or the brokenness of spirit? Jacob obtained the blessing on two lines—by the favor of God and by yielding His will. God's Spirit was working in him to bring him to a place of helplessness—God co-labored with Jacob to bring him to Bethel, the place of victory. Jacob remembered Bethel, and through all the mischievous conditions of his life, Jacob had kept his vow. When we make vows and keep them, how God helps us. We must call upon God and give Him account of the promise. "And Jacob called the name of the place Peniel: for I have seen God face to face, and my life is preserved" (Gen. 32:30).

How did he know? Do you know when God blesses you, when you have victory? But twenty years after the vision of the ladder and the angels! How did Jacob know? We must have a perfect knowledge of what God has for us. He knew that he had the favor of God and that no man could hurt him. Let us, in all our seeking, see we have the favor of God, as we walk day by day beneath an open heaven. Keep His commandments, walk in the Spirit, and stay tender in your heart. If we do so, God will appreciate us; if so, we shall he appreciated by others and our ministry will be a blessing to those who hear. God bless you. God bless— for Jesus's sake.

THE SOURCE OF DIVINE LIFE

Looking unto Jesus the author and finisher of our faith; who for the joy that was set before him endured the cross, despising the shame, and is set down at the right hand of the throne of God (Hebrews 12:2).

This is a wonderful passage; in fact all the Word of God is wonderful. It is not only wonderful, but it has power to change conditions. Any natural condition can be changed by the Word of God, which is a supernatural power. In the Word of God is the breath, the nature, and the power of the Living God, and His power works in every person who dares to believe His Word. There is life though the power of it; and as we receive the Word of faith we receive the nature of God Himself. It is as we lay hold of God's promises in simple faith that we become partakers of the divine nature. As we receive the Word of God we come right into touch with a living force, a power that changes nature into grace, a power that makes dead things live, a power that is of God, that will be manifested in our flesh. This power has come forth with its glory to transform us by divine act into sons of God, to make us like *the* Son of God, by the Spirit of God who moves us on from grace to grace and from glory to glory, as our faith rests in this living Word.

It is important that we have a foundation truth, something greater than ourselves, on which to rest. There is only one Book that has life. When we come into this life by divine faith (and we must realize that it is by grace we are saved through faith, and that it is not of ourselves, but is the gift of God), we become partakers of this life. This Word is greater than anything else. There is no darkness at all in it. Anyone who dwells in this Word is able under all circumstances to say that he is willing to come to the light so that his deeds may be made manifest. The inexpressible divine power, force, passion, and fire that we receive are of God. Drink, my beloved, drink deeply of this source of life.

MOVING WITH HIS AUTHORITY

Now faith is the substance of things hoped for, the evidence of things not seen (Hebrews 11:1).

Someone said to me one day, "I would not believe in anything I could not handle and see." Everything you can handle and see is temporary and will perish with use. But the things not seen are eternal and will not fade away. Are you dealing with tangible things or with the things that are eternal, the things that are facts, and the things that are made real to faith? Thank God that through the knowledge of the truth of the Son of God we have within us a greater power, a mightier working, an inward impact of life, of power, of vision, and of truth more real than anyone can know who lives in the realm of the tangible.

God manifests Himself to the person who dares to believe. But there is something more beautiful than that. As we receive divine life in the new birth, we receive a nature that delights to do the will of God. As we believe the Word of God, a well of water springs up within our heart. A spring is always better than a pump. But I know that a spring is apt to be outclassed when we get to the baptism of the Holy Ghost. It was a spring to the woman at the well, but with the person who has the Holy Ghost it is flowing rivers. Have you these flowing rivers? To be filled with the Holy Ghost is to be filled with the Executive of the Godhead, who brings to us all the Father has and all the Son desires; and we should be so in the Spirit that God can cause us to move with His authority and reign by His divine ability.

Brought Into Sonship

[God] hath in these last days spoken unto us by his Son, whom he hath appointed heir of all things, by whom also he made the worlds (Hebrews 1:2).

I thank God He baptizes with the Holy Ghost. It is a scriptural work and I don't want anything else, because I must be the epistle of God. There must be emanating through my body a whole epistle of the life, of the power, and of the resurrection of my Lord Jesus. There are wonderful things happening through this divine union with God Himself. By this divine Person, this Word, this Son, God made all things. God's divine Son made everything we see. I want you to see that as you receive the Son of God, and as Christ dwells in your heart by faith, there is a divine force, the power of limitless possibilities, within you, and that as a result of this incoming Christ God wants to do great things through you.

By faith, if we receive and accept His Son, God brings us into sonship, and not only into sonship but also into being joint heirs, into sharing together with Him all that the Son possesses. Very few of us who are saved by the grace of God realize how great their authority is over darkness, demons, death, and every power of the enemy. It is a real joy when we realize our inheritance on this line.

Many people do not receive the Holy Ghost because they are continually asking and never believing. Everyone who asks, receives. Believe that asking is receiving, seeking is finding, and to he who is knocking the door is being opened. Faith is the evidence of things hoped for. As sure as you have faith, God will give you the overflowing Holy Ghost, and when He comes in you will speak as the Spirit gives utterance.

FILLED WITH HIS FULLNESS

And be not drunk with wine, wherein is excess; but be filled with the Spirit (Ephesians 5:18).

God wants to flow through you with measureless power of divine utterance and grace till your whole body is a flame of fire. God intends each soul in Pentecost to be a live wire. Not a monument, but a movement. So many people have been baptized with the Holy Ghost; there was a movement of Holy Ghost believers, but they have become monuments and you cannot move them. God, wake us out of sleep, lest we should become indifferent to the glorious truth and the breath of the almighty power of God. We must be the light and salt of the earth, with the whole armor of God upon us.

It would be a serious thing if our enemies were near and we had to go back and get our sandals. It would be a serious thing if we had on no breastplate. How can we be furnished with the armor? Take it by faith. Jump in, stop in, and never come out, for this is a baptism to be lost in, where you only know one thing and that is the desire of God at all times. The baptism in the Spirit should be an ever-increasing endowment of power, an ever-increasing enlargement of grace.

Oh, Father, grant unto us a real look into the glorious liberty You have designed for the children of God, who are delivered from this present world, separated, sanctified, and made ready for Your use, whom you have designed to be filled with all Your fullness.

THE FULFILLED PROMISE

But he was wounded for our transgressions, he was bruised for our iniquities: the chastisement of our peace was upon him; and with his stripes we are healed (Isaiah 53:5).

Jesus took our infirmities. He bore our sickness. He came to heal our broken heartedness. Jesus desires that we come forth in divine likeness, in resurrection force, in the power of the Spirit, and to walk in faith and understand His Word and what He meant when He said He would give us power over all the power of the enemy. He will subdue all things till everything comes into perfect harmony with His will.

Is He reigning over your affections, desires, will? If so, when He reigns you will be subject to His reigning power. He has authority over the whole situation. When He reigns, everything must be subservient to His divine plan and will for us. See what the Word of God says: "…No man can say that Jesus is the Lord, but by the Holy Ghost" (1 Cor. 12:3). "Lord!"

Bless God forever. Oh, for Him to be Lord and Master! For Him to rule and control! For Him to be filling your whole body with the plan of truth! Because you are in Christ Jesus all things are subject to Him. It is lovely, and God wants to make it lovely to you. When you get there, you will find divine power continually working. I absolutely believe that no man comes into the place of revelation and activity of the gifts of the Spirit but by this fulfilled promise of Jesus that He will baptize us in the Holy Ghost.

CLOTHED WITH ALMIGHTY GOD

Submit yourselves therefore to God. Resist the devil, and he will flee from you (James 4:7).

What would happen right now if everybody believed God? I love the thought that God the Holy Ghost wants to emphasize the truth that if we will only yield ourselves to the divine plan, He is right there to bring forth the mystery of truth. How many of us believe the Word? Matthew, Mark, Luke, John—they are the best tracts on healing. They are full of incidents about the power of Jesus. They will never fail to accomplish the work of God if people will believe them.

This is where men lack. All lack of faith is due to not feeding on God's Word. You need it every day. How can you enter into a life of faith? Feed on the living Christ of whom this Word is full. As you get taken up with the glorious fact and the wondrous presence of the living Christ, the faith of God will spring up within you. "Faith cometh by hearing, and hearing by the Word of God" (Rom. 10:17).

Faith is the substance of things hoped for. Faith is the Word. You were begotten of the Word, the Word is in you, the life of the Son is in you, and God wants you to believe. Who shall interfere with the divine mind of the Spirit, which has all revelation, who understands the whole condition of life? For the Word of God declares He knows all things, is well acquainted with the manifestation of your body, for everything about us is naked and open before Him. Because we have the mind of the Spirit, we understand what the will of God is. When shall we come into the knowledge of God? When we cease from our own mind and allow ourselves to become clothed with the mind and authority of the mighty God.

BE FILLED WITH DIVINE POWER

That the blessing of Abraham might come on the Gentiles through Jesus Christ; that we might receive the promise of the Spirit through faith (Galatians 3:14).

These are the days of the dispensation of the Holy Ghost. There is a very blessed way to receive the Holy Ghost. And when you are in the right attitude, faith becomes remarkably active. But it can never be remarkably active in a dead life. It is when sin is out and the body is clean and the life is made right that the Holy Ghost comes, and faith brings the evidence. Why should we tarry for the Holy Ghost? Why should we wrestle and pray in a living faith to be made ready? In John 16:7-8 we find the reason:

> *...It is expedient for you that I go away: for if I go not away, the Comforter will not come unto you; but if I depart, I will send him unto you. And when he is come, he will reprove the world of sin, and of righteousness, and of judgment.*

That is why the Holy Ghost is to come into your body. First of all, your sin is gone, and then you can see clearly to speak to others. But Jesus does not want you to take the speck out of somebody else's eye while the beam is in your own. When your own sins are gone, then the Holy Ghost can convince the world of sin, of righteousness, and of judgment. Now, how dare you resist coming into the place that you are filled with the life and power of the Holy Ghost?

I call you to halt, and then to march. Halt! Think! What is the attitude of your life? Are you thirsty? Are you longing? Are you willing to pay the price? Are you willing to forfeit in order to have? Are you willing to allow yourself to die that He may live? Are you willing for Him to have the right of way to your heart, your conscience, and all you are? Are you ready to have God's deluge of blessing upon your soul? Are you ready? You say, "What for?" That you may be changed forever. Receive the Holy Ghost. Be filled with divine power forever.

THE REVELATION OF HIS WILL

I beseech you therefore, brethren, by the mercies of God, that ye present your bodies a living sacrifice, holy, acceptable unto God, which is your reasonable service. And be not conformed to this world: but be ye transformed by the renewing of your mind, that ye may prove what is that good, and acceptable, and perfect, will of God (Romans 12:1-2).

You ask, "How do you know when the Holy Spirit is speaking?" Well, hundreds of people are in this dilemma of trying to get the mind of God. The first thing you must always keep in mind is that when you are living in the perfect will of God, you only will that which is purposed in His will. If you are not living in that perfect attitude toward God, you may have any amount of thoughts of your own nature, which you will find brings you into difficulty. It is the easiest thing to get the mind of the Lord when your whole heart only desires the will of the Lord. That will save you from a thousand troubles.

Are you so in touch with God that the desire of your mind is purity regarding that thing you want to be done? Has it the sanction of purity? Would Christ desire that thing? If so, the moment you pray, you will have the witness of the Spirit and it will coincide with the will of God. But the difficulties are that people want the Lord's revelation in a carnal manner or a carnal life or where there is some human thing. Ask yourself these things: why do you want to live, why do you want to go to the conventions, why do you want to be a pastor, and why are you anxious? If I realize that I want to preach for any reason other than for the glory of God and the extension of His Kingdom, then I am in sin. If I want to be heard, I am wrong. If I want to be seen, I am wrong. If I want to be honored, I am wrong. But if I want Christ, if I want to preach because I want to advocate His glorious Gospel, if I want to be seen only because I want to exhibit His Spirit, if I am here for the advancement of the glory of Christ, then things are as easy as possible.

A BANQUET OF
ABUNDANCE IN THE SPIRIT

He brought me to the banqueting house, and his banner over me was love (Song of Solomon 2:4).

Let the Spirit cover you today that you may be intensely in earnest about the deep things of God. You should be so in the order of the Spirit that you may know that your will, your mind, and your heart may be so centered in God that He may lift you into the pavilion of splendor where you hear His voice, the place where the breath of the Almighty can send you to pray and to preach.

You are at a banquet of multiplication, a banquet of no separation, a banquet where you increase, where God has riches for you beyond all things—not fleshly things, not carnal things, but spiritual manifestations, gifts, fruits of the Spirit, beautiful beatitudes, and where God's blessings are always on you. Are you ready for this glorious place where you are dismissed and God takes place? Are you ready to be sent on your eternal race to win thousands of people that they may enter into eternal grace?

There is power in the Holy Ghost to transform, renew, and change the whole circumstance of life. You have to submit and let God take hold of you. Don't be troubled because you have not reached the place. You have reached somewhere, but the best is in store. Only yield so that He may have full control of all you are.

People are never safe until they are baptized with the Holy Ghost, and that is why the apostles pressed that fact upon believers, and that is why Jesus was always pointing to the time when they should be filled with the unction and power of the Spirit, which would empower them to carry on.

Victorious in Battle

James, a servant of God and of the Lord Jesus Christ, to the twelve tribes which are scattered abroad, greeting. My brethren, count it all joy when ye fall into divers temptations (James 1:1-2).

No person is ever able to talk about victory over temptation unless he has been tempted. All the victories are won in battles. There are tens of thousands of people in the old land and also in America and other parts of the world who are wearing badges to show they have been in the battle, and they rejoice in it. They would be ashamed to wear a badge if they had not been in the battle. It is the battle that causes them to wear the badge. It is those people who have been in the fight who tell about the victories. It is those people who have been tried beyond all things who can come out and tell you a story. It is only James and Peter and Paul, those who were in the front of the battle, who tell you how we have to rejoice in the trial because there is wonderful blessing coming out of the trial. It is in the trial that we are made.

When the trial is severe, when you think that no one is tried as much as you, when you feel that some strange thing has so happened that you are altogether in a new order, or that the trial is so hard you cannot sleep, and you do not know what to do, count it all joy. He has some plan in it, something of a divine nature. You are in a good place when you do not know what to do. After Abraham was tried, then he could offer Isaac—not before he was tried. God put him through all kinds of tests. For twenty-five years he was tested, and he is called "the father of the faithful" because he would not give in. We have blessing today because one man dared believe God without evidence of fulfillment for twenty-five years (see Gen. 12:1-4; 17:17).

MORE PRECIOUS THAN GOLD

But if the Spirit of him that raised up Jesus from the dead dwell in you, he that raised up Christ from the dead shall also quicken your mortal bodies by his Spirit that dwelleth in you (Romans 8:11).

Some of you people, because you are not healed in a moment, wonder what is up. God never breaks His promise. The trial of your faith is much more precious than gold. God has you in the earth trying to bring out His character in you. He wants to destroy the power of the devil, and He wants to move you so that in the face of difficulties and hardships you will praise the Lord. "Count it all joy." You have to take a leap today. You have to leap into the promises; you have to believe God never fails you. You have to believe it is impossible for God to break His Word. He is from everlasting to everlasting.

We must understand that there will be testing times, but they are only to make us more like the Master. He was tempted in all points as we are, yet He did not sin. He endured all things. He is our example. Oh, that God shall give us an earnest, intent position where flesh and blood have to yield! We will go forward. We will not be moved by our feelings.

What does a man do when he is prayed for at a meeting and gets a blessing, only to wake up and not feel exactly as he ought to in the morning? Often, he begins murmuring doubts. He changes the Word of God for his feelings. What an awful disgrace it is for you to change the Word of God because of your feelings. Let Him have His perfect work and stand firm on the Word of God, for it is life to your soul and body.

PRAISE IN TRIALS

My brethren, count it all joy… (James 1:2).

James did not say, "Count a bit of it joy," but, "Count it all joy." It doesn't matter what area trials come in, whether it is your business or your home or what, count it all joy. Why? "All things work together for good to them which are called according to His purpose" (see Rom. 8:28). That is a great word. It means that God is electrifying your very position, so that the devil will see there is a character about you and he will have to say something about you as he said about Job. "Satan, what is your opinion about Job?" Then the Lord goes on and says, "Don't you think he is wonderful? Don't you think he is the most excellent of all the earth? Isn't he beautiful?" "Yes—but You know, You are keeping him."

Praise the Lord! I am glad the devil has to tell the truth. And don't you know He can keep you? "If You touch his body," the devil said, "he will curse You to Your face." "You do it, but you cannot touch his life," said God. The Scripture says that Jesus was dead, but He is alive again and has power over death and hell. And then there is a big "Amen." So the devil cannot take your life without the Lord allowing it. God told satan, "Thou shalt not touch his life." Satan thought he could do it, and you know the calamity. But Job said, "Naked came I into the world and naked shall I go out. Blessed be the name of the Lord!" (See Job 1.)

Oh, it is lovely! The Lord can give us that language of praise. It is not a language of the head. This is divine language. This is the acquaintance of the heart. I want you to know that we can have heart acquaintance with God. It is far greater for me to speak out of the abundance of my heart than out of the abundance of my head. I learned a long time ago that nothing but libraries make swelled heads. You are to have swelled hearts, because out of the heart, full of the fragrance of the love of God, issues forth the living life of the Lord.

BE PERFECT

But let patience have her perfect work, that ye may be perfect…(James 1:4).

O h, is that possible? Certainly it is possible. Who is speaking? It is the breath of the Spirit, it is the hidden heart of a man who was like his brother—this is James, the Lord's brother. He speaks very much like his brother. We might expect when we read these wonderful words that we have a real touch with a kindred spirit. James had to learn patience. It was not an easy thing for him to understand how his brother could be the Son of God and be in the same house with his other brothers. It was not an easy thing for him, and he had to learn to be patient to see how it worked out.

There are many things in your life that you cannot understand, but be patient, for when the hand of God is upon the thing, it may grind very slowly, but it will form the finest thing possible if you dare wait till the end of it. Do not kick until you are through—and when you are dead enough, you will never kick at all. It is a death so that we might be alive unto God. It is only by the deaths we die that we are able to be still. Jesus withstood it all: "The cross? I can despise the cross. The shame? I can despise it. The bitter language spoken round, 'If thou be the Christ, come down and we will believe'" (see Luke 23:37). They smote Him, but He did not respond. He is the picture for us. Why did He do it? He was patient. Why? He knew that as He came to the uttermost end of the cross, He saved all people forever. You cannot tell what God has in mind for you. As you are still, pliable in the hands of God, He will be working out a greater vessel than you can probably imagine in all your life.

WANTING NOTHING

Let patience have her perfect work, that ye may be perfect and...wanting nothing (James 1:4).

Wanting nothing means you are not moved by anything; you are only living in the divine position of God. It means you are not changed by what people say. There is something about divine acquaintance that is instilled by Almighty God. The new life of God is not superficial. It builds the character in purity till the inward heart is filled with divine love and has nothing but the thoughts of God.

The Spirit of the Lord is moving us mightily to see resurrection power. We were planted with Him, and we have risen with Him. We are from above. We do not belong to the earth. God's life is manifest in our body. It is a wonderful thing to get in touch with the Living God. It is a glorious thing.

Oh, if you won't resist the Holy Ghost, the power of God will melt you down. The Holy Ghost will so take charge of you that you will be filled to the uttermost with the overflowing of His grace.

He does not want any of us to be thirsty, famished, naked, full of discord, full of evil, full of carnality, or full of sensuality. And so He sends out in His own blessed way the old prophetic cry: "Ho, every one that thirsteth, come ye to the waters, and he that hath no money; come ye, buy, and eat..." (Isa. 55:1).

ASK GOD FOR WISDOM

If any of you lack wisdom, let him ask of God, that giveth to all men liber-ally, and upbraideth not; and it shall be given him (James 1:5).

This is a very remarkable word. Many people come to me and ask if I will pray for them to have faith. I want to encourage them, but I cannot go away from God's Word. I cannot grant people faith. But by the power of the Spirit I can stimulate you until you dare to believe and rest on the authority of God's Word. The Spirit of the Living God quickens you, and I see that "Faith cometh by hearing, and hearing by the Word of God." This is a living word of faith, "If any of you lack wisdom, let him ask of God, that giveth to all men liberally." One thing you cannot find is that God ever judged you for the wisdom He gave you or for the blessing He gave. He makes it so that when you come again He gives again, never asking what you did with the last. That is the way God gives. God gives liberally and does not find fault with us.

So you have a chance today to come for much more. Do you want wisdom? Ask of God. You have to be in the order of asking. This is the order: "But let him ask in faith, nothing wavering…" (James 1:6). I am satisfied that God, who is the builder of divine order, never brings confusion in His order. There is a way into the Kingdom of Heaven, and it is through the blood of the Lord Jesus Christ. If you want this divine order in your life, if you want wisdom, you have to come to God believing. If you really believe, you will ask God only once, and that is all you need, because He has abundance for your every need. But if you go right in the face of asking once and ask six times, He knows very well you do not mean what you ask, so you do not get it. God does not honor unbelief. He honors faith.

ASK AND BELIEVE

Ask, and it shall be given you; seek, and ye shall find; knock, and it shall be opened unto you: for every one that asketh receiveth; and he that seeketh findeth; and to him that knocketh it shall be opened (Matthew 7:7-8).

If you would get to business about the baptism of the Holy Ghost and ask God definitely and once to fill you, and believe it, what would you do? You would begin to praise Him for it because you knew He had given it. If you ask God once for healing, you will get it. But if you ask a thousand times a day till you did not know you were asking, you would get nothing. If you would ask God for your healing now and begin praising Him, because He never breaks His Word, you would go out perfect. Only believe.

God wants to promote us. He wants us to get away from our own thoughts, our own foolishness, and to get to a definite place, believing that He is and that He is a rewarder of those who seek Him diligently. Have you got to the place that you dare? Have you got to the place that you are going to murmur no more when you are in the trial? Are you going to be weeping around, telling people about it, or are you going to say, "Thank You, Lord, for putting me on the top"?

There are any number of people who do not get checks sent to them because they didn't thank the donor for the last. There are many people who get no blessing because they did not thank God for the last. A thankful heart is a receiving heart. God wants to keep you in the place of constant believing.

> *Keep on believing, Jesus is near,*
> *Keep on believing, there's nothing to fear;*
> *Keep on believing, this is the way,*
> *Faith in the night, the same as the day.*

ENDURING TEMPTATION
BRINGS THE CROWN

Blessed is the man that endureth temptation: for when he is tried, he shall receive the crown of life.... Let no man say when he is tempted, I am tempted of God: for God cannot be tempted with evil, neither tempteth he any man: but every man is tempted, when he is drawn away of his own lust, and enticed. Then when lust bath conceived, it bringeth forth sin: and sin, when it is finished, bringeth forth death. Do not err, my beloved brethren (James 1:12-16).

People do not know what they are getting when they are in a great place of temptation. Enduring temptation brings the crown of life, which the Lord has promised to those who love Him. There is nothing outside of purity but sin. All unbelief is sin. God wants you to have a pure, active faith so that all the time you will be living in an advanced place of believing God, and you will be on the mountaintop and singing when other people are crying.

I want to speak to you now about lust. I am speaking about that which has turned you aside to some other thing instead of God. God has been offering you better things all the time, and you have missed it.

There are three things in life, and I notice many people are satisfied with one. There is blessing in justification, there is blessing in sanctification, and there is blessing in the baptism of the Holy Ghost. Salvation is a wonderful thing and we know it. Sanctification is a process that takes you to a higher height with God. Salvation, sanctification, and the fullness of the Spirit are processes. Many are satisfied with good—that is salvation. Other people are satisfied with better—that is a sanctified life, purified by God. Other people are satisfied with the best—that is the fullness of God with revelation from on high. So I pray that you would see there is no lustful thing in you that would rob you of the glory, so God would take you to the very summit of the blessing where you can be increased day by day into all the fullness of God.

KNOWING THE PROMISE FULFILLER

For all the promises of God in him are yea, and in him Amen, unto the glory of God by us (Second Corinthians 1:20).

God has never changed His mind concerning His promises. They are yea and amen to those who believe. God is the same yesterday and forever. To doubt Him is sin. All unbelief is sin. So we have to believe He can heal, save, fill with the Holy Ghost, and transform us altogether.

Are you ready? What for? That you might be so chastened by the Lord, so corrected by Him, that as you pass through the fire, as you pass through all temptations, you may come out as Jesus came out of the wilderness, filled with the Spirit. Are you ready? What for? That you may be so brought in touch with the Father's will that you may know that whatsoever you ask and believe, you will receive. This is the promise; this is the reality God brings to us. Are you ready? What for? That you might not yield to the flesh, but be quickened by the Spirit, and live in the Spirit without condemnation while your testimony is bright, cheerful, and full of life. This is the inheritance for you today.

God has worked out the whole plan of our inheritance, and He is showing us that the whole thing is so beautiful, that we are brought into existence in the spiritual order through the Word. Do not neglect the Word of God. Take time to think about the Word of God. It is the only place of safety. Everything is possible to those who believe. God will not fail His Word. Suppose that all the people in the world did not believe—it would make no difference to God's Word; it would be the same. You cannot alter God's Word. It is from everlasting to everlasting, and they who believe in it shall be like Mount Zion, which cannot be moved.

DISCIPLINED AS SONS

...My son, despise not thou the chastening of the Lord, nor faint when thou art rebuked of him: for whom the Lord loveth he chasteneth, and scourgeth every son whom he receiveth (Hebrews 12:5-6).

God is dealing with us as sons. What shall hinder us? Human nature. That has a lot to do with hindering God—when the human will is not wholly surrendered, when there is some mixture, part spirit and part of flesh, when there is a division in your own heart. Do not forget that the Word of God is very clear on this line. The Scriptures distinctly say there are children of obedience and children of disobedience, and they are both children, both saved. Both know it. One lives in obedience, another in disobedience, and the disobedient always gets the whip.

In a house where there are two children, one may be desirous to obey the father and mother, and he or she is loved and is very well treated. The other is loved just the same, but the difficulty is this: the wayward boy who will have his own way does many things to grieve the parents, and he gets the whip. They are both children in the house; one is getting the whip, the other is getting the blessing without the whip.

Many of God's children who are getting the whip know better. So I want you to wake up to do what you know ought to be done, because there are stripes for those who won't obey. Sin can only be removed by repentance. When you repent deep enough, you will find that thing goes forever. Never cover up sin. Sins must be judged. Sins must be brought to the blood. When you have a perfect confidence between you and God, it is amazing how your prayers rise, you catch fire, you are filled with zeal, your inspiration is tremendous, and you find out that the Spirit prays through you and you live in a place of blessing.

Baptized Into the Richness of His Grace

...According to the riches of his grace (Ephesians 1:7).

Beloved, one thing is certain this morning: God can do it. I pray God will so unfold to us the depths of His righteousness that we may no longer be poor but very rich in God by His Spirit. Beloved, it is God's thought to make us all very rich in grace, and in the knowledge of God through our Lord Jesus Christ. We have before us a message that is full of heights and depths, and lengths, and breadths; a message that came out of brokenness of spirit, the loss of all things, enduring all things; a message where flesh and all that pertains to this world had to come to nothing. We can never worship God only in the Spirit. We must also worship in truth.

When the Spirit lifts you, when God takes you on, all things come into perfect harmony and you go forth right in to victory. It is a grand place to come to where we "rejoice in Christ Jesus, and have no confidence in the flesh" (Phil. 3:3). Oh, that is the greatest of all, when the Lord Jesus has the reins. Oh, it is beautiful as we gaze upon the perfect Jesus! Jesus so outstrips everything else. For this reason Paul felt that everything must become as dross—whatever he was, whatever he had been. There was no help for anything in him. There is no help for us only on the lines of helplessness and nothingness.

I know nothing like travail in the Spirit. Oh, it is a burden till you are relieved. Brother, sister, unless God brings us into a place of brokenness of spirit, unless God remolds us in the great plan of His will for us, the best of us shall utterly fail. But when we are absolutely taken in hand by Almighty God, God makes even weakness strength. He makes even that barren, helpless, groaning cry come forth, so that men and women are born in the travail. There is a place where the helplessness is touched by the almightiness of God and where you come out shining as gold tried in the fire.

BE MADE NEW

But call to remembrance the former days, in which, after ye were illuminated, ye endured a great fight of afflictions (Hebrews 10:32).

Every day there must be a revival touch in our hearts. Every day must change us after His fashion. We are to be made new all the time. I am positive that no man can attain like-mindedness with God except by the illumination of the Spirit. I see unlimited grace in the baptism of the Holy Ghost. There is endurance in that revelation by the Spirit. The excellence of Christ can never be understood except by illumination. And I find the Holy Ghost is that great Illuminator who makes me understand all the depths of Him. I must witness Christ.

Jesus said to Thomas, "Thomas, because thou hast seen me, thou hast believed: blessed are they that have not seen, and yet have believed" (John 20:29). So I can see there is a revelation which brings me into touch with Him, where we see right into the fullness of Christ. I can see that Paul, as he saw the depths and heights of the grandeur, longed that he might win Him. Before his conversion, in his passion and zeal, Paul would do anything to bring Christians to death. And that passion that was in him raged like a mighty lion. As he was going on the way to Damascus, he heard the voice of Jesus saying, "Saul, Saul, why persecutest thou me?" (Acts 9:4). What broke him up was the tenderness of God.

Brother, it is always God's tenderness over our weakness and depravity that has us broken all the time. Oh, to win Him, my brother! There are a thousand things in the nucleus of a human heart that need softening a thousand times a day. But God will do it. Oh, this transforming regeneration by the power of the Spirit makes me see there is a place to win Him, that I may stand complete. As He was, so am I to be. The Scriptures declare it, and it shall be.

Found in Him

And be found in him, not having mine own righteousness, which is of the law, but that which is through the faith of Christ, the righteousness which is of God by faith (Philippians 3:9).

The Scriptures declare unto us that we are in Christ and Christ is in God. What is able to move you from the place of omnipotent power? Shall tribulation, or persecution, or nakedness, or peril, or sword? Ah, no! Shall life, or death, or principalities, or powers? No, we are more than conquerors through Him who loved us.

Oh, but I must be found in Him! There is a place of seclusion, a place of rest and faith in Jesus where there is nothing else like it. Jesus came to them on the water and they were terrified, but He said, "It is I; be not afraid" (Mark 6:50). My brother, He is always there. He is there in the storm as well as in the peace; He is there in the adversity. When shall we know He is there? When we are "found in Him," resting in the omnipotent plan of God. Oh, is it possible for the child of God to fail? It is not possible. "He that keepeth Israel shall neither slumber nor sleep" (Ps. 121:4). He shall watch over you continually.

Oh, but we must be found *in Him.* My brother, my sister, sometimes you thought you would never get out of this place of difficulty, but you have no idea that behind the whole thing God has been working a plan greater than all. "That I may know Him, and the power of His resurrection" (Phil. 3:10). Jesus said to Martha, "I am the resurrection, and the life" (John 11:25). Today is a resurrection day. We must know the resurrection of His power in brokenness of spirit. Oh, to know this power of resurrection, to know the rest of faith!

OH, SPIRIT, BLOW ON US

...What things soever ye desire, when ye pray, believe that ye receive them, and ye shall have them (Mark 11:24).

Ah, there is something different between saying you have faith and then being pressed into a tight corner and proving that you have faith. If you dare believe, it shall be done according to your faith. Jesus is the resurrection and the life, and I say, we must attain to it. God, help us to attain. We gain divine life in the knowledge that He made us white as snow, pure, and holy, so that we may go with boldness unto the Throne of Grace. Boldness is in His holiness. Boldness is in His righteousness. Boldness is in His truth. You cannot have the boldness of faith if you are not pure.

The Lord wants us to understand that we must come to a place where our natural life ceases, and by the power of God we rise into a life where God rules, where He reigns. Do you long to know Him? Do you long to be found in Him? Your longing shall be satisfied this day. This is a day of putting on and being clothed upon in God. Fall in the presence of God. You who want to know God, yield to His mighty power and obey the Spirit.

When the Spirit of the Lord blows upon you, you will be broken down and then built up. Jesus came forth in the glory of the Father, filled with all the fullness of God. It was the thought of God before the foundation of the world, with such love over the entire fearful, helpless human race, with all its blackness and hideousness of sin, and God loved and God brought redemption. Beloved, yield to the Him now.

Are you ready? What for? To know Him in the depths of your being. Are you ready? What for? To know the richness of His grace and the fellowship of His suffering. Are you ready? What for? To walk in the fullness of Christ. Salvation, beloved, has prepared the way for you to draw nigh unto God.

FIRE, LOVE, ZEAL, AND FAITH

Bless the Lord, O my soul: and all that is within me, bless his holy name (Psalm 103:1).

When we are filled with the joy of the Lord, then there comes forth a glad, "Praise the Lord!" David knew that, and he wished all the powers had breath to praise the Lord. It is a tragedy if there is not a divine spring within you pressing forth praise. God wants you so in the Spirit that your whole life is praise. How my soul longs for you to catch fire! There are four things that are emblematic, divinely ascertained, or revealed by the Lord—fire, love, zeal, and faith. Fire makes us burn intensely so that we are full of activity with God. Love causes us to walk in purity so that we are willing and yielded to God and not afraid to sacrifice. Zeal pushes us into the will and mighty power of God until we press beyond measure into that which pleases God. Faith laughs at impossibilities and cries, "It shall be done!" May God make these things immediately real before our eyes and give us these emblematic displays of inward flame!

We have seen that the Word could transmit the nature of the Son of God unto us. As the Spirit fills our vessel, the Word is made life in us, till the body becomes quickened by the same nature of Jesus, with the same power over all weaknesses. The Spirit of God fills us with an incorruptible force, pressing through human order, changing human order, bringing it to the place where it is resurrection life, eternal life, quickened by the Spirit, and changed from one state of grace to another, even from glory to glory. Hallelujah! Amen.

RENEWED DAILY

...Though our outward man perish, yet the inward man is renewed day by day (Second Corinthians 4:16).

Many people are receiving a clear knowledge of an inward working of the power of the Spirit that is not only quickening their mortal bodies but also pressing into that same natural body an incorruptible power that is manifesting itself. The divine teaching of the Lord has revealed unto us that the nature of the Christian life is the inward working of the Spirit, the new man in the old man, the new nature in the old nature, the resurrection power in the dead form, the quickening of all, and the divine order of God manifested in the human.

Do not be afraid to claim it: power over all sin, power over all disease. Christ is quickening your body until every vestige of natural order is eaten up by the divine life. The former law was of the natural man. Now the new law is the life of the Spirit, or the manifestation of the new creation, which is Christ in us, the manifested power of the glory. Glory is a manifestation of the divine nature in the human body.

You are justified; you are made at peace with God. And remember the peace of God is different from any other peace—it passes all understanding; it takes you away from being disturbed so that earthly things do not move you. It is a deep peace, created by the knowledge of a living faith that is the living principle of the foundation of all truth.

ACCESS INTO THE SPIRIT

Beloved...know ye the Spirit of God (First John 4:1-2).

The great need today is more of the Word. There is no foundation apart from the Word. The Word not only gives you foundation, but it puts you in a place where you can stand, and after the battle keep on standing. Nothing else will do it. When the Word is in your heart, it will preserve you from desiring sin. The Word is the living presence of that divine power that overcomes the world. You need the Word of God in your hearts that you might be able to overcome the world. *Beloved.* That is a good word. It means to say we are now in a place where God has set His love upon us. He wants us to hearken to what He has to say to us, because when His beloved is hearing His voice, then they understand what He has for them.

Beloved, I want you to see how rich you are. By faith, we have access into this grace wherein we stand, and we rejoice in the hope of the glory of God (see Rom. 5:2). This is perhaps the greatest of all thoughts we have reached: faith enables us access through Jesus Christ into all the fullness of God. It was by grace first. You were saved through grace. But now another grace, a grace of access, a grace of entering in, a grace of understanding the unfolding of the mystery, a grace which shall bring us into a place of knowledge of God is also poured out on us by the Spirit of God. We have tremendous access to the vastness of God's Spirit.

THE BREATH OF NEW LIFE

...To them that have obtained like precious faith with us through the righteousness of God and our Saviour Jesus Christ: Grace and peace be multiplied unto you through the knowledge of God, and of Jesus our Lord (Second Peter 1:1-2).

We have received like precious faith of all that have passed through. We have access into all that the Father has, all that Jesus has, and all the Holy Ghost has. Nothing can keep us out of the fullness of God. Jesus Christ is the Alpha and Omega for us, so that we may know grace, favor, and mercy.

You want grace multiplied this morning? You want peace multiplied? You have it here if you dare to believe. We have access. We have a right to it.

According as his divine power hath given unto us all things that pertain unto life and godliness, through the knowledge of him that hath called us to glory and virtue: whereby are given unto us exceeding great and precious promises: that by these ye might be partakers of the divine nature... (2 Peter 1:3-4).

It is true that He came to us in grace, He met us in need, and He transformed us by His power. It is right to say that now we have within us an inheritance, right to say it is incorruptible and undefiled. We have a right to say it is filled with glory and virtue. We have a right to say we have the same nature as the Lord Jesus Christ. All human weakness in believers is spoiled when it is a mixture. If your faith is not perfect, your victories are uncertain, your prayers have lost the anointing, your pressing into the Kingdom of God is somewhat veiled, and your personality of divine power is hindered. Why? God comes to us, breathes into us a new life, shows us we have access into this grace where we stand, that we may have a new nature that has no variableness, no shadow of turning, but believes all things, hopes all things, endures all things, and is all the time being changed.

Christ Arose

...And rejoice in hope of the glory of God (Romans 5:2).

The Holy Ghost is the manifestation of God's Son. The Holy Ghost is always revealing God to us as divine, as so uniquely divine that He has overcoming power. His power is pure and has no measure. Now that we have received salvation, He wants to open our eyes to understand what Christ really did for us. In due time, at the end of the weeks of the law, when there was no arm to save, when there was no hope, when law had failed, Christ took our place, delivered us from all the powers of human weaknesses and failure, and so came to us in our sins. When we were in sin, Christ died for us. In due time, at the end of failure, at the right moment, He died for us and delivered us from the power of the devil—delivered us from death, delivered us from sin, delivered us from the grave—and gave us a hope of immortality through His life. We are saved by His life.

Jesus had eternal properties. Jesus had power to impart eternal gifts. He has delivered us from the curse of the law and set us free. What is the Gospel? It is the power of God unto salvation. The Gospel has power to bring immortality and life. Immortality and life are the nature of the Lord Jesus, and through this life we are delivered from all things and prepared for the glorious hope of the coming of the Lord.

> *Christ arose, a victor over death's domain.*
> *He arose, forever with His saints to reign;*
> *He arose! He arose!*
> *Hallelujah, Christ arose!*

ATONEMENT

But if the Spirit of him that raised up Jesus from the dead dwell in you, he that raised up Christ from the dead shall also quicken your mortal bodies by his Spirit that dwelleth in you (Romans 8:11).

How did He rise? Out of death. He was victorious over death. Were we not planted with Him? Were we not risen with Him? Then the only thing that can happen is to be seated with Him. The past is under the blood; the whole thing is finished. Now entering into another step of this divine order, the Lord will speak to us.

And not only so, but we also joy in God through our Lord Jesus Christ, by whom we have now received the atonement (Romans 5:11).

Atonement—*at-one-ment*. When we are one with the Lord, we are in perfect association with Him. Whatever His appointment in the earth, whatever He was, we have been joined up to Him as one, meaning that He has absolutely taken every vestige of human deformity, depravity, lack of comprehension, and inactivity of faith and has nailed it to the cross. It is forever on the cross. You died with Him on the cross and, if you will only believe you are dead with Him, you are dead indeed to sin and alive to righteousness.

The atonement is the wonderful regenerative power of God, and it means, "I am complete in His oneness." There is not a vestige of human weakness. If I dare believe, I am so in order with God's Son that He makes me perfect—at one with Him, no sin, no blemish, no failure, absolutely perfect. Dare you believe it? It may not be easy for you, but I want to make it easy. If you dare believe now, oneness, purity, power, and eternity are working through you. He has made us whole and complete in Him through the blood.

COVERED WITH ATONEMENT

Wherefore, as by one man sin entered into the world, and death by sin; and so death passed upon all men, for that all have sinned: (For until the law sin was in the world: but sin is not imputed when there is no law. Nevertheless death reigned from Adam to Moses, even over them that had not sinned after the similitude of Adam's transgression, who is the figure of him that was to come. But not as the offence, so also is the free gift. For if through the offence of one many be dead, much more the grace of God, and the gift by grace, which is by one man, Jesus Christ, hath abounded unto many) (Romans 5:12-15).

Through one man's disobedience, through one man's sin, death came and reigned. As sin and death reigned because of Adam, so now the new Man, Christ, shall make us so awake to righteousness, to peace, to abundance in God. Just as death had its power, life has to have its power and victory through a new man.

Christ's mind has been replanted in your natural order so that you may see what you cannot understand. God thoroughly understands what you will never understand, and overflows blessing to you and says, "Only believe, brother, and it shall be overflowing to you." God will make it rich to you. You know how sin was abounding, how we were held, how we were defeated, how we groaned and travailed. Now grace, life, and ministry abound to us.

Brother, sister, take a leap that you may never know what defeat is any more. This is the real power of resurrection. It covers you with atonement. And now it reveals to you all that all that Christ ever had or will have abounds toward you to liberate you from all human nature and to bring you into all divinity. This is the glorious liberty of the Gospel of Christ.

THE WONDERFUL
PROVISION OF GRACE

And not as it was by one that sinned, so is the gift: for the judgment was by one to condemnation, but the free gift is of many offenses unto justification (Romans 5:16).

We have been condemned and lost. How human nature destroys! We all know sin had its reign, but there is a justification for our sin. Jesus touches human weaknesses with His touch of infinite, glorious resurrection power. He transforms you.

For if by one man's offence death reigned by one; much more they which receive abundance of grace and of the gift of righteousness shall reign in life by one, Jesus Christ (Romans 5:17).

Oh, how rich we are! There was death, but it has been supplanted. Now there is a righteous life. You were in death, but now you have the righteous life, which reigns over death and all weaknesses. Your grace ran out years ago. My grace was spun out years ago, but the revelation of the Spirit taught me that His grace could take the place of my grace. His power and grace could cover me where I could not cover myself. He would stand beside me when I was sure to go down. Where sin abounded, grace abounded; His love abounded.

He stretched out His hand. He was in mercy. He never failed. He was there every time when I was sure to go down. Grace abounded. Oh the mercy, the boundless mercy of the love of God to us! I hope you are getting this grace—and I hope you are thriving in it and triumphing in it. God must give you these divine attributes of the Spirit that you may come into like-mindedness with Him in this wonderful provision.

JUSTIFIED AND RIGHTEOUS

For what the law could not do, in that it was weak through the flesh, God sending his own Son in the likeness of sinful flesh, and for sin, condemned sin in the flesh: that the righteousness of the law might be fulfilled in us, who walk not after the flesh, but after the Spirit (Romans 8:3-4).

Many people fail to access God's divine gift because they are always fearful because of their knowledge of their own imperfection. The devil has a tremendous trap. He tries all the time to catch poor people who have made a little slip or not said just the right thing. The devil tries to make mountains out of molehills.

I like the thought that God's Son is so gracious toward us. Beloved, where you fail in your righteousness, Jesus Christ has a gift of righteousness. He takes away your filthy garment and clothes you with a new garment. He even has power to take away your tongue and your thoughts of evil. If you believe. God wants to supplant your sin with His righteousness, the righteousness of the Son of God. It has no adulteration in it. It has no judgment in it. It is full of mercy and entreaty. It is the righteousness of the law of God's Spirit.

Dare you come into it? There is a lot of truth about being saved. It is a reality. There is a great deal of truth about having the peace of God. There is a great deal of knowledge in the fact that you know you are free, and there is a wonderful manifestation of power to keep you free. But I find satan dethrones some of the loveliest people because he catches them at a time when they are unaware. I find them all the time—poor souls!—deceived by the power of satan. Hear this word: When satan is the nearest, God is nearer with an abounding measure of His grace. when you feel almost as though you would be defeated, He has a banner waving over you to cover you at that moment. He covers you with His grace. He covers you with His righteousness. It is the very nature of the Son of God. It is the very life of God.

Coming into Collaboration with God

For with thee is the fountain of life: in thy light shall we see light. O continue thy lovingkindness unto them that know thee; and thy righteousness to the upright in heart (Psalm 36:9-10).

This life cannot possibly remain in the body. When you are intoxicated with the Spirit, the Spirit flows through the avenues of your mind and the keen perception of your heart with deep throbbing. You are filled with the passion of the grace of God till you may be so filled with illumination by the power of the new wine—the wine of the kingdom, the Holy Ghost—till your whole body is intoxicated. This is rapture. This will have to leave the body. There is no natural body that will be able to stand this process of going forth. It will have to leave the body. But the body will preserve it until the sons of God are marvelously manifested.

Sonship is a position of rightful heirship. Sons have a right to the first claiming of the will. I would like you to realize that redemption is so perfect and will rid you of judging yourself. God has a righteous judgment for you. Get away from all the powers of the devil. God's grace abounds liberally toward you. Grace abounds. Righteousness abounds. This life is holy and new. The Son of God is reigning in your human body. This life in you is so after the order of God that it is not ashamed in any way to say you are coming into collaboration with the Father, with the Son, and with the Holy Ghost. God has been showing me that Jesus meant that He will give us power to remit sins when He said, "Whose soever sins ye remit, they are remitted unto them; and whose soever sins ye retain, they are retained" (John 20:23).

THE POWER OF FAITH

And God, which knoweth the hearts, bare them witness, giving them the Holy Ghost, even as he did unto us; and put no difference between us and them, purifying their hearts by faith (Acts 15:8-9).

Sincere faith never wavers. It has audacity, purity, and empowers us to be sensitive to the breath of God. Faith imparts the very nature of the Son of God to us. Faith comes from the Author of faith. Faith is sight. The crooked are made straight, the lame leap with joy, and the blind are made free.

God finished creation. The Lord completed the perfect work of creation forever. We are complete in Him, belonging to the Living Head. We are His righteousness, created for His purpose, so that we might be in the world but over all the powers of the world. The Spirit lifts, the Word of Incarnation moves, the divine life operates, and the Spirit quickens. We have the fullness of God within us. You are being changed, made right and ready. Believe it. God's plan, purpose, revelation is for us to leap gloriously.

So we have to see that God, in the Holy Ghost order, is bringing us into like-mindedness of faith. I speak this to you because I know the Holy Ghost is bringing this Church through. She has passed through many dark days of misunderstanding, but God is showing us that we have power to defeat the powers of the enemy. We have power to reign in this life by another. God has mightily justified us with abounding grace, filled us with the Holy Ghost, and given us the hope of the glory.

When we were helpless, Jesus Christ came and took our place. And as we all received these evil things through Adam, Jesus gave a new impetus, so grace could be where sin was and righteousness could be where there was no righteousness. Bless God! It is not far off. It is very near, at the door. Ah, there will be a shout some day. It will not be long before He shall be here!

A GREAT SPIRITUAL MAGNET

Therefore as by the offence of one judgment came upon all men to condemnation; even so by the righteousness of one the free gift came upon all men unto justification of life. For as by one man's disobedience many were made sinners, so by the obedience of one shall many be made righteous. Moreover the law entered, that the offence might abound. But where sin abounded, grace did much more abound: that as sin hath reigned unto death, even so might grace reign through righteousness unto eternal life by Jesus Christ our Lord (Romans 5:18-21).

Eternal life is resurrection. Eternal life is with the Father and with the Son. Eternal life has come into us and as the Father is, so are we. As the Son is, so are we, and the glory itself will not be able to contain His position without the glory of the earth coming to the glory that is in heaven. This eternal life is manifested in mortal bodies, so that the life of Christ shall be so manifested in our mortal bodies that everything shall be dead indeed unto sin and alive unto God by the Spirit. We are ready; we are gloriously ready. Oh, hallelujah!

The life, the redemption, the glorious life in the Spirit! Have you got it? Have you entered into it? Is it reality to you? Do you know that it would not be possible for Him to move at all in the glory without you moving that way? It would be impossible for the Lord to come without taking you.

I saw one day a great big magnet let down amongst iron, and it picked up loads of iron and carried it away. That is a natural order, but ours is a spiritual magnet. What is in you is holy. What is in you is pure. And when the Lord of righteousness appears, who is our life, then that which is holy, which is His nature and life, shall go, and we shall be forever with the Lord.

COVET LOVE

For God so loved the world, that he gave his only begotten Son, that whoso-ever believeth in him should not perish, but have everlasting life (John 3:16).

You have not gone yet—but you are sure to go. Seeing we are here, comforting one another, building up one another in the most holy faith, we would say: "No, Lord; let it please You that we remain. But please, Father, let us be more holy, let us be more pure. Please, Father, let this life of Your Son eat up all mortality till there is nothing left but that which is to be changed in a moment, in the twinkling of an eye." Do not let one thought, one act, one thing in any way interfere with more rapture.

Ask God that every moment shall be a moment of purification, a moment of seeking the rapture, a moment of being in your body in a new order of the Spirit. Let God take you into the fullness of redemption in a wonderful way. Covet to be more holy. Covet to be more separate. Covet God. Covet gifts. Covet the graces. Covet the beatitudes. Covet earnestly. And may God show us this divine order, this divine love. Oh, breathe this holy, intense love in our bosom today—Love! Love! Love! Let it please You, Lord, that this bond of union, this holy covenant with You shall be so strong that no man shall be able to separate us from this love of God in Christ Jesus. And whom the Lord has joined together, let no power in the world put asunder. May love, love, *love* take us on to the summit of the perfection: "For God so loved!"

THE REVELATION OF CHRIST

And I say also unto thee, That thou art Peter, and upon this rock I will build my church; and the gates of hell shall not prevail against it (Matthew 16:18).

We are more confident today than we were yesterday. God is building us up in this faith, so that we are living in great expectation. He is bringing us into a place with Himself where we can say, "I have seen God." I have been asking God to send us His Word on fire, something that will live in our hearts, that will abide with us forever. It is important that every day we should lay some new foundation that can never be uprooted. Oh, for a living touch from God, and a new inspiration of power, and a deeper sense of His love! I have been thinking about the sixteenth chapter of Matthew, and Peter's answer to Jesus when He asked His disciples the question, "Whom say ye that I am?" and Peter answered saying, "Thou art the Christ, the Son of the living God" (Matt. 16:15-16).

Beloved friends, do you know Him? Has this revelation come to your heart? Do you call Him Lord? Do you find comfort in the fact that He is yours? The Master knew what was in their thoughts before He asked them. This fact makes me long more and more to be really true; God is seeing right into my heart and reads my thoughts. If you can call Jesus Lord today, it is by the Holy Ghost. And so there ought to be within us a deep response that says, "Thou art the Christ." When we can say this from our hearts, it makes us know that we are not born of flesh and blood but of the Spirit of the Living God. If you will go back to the time when you first had the knowledge that you were born of God, you will see that there was within you a deep cry for your Father; you found you had a heavenly Father. If you want to know the real success of any life it will be because of this knowledge, "Thou art the Christ."

THE NARROW WAY

From that time forth began Jesus to shew unto his disciples, how that he must go unto Jerusalem, and suffer many things of the elders and chief priests and scribes, and be killed, and be raised again the third day. Then Peter took him, and began to rebuke him, saying, Be it far from thee, Lord: this shall not be unto thee. But he turned, and said unto Peter, Get thee behind me, Satan: thou art an offence unto me: for thou savourest not the things that be of God, but those that be of men. Then said Jesus unto his disciples, If any man will come after me, let him deny himself, and take up his cross, and follow me (Matthew 16:21-24).

We find the fundamental truths of all the ages were planted right in the life of Peter. We see evidences of the spiritual power to which he had attained, and we also see the natural power working. Jesus saw that He must suffer if He would reach that spiritual life which God intended Him to reach. So Jesus said, "I must go forward; your words, Peter, are an offense to Me." So if you seek to save yourself, it is an offense to God. God has impressed it upon me more and more that if I seek—at any time—the favor of men or earthly power, I shall lose favor with God, and I cannot have faith. Jesus said, "How can ye believe if ye seek honor one of another?"

God is speaking to us, every one, and trying to get us to cut the shorelines. There is only one place where we can get the mind and will of God—it is alone with God; if you look to anybody else you cannot get it. We must get out on the water in faith. If we seek to save ourselves, we shall never reach the place where we will be able to bind and loose. There is a close companionship between you and Jesus that nobody knows about, where every day you have to choose or refuse. It seems to me that God wants to get every one of us separated to Himself in this holy war, and we are not going to have faith if we do not give ourselves wholly up to Him. Beloved, it is in these last days that I cannot have the power I want to have unless I am willing to shear myself; it is a narrow way.

Stand on the Rock

And I appoint unto you a kingdom, as my Father hath appointed unto me; that ye may eat and drink at my table in my kingdom, and sit on thrones judging the twelve tribes of Israel (Luke 22:29-30).

Do you believe that the Father in heaven would make you a judge over a kingdom if there was anything crooked in you? Do you believe you will be able to bind unless you are free yourself? But every man that has this living Christ within him has the power that will put to death all sin. With Jesus's last words on earth He gave the disciples a commission; the discipleship has never ceased. The churches are weak today because Christ the rock is not abiding in them in the manifestations of the power of God. This is not because it is a special gift—this power to loose and to bind—but it is whether you have the rock foundation in you.

In the name of Jesus you will loose, and in the name of Jesus you will bind, and if He is in you, it ought to bring forth evidences of that power. One can see that Peter had great sympathy in the natural, and he did not want Jesus to be crucified; it was perfectly natural for Peter to say what he did, but Jesus said, "Get thee behind me" (Matt. 16:23). He knew He must not be turned aside by any human sympathy.

The only way we can retain our humility is by keeping on this narrow line and saying, "Get thee behind me, satan." If you try to go the easy way you cannot be Jesus's disciple. Beloved, we are now living in the fact that Jesus is the Rock. It makes me glad because we are in the reach of wonderful possibilities because of this Rock. Take a stand on the fact that this Rock cannot be overthrown.

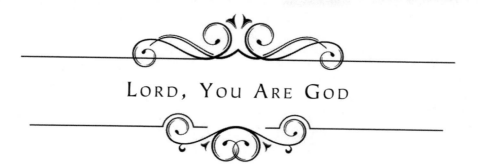

Lord, You Are God

…Thou art the Christ, the Son of the living God (Matthew 16:16).

When shall we see all the people filled with the Holy Ghost, and the things done as they were in the Acts of the Apostles? It will be when all the people shall say, "Lord, You are God." I want you to come into a place of such relationship with God that you will know your prayers are answered, because He has promised.

I believe God is ever opening the door of opportunity, but we must be ready to enter that door. John the Baptist opened the door for the Lord Jesus. He said of Him "Behold the Lamb of God," and I have cried to God that it may come to my lot to have the same cry that John had. I am more than ever, impressed as I read the Word of God and think over John the Baptist's Gospel, that neither his father nor his mother ever really understood their son, although they knew he was filled with the Holy Ghost. I believe the great plan of his father was to make him a priest, but it would not do. A man filled with the Holy Ghost must have nothing of the old order about him.

John the Baptist was full of the power of the Spirit in the wilderness, feeding on locusts and wild honey. God was with him all the time. He was in a new order of things. He could not keep still, and so he went forth by the mighty power of God and cried in the wilderness, and it was a cry of the Spirit that moved all who came to the Jordan to be baptized by him. He opened the door for the Master, and how lovely it was that he was ready to prepare the way of the Lord.

Beloved, may the Lord get us ready for any door that He may open for us.

About Smith Wigglesworth

Smith Wigglesworth, often referred to as "the Apostle of Faith," was a British evangelist who helped pioneer the Pentecostal revival that occurred a century ago. Smith was born in Yorkshire, England in 1859. He became a born-again Christian when he was 8 years old and grew up sharing the gospel with family, friends, and co-workers. He married Mary Jean "Polly" Featherstone, a Salvation Army minister, in 1882. They had five children together, Alice, Seth, Harold, Ernest, and George.

After encountering the baptism of the Holy Spirit in 1907, Smith began preaching a gospel that includes divine healing, signs and wonders, and speaking in tongues. His ministry quickly grew and soon he abandoned his plumbing profession to focus on ministering the Gospel. Smith's meetings were known for great miracles. Many received the baptism of the Holy Spirit and encountered physical healings and spiritual transformation through his ministry. Smith visited many pockets of revival around the world and preached a gospel of power and fire. He also raised several people from the dead.

While many ministers associated with the Pentecostal revival of the 1900s came and went, Smith's steady faith and enduring ministry made him one of the most influential evangelists in the early history of Pentecostalism. His teachings on communion with God and the gifts of the Spirit laid the foundation for the modern Charismatic Church. Smith continued to minister until his death in 1947.